THE CASSELL

Atlas of the 19TH CENTURY WORLD

1783–1914

John Haywood

with

Brian Catchpole

CASSELL

Project director   Peter Furtado

Cartographic manager   Richard Watts

Advisory editors   Jeremy Black
Professor of History, University of Exeter, UK

K.M. Chaudhuri
Vasco da Gama Professor of European Exploration, European University Institute, Florence, Italy

Barry Cunliffe
Professor of European Archaeology, University of Oxford, UK

Brian M. Fagan
Professor of Anthropology, University of California, Santa Barbara, USA

J.E. Spence
Associate Fellow, Royal Institute of International Affairs, UK

Academic advisors   J.I. Catto
Oriel College, University of Oxford, UK

Professor Robin Cohen
University of Warwick, UK

Professor J.H. Elliott
Regius Professor of Modern History, University of Oxford, UK

Professor Harold James
Princeton University, New Jersey, USA

Professor Maldwyn A. Jones
University of London, UK

Dr Stuart Kewley
University of Cambridge, UK

Dr Stewart Lone
Australian Defence Force Academy

Dr Oswyn Murray
Balliol College, University of Oxford, UK

Professor A.J.S. Reid
The Australian National University

Professor Francis Robinson
Royal Holloway, University of London, UK

Professor John K. Thornton
Millersville University, Pennsylvania, USA

This page:
Portrait of Simon Bolivar

Opposite above left:
King George V of Britain and Queen Mary

Opposite centre right:
Cartoon of the Japanese emperor and the "Russian bear"

Opposite below left:
Jamaican runaway slave

Following page:
Yoruba carving of Queen Victoria of Britain

Art director	Ayala Kingsley
Art editor	Martin Anderson
Cartographic editor	Tim Williams
Editors	Susan Kennedy
	Peter Lewis
(Encyclopedic dictionary)	BCS Publishing
Cartographer	Nathalie Johns
Picture research	Claire Turner
Production	Clive Sparling
Editorial assistance	Marian Dreier
Typesetter	Brian Blackmore
Illustrations	Charles Raymond
Proof reader	Lynne Elson
Index	Ann Barrett

AN ANDROMEDA BOOK

Produced and prepared by
Andromeda Oxford Ltd
11–15 The Vineyard
Abingdon
Oxfordshire OX14 3PX

© Andromeda Oxford Ltd 1998

First published in the UK
by Cassell plc
Wellington House
125 Strand
London WC2R 0BB

ISBN 0-304-35048-6

Printed in Italy Petruzzi Città di Castello - PG

Contents

INTRODUCTION

In 1783 Britain disconsolately accepted the independence of its thirteen colonies in North America. Yet, in the century and a quarter after the emergence of the United States, European powers still dominated the world. Their armies spread their authority, their navies charted the seas and their merchants built a network of trade and investment. A genuinely global economy was the result.

The only part of the world effectively to resist the European powers was North America, but the United States itself was a state ruled by people of European descent, its economy closely linked to and partly financed by Europe, and its culture shaped by European influences. The railroads that effectively made the United States by linking the Atlantic and Pacific coasts owed much to British investment and technology. By 1900, though, the United States had challenged and overtaken much of Europe's economic and technological lead, and was poised to become the most powerful state in the world.

The United States was sustained by migration. Between 1815 and 1901, the United States took over eight million immigrants from the British Isles alone, and many more from Germany, Scandinavia and eastern and southern Europe. European migrants also totally altered the politics, economy and ethnic composition of Australasia and Canada.

Europeans were not the only people to move, but those non-whites who journeyed long distances in pursuit of work – Chinese, Japanese, Indians, Malays as well as Africans – did so only with the consent of the European or North American states. Unlike Europeans who were generally welcomed, despite their poverty, to assist in populating the new lands and building a new society, these non-Europeans were often contract laborers or worse, controlled by strict racial barriers.

The age of migrations reflected the potency of the new technologies of the age. Thanks to the steamship, the oceans shrank; long voyages became faster, safer, cheaper, more comfortable. Barbed wire, invented in the United States in 1873, made possible the fencing in of the prairies and thus the establishment of vast ranches on what had been virgin land.

Refrigerated shipholds allowed fresh meat grown on these ranches to be shipped to cities on the other side of the globe. Railroads, too, brought foodstuffs and other raw materials quickly and efficiently to the urban centers.

Trade was not restricted to raw materials. The heavy industry, light engineering, chemicals and textile manufacture that now drove Europe's economy also provided products for the rest of the world. European investment capital acted as the engine of this global economy, financing the creation of the infrastructure for the new trade on every continent. The British empire, which encompassed more than a fifth of the Earth's landmass by 1914 (its political and financial influence pervaded much of the rest) was dominant in this flow of capital, though increasingly challenged by its cultural and political offspring, the United States. As a result English became the international language of business across most of the globe.

The spread of European influence was not always peaceful. There was violent resistance, especially in Africa and China. Yet there was frequently also emulation. This was most apparent in Japan, which embarked on a process of westernization from the 1870s. Similar choices were made in Egypt, Persia and Siam, which saw the benefits of adopting western ways.

The formal European empires ensured that their colonies were educated in European ways of government, law and culture as much as in technology and commerce. This cultural imperialism was often conducted with little thought for the indigenous civilizations, and was barely questioned by the Europeans. The *pax Britannica* was maintained across the globe by a combination of British gunboats and diplomats, but the introduction of British education, religion and the political institutions of Westminster was thought to bring undeniable benefits to the "poor benighted heathen". Although advantages undoubtedly accrued, the forcible imposition of western civilization built up resentments that would grow throughout the first half of the twentieth century and explode after 1945.

In the nineteenth century, humanity sought to use advances in knowledge to mould the environment. Science – conducted mainly in Germany, France, Britain and the United States – made massive advances and its power to change the world became undeniable. Scientific breeding and a thorough knowledge of the needs of plants and animals transformed national economies: Malaya, for example, was changed utterly when the British introduced the rubber tree from South America. Science seemed to hold the key to the future, to the creation and use of goods, new sources of power (electricity, turbines, internal-combustion engines) and new materials (alloys, dyes, fertilizers, explosives). Equally revolutionary were the telegraph, telephone and radio, which shrank dis-

tance even more than had railroad and steamships: in 1901 Marconi transmitted radio signals across the Atlantic. Two years later the Wright brothers made the world's first heavier-than-air flight, giving the industrial countries access to a new medium that would have great implications, civil and military.

Every such innovation helped dissolve former certainties, and in 1914, when Europe began the conflict that engulfed the continent, the assumptions of the previous century were destroyed. To survive, the powers drew on the resources of their old colonies in ways that changed the relationships between them for ever ■

USING THIS ATLAS

This atlas is part of a six-volume chronological set covering the Ancient (1), Classical (2), Medieval (3), Early Modern (4), 19th Century (5), and Modern (6) worlds. To help the user pinpoint straight away which era any particular map relates to, pages are numbered first by volume, and then by 2-page spread within that volume. Thus, map spread 14 in volume 5 is identified by the page number 5.14.

World map spreads outline global history on the date shown. Different typographical categories (see table opposite) denote different kinds of political or social entity. The text on these spreads includes many cross-references to other relevant spreads. The timelines here are organized by region.

Regional map spreads cover a part of the world over a specific period. Maps for a continent or major region are grouped in a section, named in the heading on the right-hand side of the spread. These sections also appear in the Contents page.

Maps are shown in true cartographic projections. North is generally at the top of the page. Some distortion is evident in those maps that cover huge areas of the world (e.g. Asia). Where necessary location maps have been included.

Each regional map has certain standard features: thick grey lines denote major borders, thin grey lines internal borders. Campaigns or journeys are shown by lines with arrowheads; thicker grey arrows are used for mass movements of people. Trade routes are thinner lines, with arrowheads when the trade is one-way. All map-key items are referred to in text. The main text explains and amplifies the information on the map.

The timelines on regional maps are arranged in geographical or thematic sections. Civilizations, cultures, and dynasties are shown with colored bands; broad historical phases (such as "Bronze Age") are indicated with grey bands. Every regional map also has several numbered "pointers", whose captions offer further historical detail on the places marked. Finally, the panel bottom right cross-refers to other spreads with related information, listing their numbers and themes.

A substantial encyclopedic section at the end of the book contains an A–Z guide to the people, places, and events of the period. It is cross-referenced both within the section and to the information that appears on the map spreads.

The index provides detailed references to the text, timelines, pointer captions and map keys. Space constraints have precluded indexing every location on the maps themselves.

TYPOGRAPHICAL CONVENTIONS	
World maps	
FRANCE	state or empire
Belgian Congo	dependency or territory
Mongols	tribe, chiefdom or people
Anasazi culture	cultural group
Regional maps	
HUNGARY	state or empire
Bohemia	dependency or territory
Slavs	tribe, chiefdom or people
ANATOLIA	geographical region
✕	battle
•	site or town

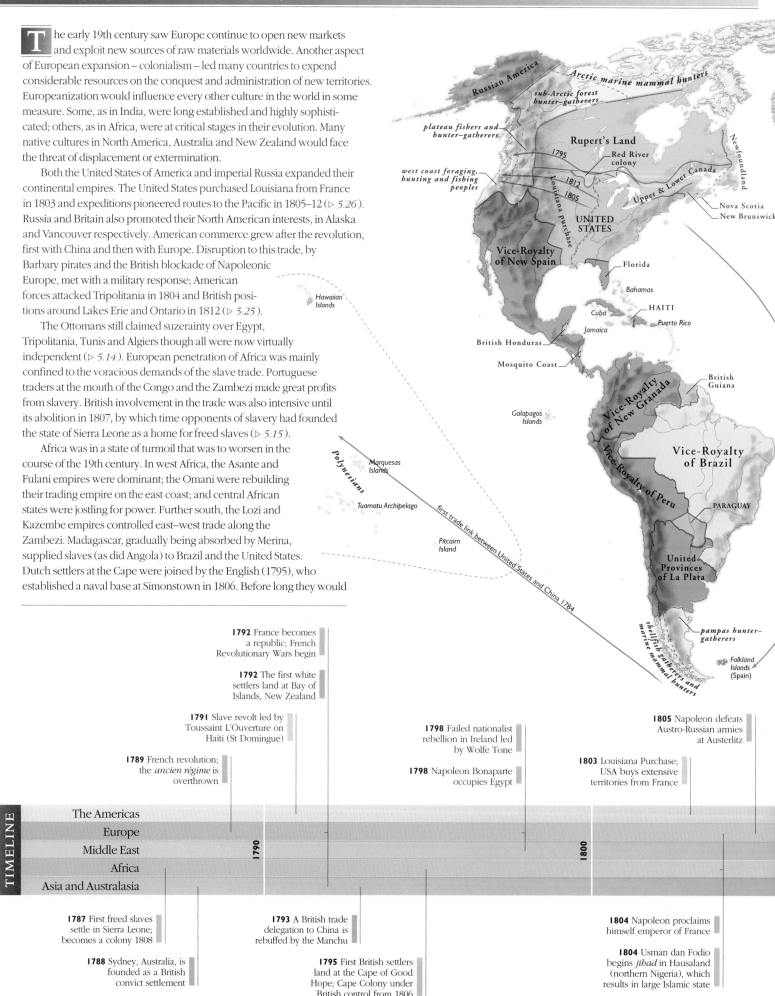

T he early 19th century saw Europe continue to open new markets and exploit new sources of raw materials worldwide. Another aspect of European expansion – colonialism – led many countries to expend considerable resources on the conquest and administration of new territories. Europeanization would influence every other culture in the world in some measure. Some, as in India, were long established and highly sophisticated; others, as in Africa, were at critical stages in their evolution. Many native cultures in North America, Australia and New Zealand would face the threat of displacement or extermination.

Both the United States of America and imperial Russia expanded their continental empires. The United States purchased Louisiana from France in 1803 and expeditions pioneered routes to the Pacific in 1805–12 (▷ 5.26). Russia and Britain also promoted their North American interests, in Alaska and Vancouver respectively. American commerce grew after the revolution, first with China and then with Europe. Disruption to this trade, by Barbary pirates and the British blockade of Napoleonic Europe, met with a military response; American forces attacked Tripolitania in 1804 and British positions around Lakes Erie and Ontario in 1812 (▷ 5.25).

The Ottomans still claimed suzerainty over Egypt, Tripolitania, Tunis and Algiers though all were now virtually independent (▷ 5.14). European penetration of Africa was mainly confined to the voracious demands of the slave trade. Portuguese traders at the mouth of the Congo and the Zambezi made great profits from slavery. British involvement in the trade was also intensive until its abolition in 1807, by which time opponents of slavery had founded the state of Sierra Leone as a home for freed slaves (▷ 5.15).

Africa was in a state of turmoil that was to worsen in the course of the 19th century. In west Africa, the Asante and Fulani empires were dominant; the Omani were rebuilding their trading empire on the east coast; and central African states were jostling for power. Further south, the Lozi and Kazembe empires controlled east–west trade along the Zambezi. Madagascar, gradually being absorbed by Merina, supplied slaves (as did Angola) to Brazil and the United States. Dutch settlers at the Cape were joined by the English (1795), who established a naval base at Simonstown in 1806. Before long they would

1792 France becomes a republic; French Revolutionary Wars begin

1792 The first white settlers land at Bay of Islands, New Zealand

1791 Slave revolt led by Toussaint L'Ouverture on Haiti (St Domingue)

1789 French revolution; the *ancien régime* is overthrown

1798 Failed nationalist rebellion in Ireland led by Wolfe Tone

1798 Napoleon Bonaparte occupies Egypt

1805 Napoleon defeats Austro-Russian armies at Austerlitz

1803 Louisiana Purchase; USA buys extensive territories from France

TIMELINE

The Americas
Europe
Middle East
Africa
Asia and Australasia

1790

1800

1787 First freed slaves settle in Sierra Leone; becomes a colony 1808

1788 Sydney, Australia, is founded as a British convict settlement

1793 A British trade delegation to China is rebuffed by the Manchu

1795 First British settlers land at the Cape of Good Hope; Cape Colony under British control from 1806

1804 Napoleon proclaims himself emperor of France

1804 Usman dan Fodio begins *jihad* in Hausaland (northern Nigeria), which results in large Islamic state

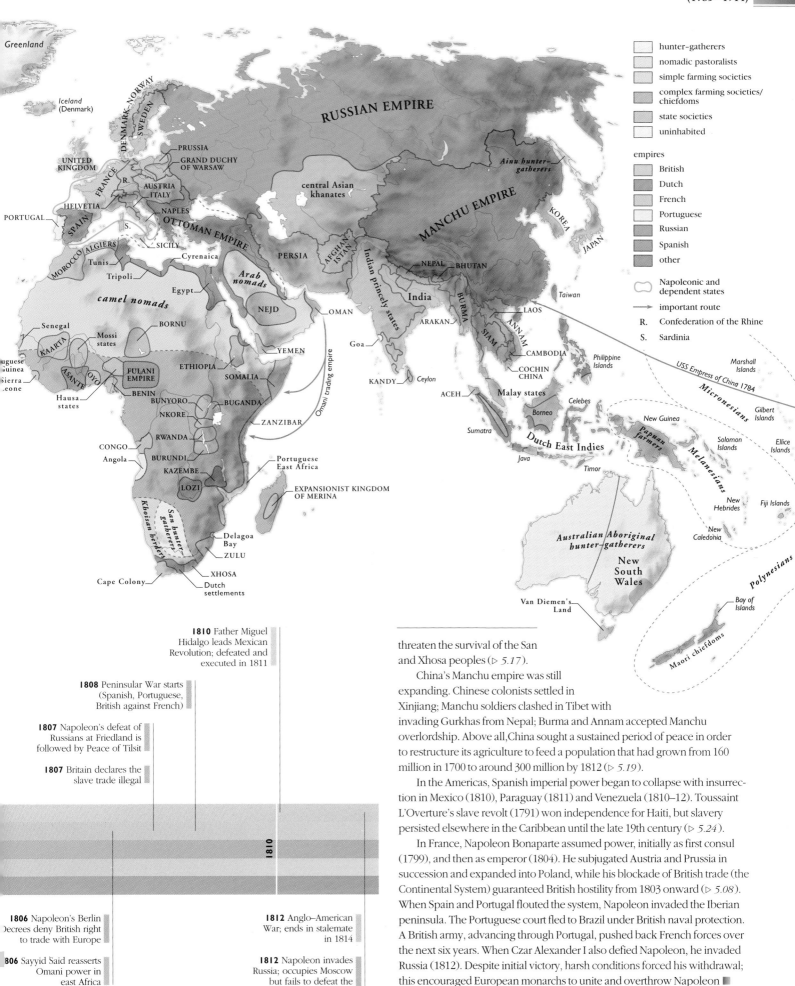

hunter-gatherers
nomadic pastoralists
simple farming societies
complex farming societies/ chiefdoms
state societies
uninhabited

empires
British
Dutch
French
Portuguese
Russian
Spanish
other

Napoleonic and dependent states
important route
R. Confederation of the Rhine
S. Sardinia

Map labels: Greenland, Iceland (Denmark), UNITED KINGDOM, DENMARK–NORWAY, SWEDEN, RUSSIAN EMPIRE, PRUSSIA, GRAND DUCHY OF WARSAW, FRANCE, R., AUSTRIA, ITALY, HELVETIA, NAPLES, PORTUGAL, SPAIN, SICILY, S., MOROCCO, ALGIERS, Tunis, Tripoli, Cyrenaica, OTTOMAN EMPIRE, Egypt, *Arab nomads*, *camel nomads*, NEJD, OMAN, YEMEN, PERSIA, AFGHANISTAN, *central Asian khanates*, *Ainu hunter-gatherers*, MANCHU EMPIRE, KOREA, JAPAN, Taiwan, NEPAL, BHUTAN, *Indian princely states*, India, BURMA, ARAKAN, SIAM, LAOS, ANNAM, CAMBODIA, COCHIN CHINA, Goa, KANDY, Ceylon, ACEH, Malay states, Sumatra, Borneo, Celebes, Java, Timor, *Dutch East Indies*, Philippine Islands, New Guinea, *Papuan farmers*, Marshall Islands, *Micronesians*, Gilbert Islands, Solomon Islands, Ellice Islands, *Melanesians*, New Hebrides, Fiji Islands, New Caledonia, *Polynesians*, *Australian Aboriginal hunter-gatherers*, New South Wales, Van Diemen's Land, Bay of Islands, *Maori chiefdoms*, USS Empress of China 1784, Senegal, KAARTA, Mossi states, ASANTE, OYO, Hausa states, BORNU, FULANI EMPIRE, BENIN, ETHIOPIA, SOMALIA, BUNYORO, BUGANDA, NKORE, RWANDA, ZANZIBAR, *Omani trading empire*, CONGO, Angola, BURUNDI, KAZEMBE, LOZI, *San hunter-gatherers*, *Khoisan herders*, Portuguese East Africa, EXPANSIONIST KINGDOM OF MERINA, Delagoa Bay, ZULU, XHOSA, Cape Colony, Dutch settlements, Portuguese Guinea, Sierra Leone, Hausa states

---

1810 Father Miguel Hidalgo leads Mexican Revolution; defeated and executed in 1811

1808 Peninsular War starts (Spanish, Portuguese, British against French)

1807 Napoleon's defeat of Russians at Friedland is followed by Peace of Tilsit

1807 Britain declares the slave trade illegal

1810

1806 Napoleon's Berlin Decrees deny British right to trade with Europe

1806 Sayyid Said reasserts Omani power in east Africa

1812 Anglo–American War; ends in stalemate in 1814

1812 Napoleon invades Russia; occupies Moscow but fails to defeat the Russians decisively

---

threaten the survival of the San and Xhosa peoples (▷ 5.17).

China's Manchu empire was still expanding. Chinese colonists settled in Xinjiang; Manchu soldiers clashed in Tibet with invading Gurkhas from Nepal; Burma and Annam accepted Manchu overlordship. Above all, China sought a sustained period of peace in order to restructure its agriculture to feed a population that had grown from 160 million in 1700 to around 300 million by 1812 (▷ 5.19).

In the Americas, Spanish imperial power began to collapse with insurrection in Mexico (1810), Paraguay (1811) and Venezuela (1810–12). Toussaint L'Overture's slave revolt (1791) won independence for Haiti, but slavery persisted elsewhere in the Caribbean until the late 19th century (▷ 5.24).

In France, Napoleon Bonaparte assumed power, initially as first consul (1799), and then as emperor (1804). He subjugated Austria and Prussia in succession and expanded into Poland, while his blockade of British trade (the Continental System) guaranteed British hostility from 1803 onward (▷ 5.08). When Spain and Portugal flouted the system, Napoleon invaded the Iberian peninsula. The Portuguese court fled to Brazil under British naval protection. A British army, advancing through Portugal, pushed back French forces over the next six years. When Czar Alexander I also defied Napoleon, he invaded Russia (1812). Despite initial victory, harsh conditions forced his withdrawal; this encouraged European monarchs to unite and overthrow Napoleon ■

The Congress of Vienna (1814–15) dismembered Napoleon's empire and transformed the map of Europe (▷ 5.08). The German Confederation was formed, an alliance of states dominated by Austria and Prussia. Wholly new nations also arose: Greece wrested sovereignty from the Ottoman empire from 1821–28; Belgium rebelled against Dutch rule (1830) and won international recognition of its independence in 1839. Yet the restoration of autocratic monarchies by the Congress in the name of stability bred resentment, which erupted in a series of revolutions that swept the continent in 1848 (▷ 5.09). Only Britain and Russia stayed unaffected; elsewhere, liberals and nationalists exploited economic hardship to foment revolts demanding representative forms of government. Internal divisions caused the revolutions to fail and conservative forces soon regained power.

In contrast, revolutions succeeded in toppling the Spanish and Portuguese empires in Central and South America. Brazil proclaimed an independent empire after King João VI returned to Portugal in 1822. The collapse of Spain during the Napoleonic Wars led to a succession of uprisings against Spanish rule in the Americas: eleven independent states were formed by 1826 (▷ 5.23). The disparate nature of the region's cultures and the diversity of the revolutionaries' aspirations prevented the development of the envisaged Hispano–American state; Simón Bolívar's Gran Colombia (comprising modern Venezuela, Colombia, and Ecuador) fragmented in 1830, only eleven years after its formation.

Spain's fall benefited the United States, which gained the territories of East and West Florida in 1819–22. US foreign policy was outlined in the Monroe Doctrine of 1823, which stipulated separate spheres of interest for Europe and the Americas to forestall any renewal of European ambition in the region. The transcontinental expansion of the United States also accelerated during this period, with the annexation of Oregon in 1844, and Texas in 1845 (▷ 5.26). War with Mexico (1846–48) led to the United States gaining California, where gold deposits were discovered soon after.

In Russia, Czar Alexander I and his successor Nicholas I maintained an implacable opposition to reform at home and abroad; an insurrection in Poland against Russian rule was suppressed (1830–31), while Russian troops were also sent to help Austria quell a Hungarian nationalist uprising in 1848–49. Russian forces

Map labels

Russian America
Arctic marine mammal hunters
sub-Arctic forest hunter–gatherers
west coast foraging, hunting and fishing peoples
plateau fishers and hunter–gatherers
Rupert's Land
Canada
Newfoundland
UNITED STATES
Nova Scotia
New Brunswick
MEXICO
Bahamas
British Honduras
Cuba
HAITI
Puerto Rico
Jamaica
DOMINICAN REPUBLIC
GUATEMALA
EL SALVADOR
HONDURAS
NICARAGUA
COSTA RICA
Hawaiian Islands
Galapagos Islands
COLOMBIA
VENEZUELA
British Guiana
Dutch Guiana
French Guiana
ECUADOR
BRAZIL
PERU
BOLIVIA
PARAGUAY
Marquesas Islands (France)
Tuamotu Archipelago (France)
Pitcairn Island (Britain)
ARGENTINA
CHILE
URUGUAY
shellfish gatherers and marine mammal hunters
pampas hunter–gatherers
Falkland Islands (Britain)

Timeline

1823 Monroe Doctrine warns against further European expansion in the Americas

1822 Brazil declares independence from Portugal

1818 Border between Canada and United States is defined as 49th Parallel

1830–31 Polish revolt against Russian rule

1815 Defeat of Napoleon by British and Prussian forces at Waterloo

1828 Greeks win War of Independence (Ottomans recognize Greece 1832)

1839–42 Britain fights the First Afghan War to stop the southern spread of Russian influence

TIMELINE			
The Americas			
Europe			
Middle East	1820	1830	
Africa			
Asia and Australasia			

1816–20 Argentina declares its independence from Spain; war of liberation lasts for four years

1820 British settlers begin to arrive at the Cape in large numbers

1833 Falkland Islands are occupied by Britain

1837 Natal Republic is founded by Afrikaners

1824–26 British fight two unsuccessful wars against the Asante of west Africa

1833 The Ottoman empire recognizes the independence of Egypt

1839 Belgian independence is internationally guaranteed

1816 Shaka, king of the Zulu, begins to expand the Zulu empire

1816 Britain begins to recruit Gurkha soldiers from Nepal

1839–42 First Opium War is fought between Britain and China

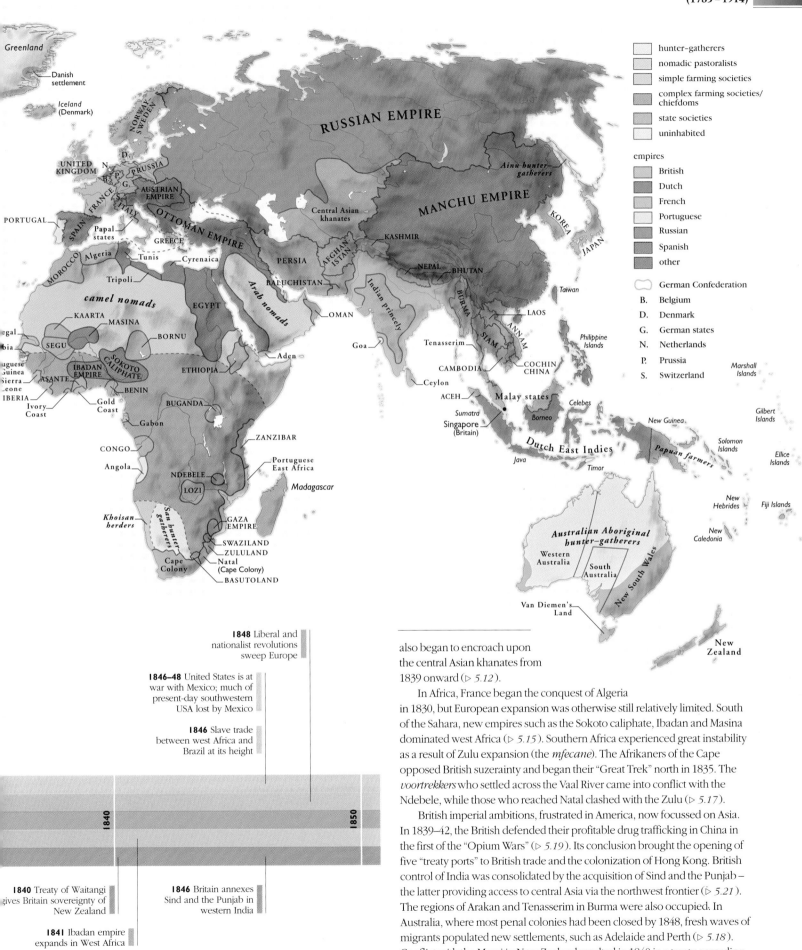

hunter-gatherers
nomadic pastoralists
simple farming societies
complex farming societies/ chiefdoms
state societies
uninhabited

empires
British
Dutch
French
Portuguese
Russian
Spanish
other

German Confederation
B. Belgium
D. Denmark
G. German states
N. Netherlands
P. Prussia
S. Switzerland

1848 Liberal and nationalist revolutions sweep Europe

1846–48 United States is at war with Mexico; much of present-day southwestern USA lost by Mexico

1846 Slave trade between west Africa and Brazil at its height

1840

1850

1840 Treaty of Waitangi gives Britain sovereignty of New Zealand

1841 Ibadan empire expands in West Africa

1846 Britain annexes Sind and the Punjab in western India

also began to encroach upon the central Asian khanates from 1839 onward (▷ *5.12*).

In Africa, France began the conquest of Algeria in 1830, but European expansion was otherwise still relatively limited. South of the Sahara, new empires such as the Sokoto caliphate, Ibadan and Masina dominated west Africa (▷ *5.15*). Southern Africa experienced great instability as a result of Zulu expansion (the *mfecane*). The Afrikaners of the Cape opposed British suzerainty and began their "Great Trek" north in 1835. The *voortrekkers* who settled across the Vaal River came into conflict with the Ndebele, while those who reached Natal clashed with the Zulu (▷ *5.17*).

British imperial ambitions, frustrated in America, now focussed on Asia. In 1839–42, the British defended their profitable drug trafficking in China in the first of the "Opium Wars" (▷ *5.19*). Its conclusion brought the opening of five "treaty ports" to British trade and the colonization of Hong Kong. British control of India was consolidated by the acquisition of Sind and the Punjab – the latter providing access to central Asia via the northwest frontier (▷ *5.21*). The regions of Arakan and Tenasserim in Burma were also occupied. In Australia, where most penal colonies had been closed by 1848, fresh waves of migrants populated new settlements, such as Adelaide and Perth (▷ *5.18*). Conflict with the Maori in New Zealand resulted in 1840 in a treaty according to which the Maori recognized Queen Victoria as their sovereign; however, the treaty left many questions of land ownership and sale unresolved ∎

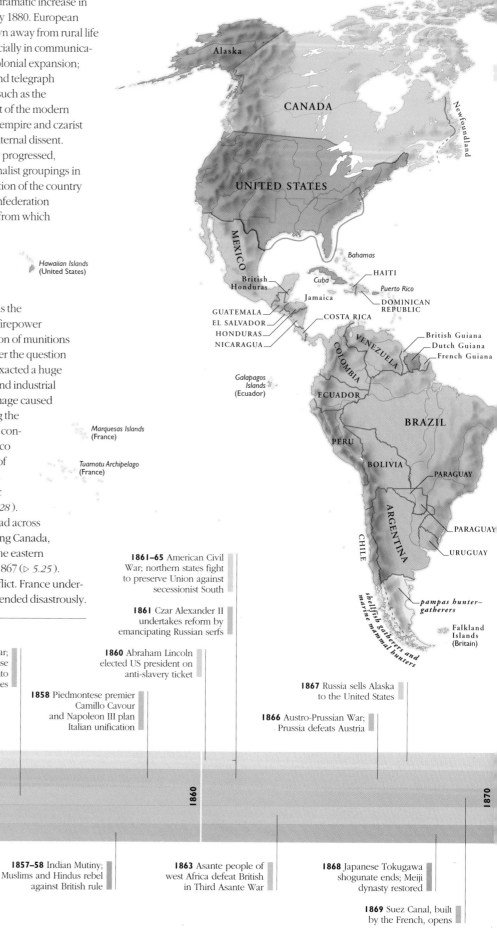

Growing urbanization and industrialization, and a dramatic increase in population, were evident throughout the world by 1880. European cities developed rapidly, as ever more people were drawn away from rural life by factory work (▷ 5.10). Technological advances, especially in communications, impelled industrial development and promoted colonial expansion; by the 1850s, the British had installed the first railroads and telegraph systems in India. Politically, while some ancient entities such as the Tokugawa shogunate in Japan did not survive the advent of the modern age, others – the Chinese Manchu dynasty, the Ottoman empire and czarist Russia – lingered into the 20th century, though torn by internal dissent.

Dynamic new nation-states arose as the 19th century progressed, changing the balance of power in Europe. In Italy, nationalist groupings in the north and south combined to bring about the unification of the country (▷ 5.09). The struggle for domination in the German Confederation between Austria and Prussia resulted in conflict in 1866, from which Prussia emerged victorious (▷ 5.11). Another crushing Prussian military victory in 1870–71 against France destroyed the empire of Napoleon III and led to Prussia forming the nucleus of the German "second empire".

Warfare was in the process of being radically altered by mechanization. The American Civil War (1861–65) was the first conflict to utilize the greatly enhanced mobility and firepower afforded respectively by railroads and the mass production of munitions (▷ 5.27). Contested between the North and the South over the question of slavery and the extent of federal jurisdiction, the war exacted a huge toll in human lives. The North's far superior manpower and industrial capacity eventually allowed it to prevail. Despite the damage caused by the war, however, the United States was fast becoming the dominant power in the Western Hemisphere. Expansion continued with the purchase of the Gadsden Strip from Mexico (1853) and Alaska from Russia (1867). The inauguration of a transcontinental electric telegraph was swiftly followed by the linking of the Union Pacific and the Central Pacific railroads to form a coast-to-coast route in 1869 (▷ 5.26, 5.28). In the 1870s and 1880s, the construction of another railroad across the North American continent played a vital role in unifying Canada, joining the new western territory of British Columbia to the eastern provinces that had declared the Dominion of Canada in 1867 (▷ 5.25).

Central and South America were beset by armed conflict. France undertook an imperial adventure in Mexico in 1863–67, which ended disastrously.

1861–65 American Civil War; northern states fight to preserve Union against secessionist South

1861 Czar Alexander II undertakes reform by emancipating Russian serfs

1854–56 Crimean War; Britain and France oppose Russian expansion into Ottoman territories

1860 Abraham Lincoln elected US president on anti-slavery ticket

1867 Russia sells Alaska to the United States

1852 French second empire: Louis Napoleon emperor (Napoleon III)

1858 Piedmontese premier Camillo Cavour and Napoleon III plan Italian unification

1866 Austro-Prussian War; Prussia defeats Austria

TIMELINE			
The Americas			
Europe			
Middle East	1850	1860	1870
Africa			
Asia and Australasia			

1851–53 Gold rush in Australia

1857–58 Indian Mutiny; Muslims and Hindus rebel against British rule

1863 Asante people of west Africa defeat British in Third Asante War

1868 Japanese Tokugawa shogunate ends; Meiji dynasty restored

1853 US Commodore Matthew Perry opens up Japan to western trade

1869 Suez Canal, built by the French, opens

1870 Unification of Italy as Rome becomes part of the kingdom

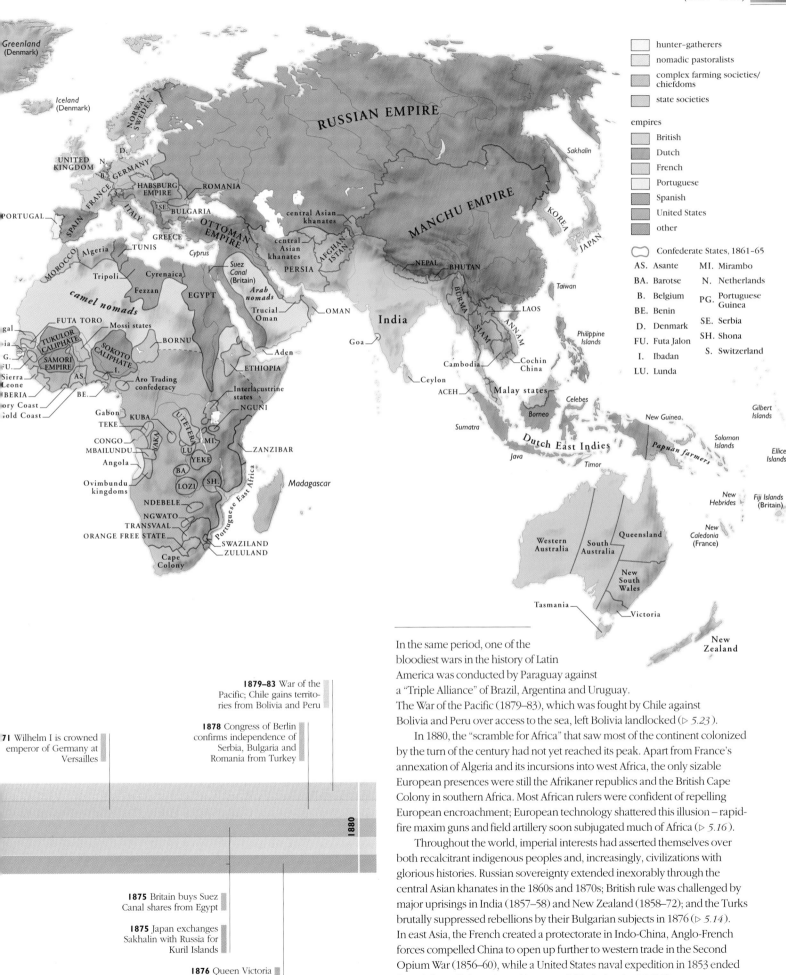

hunter-gatherers
nomadic pastoralists
complex farming societies/chiefdoms
state societies

empires
British
Dutch
French
Portuguese
Spanish
United States
other

Confederate States, 1861–65

AS. Asante
BA. Barotse
B. Belgium
BE. Benin
D. Denmark
FU. Futa Jalon
I. Ibadan
LU. Lunda

MI. Mirambo
N. Netherlands
PG. Portuguese Guinea
SE. Serbia
SH. Shona
S. Switzerland

In the same period, one of the bloodiest wars in the history of Latin America was conducted by Paraguay against a "Triple Alliance" of Brazil, Argentina and Uruguay. The War of the Pacific (1879–83), which was fought by Chile against Bolivia and Peru over access to the sea, left Bolivia landlocked (▷ 5.23).

In 1880, the "scramble for Africa" that saw most of the continent colonized by the turn of the century had not yet reached its peak. Apart from France's annexation of Algeria and its incursions into west Africa, the only sizable European presences were still the Afrikaner republics and the British Cape Colony in southern Africa. Most African rulers were confident of repelling European encroachment; European technology shattered this illusion – rapid-fire maxim guns and field artillery soon subjugated much of Africa (▷ 5.16).

Throughout the world, imperial interests had asserted themselves over both recalcitrant indigenous peoples and, increasingly, civilizations with glorious histories. Russian sovereignty extended inexorably through the central Asian khanates in the 1860s and 1870s; British rule was challenged by major uprisings in India (1857–58) and New Zealand (1858–72); and the Turks brutally suppressed rebellions by their Bulgarian subjects in 1876 (▷ 5.14). In east Asia, the French created a protectorate in Indo-China, Anglo-French forces compelled China to open up further to western trade in the Second Opium War (1856–60), while a United States naval expedition in 1853 ended Japan's long diplomatic and commercial isolation (▷ 5.20) ■

1879–83 War of the Pacific; Chile gains territories from Bolivia and Peru

1878 Congress of Berlin confirms independence of Serbia, Bulgaria and Romania from Turkey

71 Wilhelm I is crowned emperor of Germany at Versailles

1880

1875 Britain buys Suez Canal shares from Egypt

1875 Japan exchanges Sakhalin with Russia for Kuril Islands

1876 Queen Victoria is proclaimed empress of India

B y 1914 the dominion of European peoples had spread throughout the world – the imperial system was at its peak, and expeditions had explored both polar regions. Colonization was most extensive in Africa; the "scramble for Africa" that had begun among European powers after 1870 was formalized at the Berlin Conference of 1884–85, which divided virtually all of the continent between rival claimants (▷ 5.16). Africans resisted the despoliation of their homelands, but usually to no avail; the Ethiopians successfully repulsed Italian invaders in 1896, but other peoples fought in vain against European troops equipped with superior weapons. Colonial forces also clashed; France and Britain disputed control of the upper Nile, and Germany's vigorous late pursuit of an African empire presaged the conflict to come in Europe. The Second Anglo-Boer War (1899–1902) was the culmination of decades of tension between settlers of Dutch and British origin in southern Africa; the British gained supremacy in a bitter struggle, but their failure to attract mass settlement left the Afrikaners dominant in the new Union of South Africa (▷ 5.17).

The United States emerged as an imperial power, while the empires of Russia and Britain continued to grow. The British empire reached the height of its power, with important colonial possessions in every continent. The transoceanic remnants of Spain's empire – Cuba, Puerto Rico, Guam and the Philippines – fell to the United States in the Spanish–American War of 1898. In Central America, US technology succeeded in cutting the Panama Canal, which opened for navigation in 1914 (▷ 5.24). The extension of the railroad network throughout the United States by the end of the 19th century was instrumental in opening up new territories; and, as the 20th century dawned, American engineers pioneered important new forms of transport. The first powered heavier-than-air flight was made in 1903, and mass automobile ownership was a fact by 1914.

Russia's expansion to the east brought it into conflict with Japan (▷ 5.12). The industrializing and ambitious Japan routed Russian forces in 1904–05 and annexed Korea in 1910. Russia's humiliation sparked the first of a series of revolutions that led to the fall of the imperial regime in 1917.

Britain's prime interest was to protect its trade through the Suez Canal, including the new resource of oil which Britain received from the Persian Gulf. To this end, bases were developed in the Mediterranean. Egypt was also occupied in 1882. Further east, British

1889 Brazil is proclaimed a republic

1888 Wilhelm II becomes German emperor (*Kaiser*)

1885 Completion of Canadian Pacific Railway links east and west Canada

1896 Ethiopian defeat of Italians at Adowa secures 40 years of independence

1896 Klondike gold rush brings flood of prospectors to the Canadian northwest

1882 Triple Alliance formed between Germany, Austria-Hungary, and Italy

TIMELINE

The Americas

Europe

Middle East

Africa

Asia and Australasia

1885

1895

1884–85 Berlin Conference divides up Africa between European powers

1891 Construction of Trans-Siberian railroad begins

1886 Discovery of gold in Transvaal initiates intensive mining activity throughout southern Africa

1894 Franco-Russian Alliance formed to counter Triple Alliance threat

1899–1902 Second Anglo-Boer War; British overcome Afrikaners

1894–95 Sino-Japanese War; Korea independent and Taiwan is ceded to Japan on Chinese defeat

1900–01 Boxer Uprising in China against foreigners

Alaska

CANADA

Newfoundland

UNITED STATES

MEXICO

Hawaiian Islands (United States)

Bahamas

British Honduras

CUBA

HAITI

Puerto Rico (United States)

Jamaica

DOMINICAN REPUBLIC

GUATEMALA

EL SALVADOR

HONDURAS

NICARAGUA

COSTA RICA

PANAMA

VENEZUELA

British Guiana

Dutch Guiana

French Guiana

COLOMBIA

Galapagos Islands (Ecuador)

ECUADOR

BRAZIL

PERU

Marquesas Islands (France)

BOLIVIA

PARAGUAY

Tuamotu Archipelago (France)

Easter Island (Chile)

CHILE

ARGENTINA

URUGUAY

Falkland Islands (Britain)

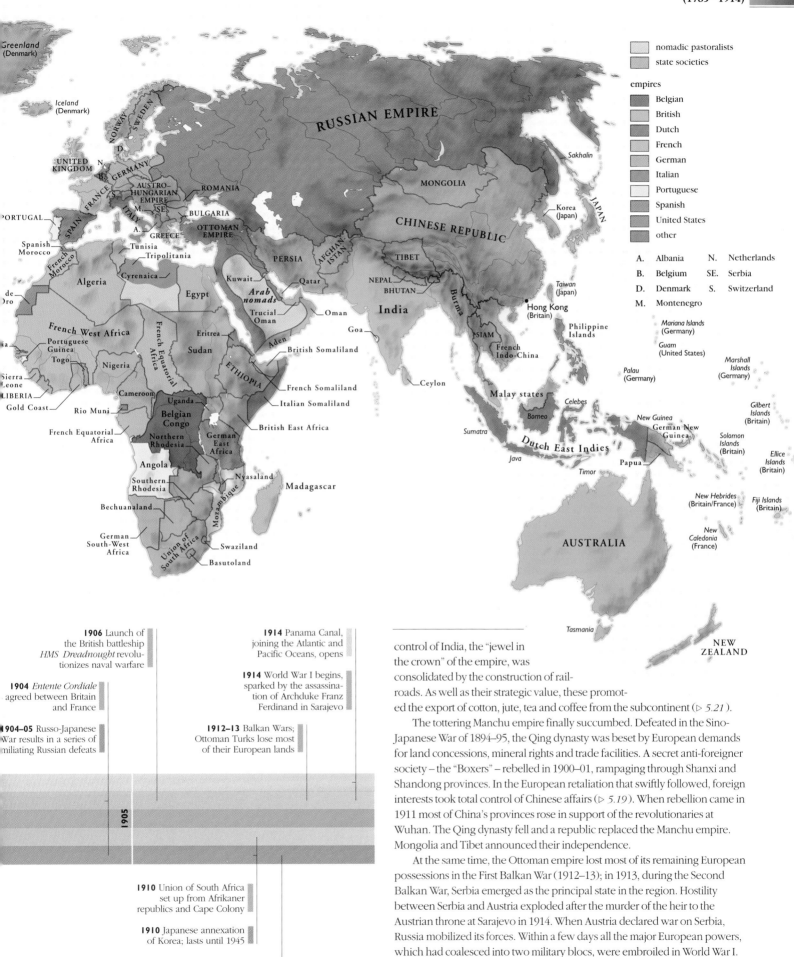

nomadic pastoralists

state societies

empires

Belgian

British

Dutch

French

German

Italian

Portuguese

Spanish

United States

other

A. Albania   N. Netherlands
B. Belgium   SE. Serbia
D. Denmark   S. Switzerland
M. Montenegro

1906 Launch of
the British battleship
HMS Dreadnought revolu-
tionizes naval warfare

1904 *Entente Cordiale*
agreed between Britain
and France

1904–05 Russo-Japanese
War results in a series of
humiliating Russian defeats

1914 Panama Canal,
joining the Atlantic and
Pacific Oceans, opens

1914 World War I begins,
sparked by the assassina-
tion of Archduke Franz
Ferdinand in Sarajevo

1912–13 Balkan Wars;
Ottoman Turks lose most
of their European lands

1905

1910 Union of South Africa
set up from Afrikaner
republics and Cape Colony

1910 Japanese annexation
of Korea; lasts until 1945

1911 Chinese Revolution
overthrows Qing dynasty;
republic established 1912

control of India, the "jewel in
the crown" of the empire, was
consolidated by the construction of railroads. As well as their strategic value, these promot-
ed the export of cotton, jute, tea and coffee from the subcontinent (▷ 5.21).

The tottering Manchu empire finally succumbed. Defeated in the Sino-
Japanese War of 1894–95, the Qing dynasty was beset by European demands
for land concessions, mineral rights and trade facilities. A secret anti-foreigner
society – the "Boxers" – rebelled in 1900–01, rampaging through Shanxi and
Shandong provinces. In the European retaliation that swiftly followed, foreign
interests took total control of Chinese affairs (▷ 5.19). When rebellion came in
1911 most of China's provinces rose in support of the revolutionaries at
Wuhan. The Qing dynasty fell and a republic replaced the Manchu empire.
Mongolia and Tibet announced their independence.

At the same time, the Ottoman empire lost most of its remaining European
possessions in the First Balkan War (1912–13); in 1913, during the Second
Balkan War, Serbia emerged as the principal state in the region. Hostility
between Serbia and Austria exploded after the murder of the heir to the
Austrian throne at Sarajevo in 1914. When Austria declared war on Serbia,
Russia mobilized its forces. Within a few days all the major European powers,
which had coalesced into two military blocs, were embroiled in World War I.
This devastating global conflict was to bring the collapse of the Russian,
German and Austro-Hungarian empires ■

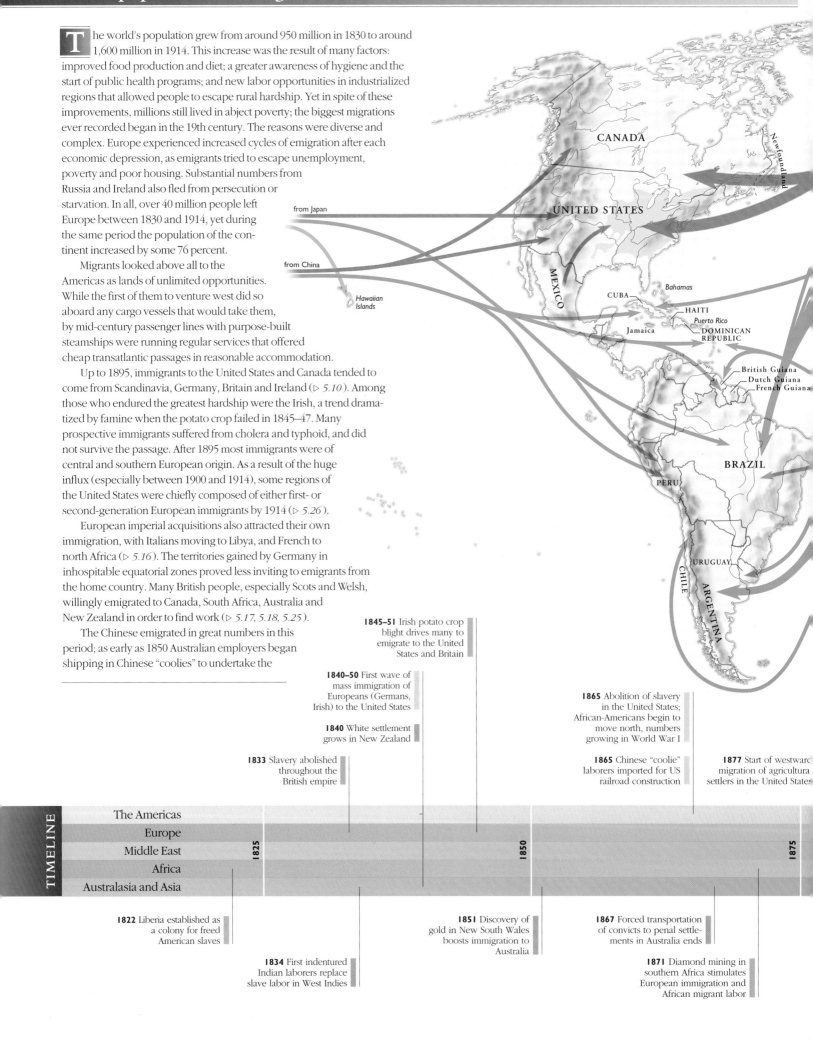

The world's population grew from around 950 million in 1830 to around 1,600 million in 1914. This increase was the result of many factors: improved food production and diet; a greater awareness of hygiene and the start of public health programs; and new labor opportunities in industrialized regions that allowed people to escape rural hardship. Yet in spite of these improvements, millions still lived in abject poverty; the biggest migrations ever recorded began in the 19th century. The reasons were diverse and complex. Europe experienced increased cycles of emigration after each economic depression, as emigrants tried to escape unemployment, poverty and poor housing. Substantial numbers from Russia and Ireland also fled from persecution or starvation. In all, over 40 million people left Europe between 1830 and 1914, yet during the same period the population of the continent increased by some 76 percent.

Migrants looked above all to the Americas as lands of unlimited opportunities. While the first of them to venture west did so aboard any cargo vessels that would take them, by mid-century passenger lines with purpose-built steamships were running regular services that offered cheap transatlantic passages in reasonable accommodation.

Up to 1895, immigrants to the United States and Canada tended to come from Scandinavia, Germany, Britain and Ireland (▷ 5.10). Among those who endured the greatest hardship were the Irish, a trend dramatized by famine when the potato crop failed in 1845–47. Many prospective immigrants suffered from cholera and typhoid, and did not survive the passage. After 1895 most immigrants were of central and southern European origin. As a result of the huge influx (especially between 1900 and 1914), some regions of the United States were chiefly composed of either first- or second-generation European immigrants by 1914 (▷ 5.26).

European imperial acquisitions also attracted their own immigration, with Italians moving to Libya, and French to north Africa (▷ 5.16). The territories gained by Germany in inhospitable equatorial zones proved less inviting to emigrants from the home country. Many British people, especially Scots and Welsh, willingly emigrated to Canada, South Africa, Australia and New Zealand in order to find work (▷ 5.17, 5.18, 5.25).

The Chinese emigrated in great numbers in this period; as early as 1850 Australian employers began shipping in Chinese "coolies" to undertake the

1845–51 Irish potato crop blight drives many to emigrate to the United States and Britain

1840–50 First wave of mass immigration of Europeans (Germans, Irish) to the United States

1840 White settlement grows in New Zealand

1833 Slavery abolished throughout the British empire

1865 Abolition of slavery in the United States; African-Americans begin to move north, numbers growing in World War I

1865 Chinese "coolie" laborers imported for US railroad construction

1877 Start of westward migration of agricultural settlers in the United States

TIMELINE

The Americas
Europe
Middle East
Africa
Australasia and Asia

1825
1850
1875

1822 Liberia established as a colony for freed American slaves

1851 Discovery of gold in New South Wales boosts immigration to Australia

1867 Forced transportation of convicts to penal settlements in Australia ends

1834 First indentured Indian laborers replace slave labor in West Indies

1871 Diamond mining in southern Africa stimulates European immigration and African migrant labor

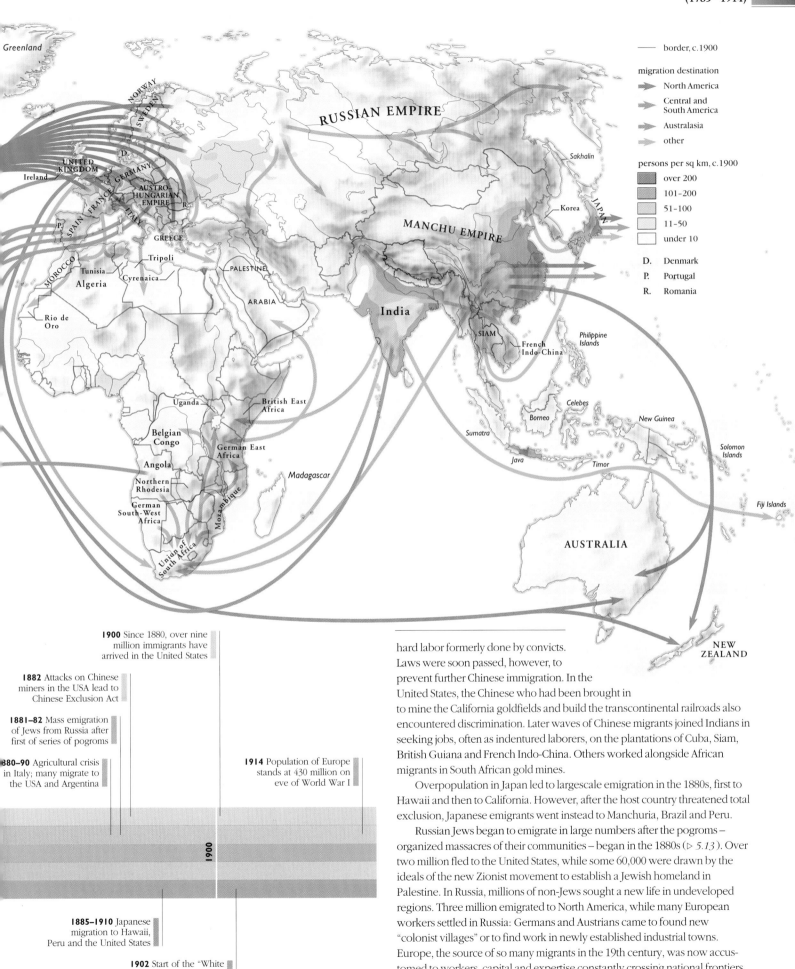

1900 Since 1880, over nine million immigrants have arrived in the United States

1882 Attacks on Chinese miners in the USA lead to Chinese Exclusion Act

1881–82 Mass emigration of Jews from Russia after first of series of pogroms

1880–90 Agricultural crisis in Italy; many migrate to the USA and Argentina

1914 Population of Europe stands at 430 million on eve of World War I

1900

1885–1910 Japanese migration to Hawaii, Peru and the United States

1902 Start of the "White Australia" policy; non-European immigrants excluded for over 60 years

hard labor formerly done by convicts. Laws were soon passed, however, to prevent further Chinese immigration. In the United States, the Chinese who had been brought in to mine the California goldfields and build the transcontinental railroads also encountered discrimination. Later waves of Chinese migrants joined Indians in seeking jobs, often as indentured laborers, on the plantations of Cuba, Siam, British Guiana and French Indo-China. Others worked alongside African migrants in South African gold mines.

Overpopulation in Japan led to largescale emigration in the 1880s, first to Hawaii and then to California. However, after the host country threatened total exclusion, Japanese emigrants went instead to Manchuria, Brazil and Peru.

Russian Jews began to emigrate in large numbers after the pogroms – organized massacres of their communities – began in the 1880s (▷ 5.13). Over two million fled to the United States, while some 60,000 were drawn by the ideals of the new Zionist movement to establish a Jewish homeland in Palestine. In Russia, millions of non-Jews sought a new life in undeveloped regions. Three million emigrated to North America, while many European workers settled in Russia: Germans and Austrians came to found new "colonist villages" or to find work in newly established industrial towns. Europe, the source of so many migrants in the 19th century, was now accustomed to workers, capital and expertise constantly crossing national frontiers, a situation that would end abruptly with the outbreak of war in 1914 ∎

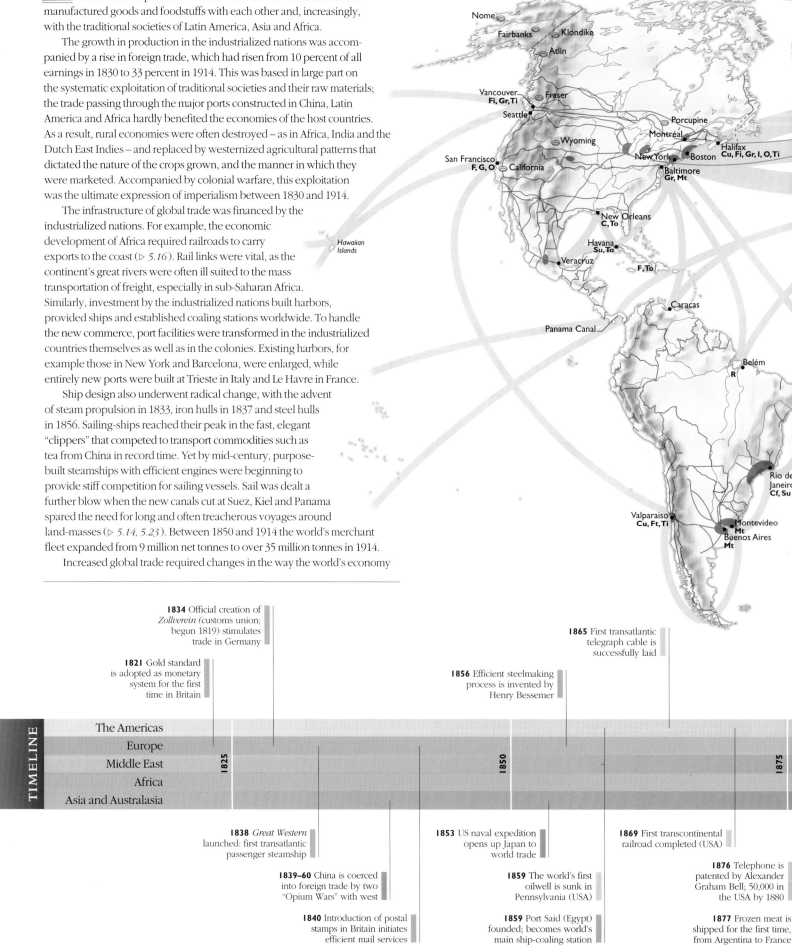

Between 1830 and 1914 world trade was dominated by the industrialized nations of Europe and the United States. These countries traded manufactured goods and foodstuffs with each other and, increasingly, with the traditional societies of Latin America, Asia and Africa.

The growth in production in the industrialized nations was accompanied by a rise in foreign trade, which had risen from 10 percent of all earnings in 1830 to 33 percent in 1914. This was based in large part on the systematic exploitation of traditional societies and their raw materials; the trade passing through the major ports constructed in China, Latin America and Africa hardly benefited the economies of the host countries. As a result, rural economies were often destroyed – as in Africa, India and the Dutch East Indies – and replaced by westernized agricultural patterns that dictated the nature of the crops grown, and the manner in which they were marketed. Accompanied by colonial warfare, this exploitation was the ultimate expression of imperialism between 1830 and 1914.

The infrastructure of global trade was financed by the industrialized nations. For example, the economic development of Africa required railroads to carry exports to the coast (▷ 5.16). Rail links were vital, as the continent's great rivers were often ill suited to the mass transportation of freight, especially in sub-Saharan Africa. Similarly, investment by the industrialized nations built harbors, provided ships and established coaling stations worldwide. To handle the new commerce, port facilities were transformed in the industrialized countries themselves as well as in the colonies. Existing harbors, for example those in New York and Barcelona, were enlarged, while entirely new ports were built at Trieste in Italy and Le Havre in France.

Ship design also underwent radical change, with the advent of steam propulsion in 1833, iron hulls in 1837 and steel hulls in 1856. Sailing-ships reached their peak in the fast, elegant "clippers" that competed to transport commodities such as tea from China in record time. Yet by mid-century, purpose-built steamships with efficient engines were beginning to provide stiff competition for sailing vessels. Sail was dealt a further blow when the new canals cut at Suez, Kiel and Panama spared the need for long and often treacherous voyages around land-masses (▷ 5.14, 5.23). Between 1850 and 1914 the world's merchant fleet expanded from 9 million net tonnes to over 35 million tonnes in 1914.

Increased global trade required changes in the way the world's economy

1834 Official creation of *Zollverein* (customs union; begun 1819) stimulates trade in Germany

1821 Gold standard is adopted as monetary system for the first time in Britain

1865 First transatlantic telegraph cable is successfully laid

1856 Efficient steelmaking process is invented by Henry Bessemer

TIMELINE

| The Americas |
| Europe |
| Middle East |
| Africa |
| Asia and Australasia |

1825   1850   1875

1838 *Great Western* launched: first transatlantic passenger steamship

1839–60 China is coerced into foreign trade by two "Opium Wars" with west

1840 Introduction of postal stamps in Britain initiates efficient mail services

1853 US naval expedition opens up Japan to world trade

1859 The world's first oilwell is sunk in Pennsylvania (USA)

1859 Port Said (Egypt) founded; becomes world's main ship-coaling station

1869 First transcontinental railroad completed (USA)

1876 Telephone is patented by Alexander Graham Bell; 50,000 in the USA by 1880

1877 Frozen meat is shipped for the first time, from Argentina to France

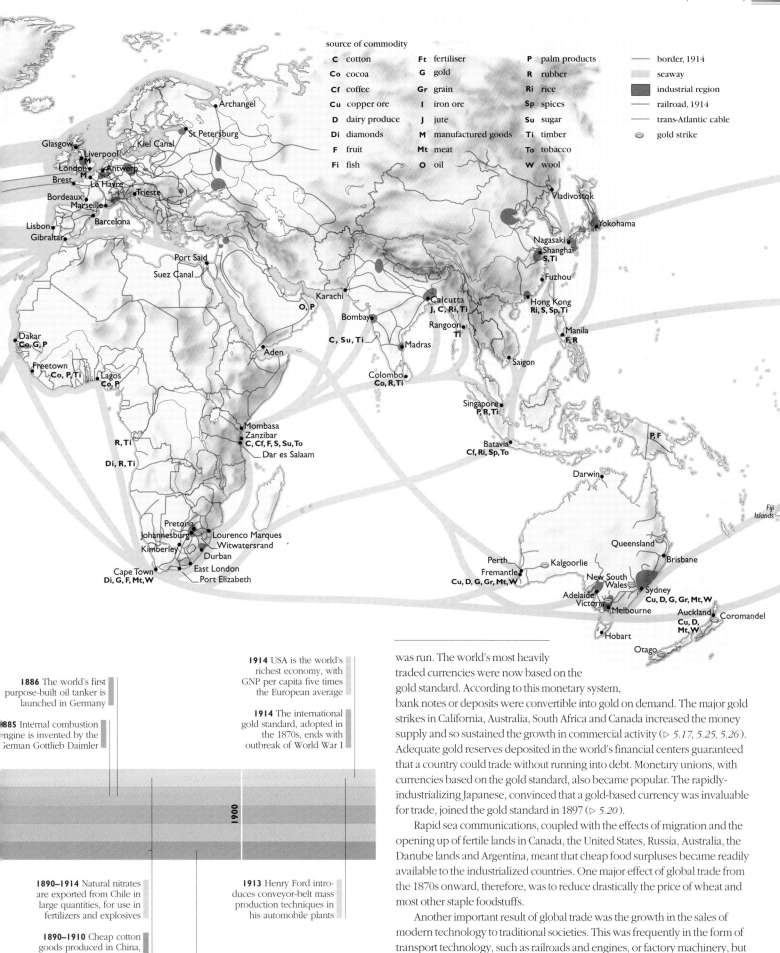

source of commodity

C	cotton	**Ft**	fertiliser	**P**	palm products	
Co	cocoa	**G**	gold	**R**	rubber	
Cf	coffee	**Gr**	grain	**Ri**	rice	
Cu	copper ore	**I**	iron ore	**Sp**	spices	
D	dairy produce	**J**	jute	**Su**	sugar	
Di	diamonds	**M**	manufactured goods	**Ti**	timber	
F	fruit	**Mt**	meat	**To**	tobacco	
Fi	fish	**O**	oil	**W**	wool	

—— border, 1914
▭ seaway
▮ industrial region
------ railroad, 1914
—— trans-Atlantic cable
◉ gold strike

Map labels: Archangel, Glasgow, Kiel Canal, St Petersburg, Liverpool, London, M, Antwerp, Brest, Le Havre, Bordeaux, Trieste, Marseille, Lisbon, Barcelona, Gibraltar, Vladivostok, Yokohama, Nagasaki, Shanghai S,Ti, Fuzhou, Port Said, Suez Canal, Karachi, O,P, Calcutta J, C, Ri, Ti, Hong Kong Ri, S, Sp, Ti, Bombay, Rangoon Ti, Manila F, R, C, Su, Ti, Madras, Aden, Saigon, Colombo Co, R, Ti, Dakar Co, G, P, Freetown Co, P, Ti, Lagos Co, P, Singapore P, R, Ti, Mombasa, Zanzibar C, Cf, F, S, Su, To, Dar es Salaam, Batavia Cf, Ri, Sp, To, R, Ti, Di, R, Ti, P, F, Darwin, Fiji Islands, Pretoria, Johannesburg, Lourenco Marques, Kimberley, Witwatersrand, Durban, Cape Town Di, G, F, Mt, W, East London, Port Elizabeth, Queensland, Brisbane, Perth, Kalgoorlie, Fremantle, New South Wales, Cu, D, G, Gr, Mt, W, Adelaide, Victoria, Sydney Cu, D, G, Gr, Mt, W, Melbourne, Auckland Cu, D, Mt, W, Coromandel, Hobart, Otago

1886 The world's first purpose-built oil tanker is launched in Germany

1885 Internal combustion engine is invented by the German Gottlieb Daimler

1914 USA is the world's richest economy, with GNP per capita five times the European average

1914 The international gold standard, adopted in the 1870s, ends with outbreak of World War I

1900

1890–1914 Natural nitrates are exported from Chile in large quantities, for use in fertilizers and explosives

1890–1910 Cheap cotton goods produced in China, India and Japan undercut European cotton industry

1895 Malayan rubber plantations begin production

1913 Henry Ford introduces conveyor-belt mass production techniques in his automobile plants

was run. The world's most heavily traded currencies were now based on the gold standard. According to this monetary system, bank notes or deposits were convertible into gold on demand. The major gold strikes in California, Australia, South Africa and Canada increased the money supply and so sustained the growth in commercial activity (▷ 5.17, 5.25, 5.26). Adequate gold reserves deposited in the world's financial centers guaranteed that a country could trade without running into debt. Monetary unions, with currencies based on the gold standard, also became popular. The rapidly-industrializing Japanese, convinced that a gold-based currency was invaluable for trade, joined the gold standard in 1897 (▷ 5.20).

Rapid sea communications, coupled with the effects of migration and the opening up of fertile lands in Canada, the United States, Russia, Australia, the Danube lands and Argentina, meant that cheap food surpluses became readily available to the industrialized countries. One major effect of global trade from the 1870s onward, therefore, was to reduce drastically the price of wheat and most other staple foodstuffs.

Another important result of global trade was the growth in the sales of modern technology to traditional societies. This was frequently in the form of transport technology, such as railroads and engines, or factory machinery, but also increasingly came to comprise advanced military hardware. The balance of power in regional conflicts was radically altered by this development ▮

Enlightenment thinkers of the mid-18th century often emphasized people's right to self-determination through a system of representative government. In this they expressed a hostility to the repressive forces – clerics, aristocrats and absolute monarchs – that still reigned supreme throughout Europe in the 18th century. Fueled by poverty, inflation and food shortages, and inspired by the successful revolution of American colonists against the British, this discontent was soon to erupt.

Uprisings occurred in 1784, when the Patriot party in the Dutch Netherlands tried to democratize government, and in 1787, when citizens of the neighboring territory of the Austrian Netherlands (Belgium) attempted to establish an independent republic. Neither insurrection achieved its goals.

A more widely based protest began against the *ancien régime* (autocratic royal government) in France when Louis XVI tried to raise taxes to avert state bankruptcy. He summoned the Estates-General – a periodic assembly of deputies from the three "Estates" (clergy, nobility, and commoners) – to approve his plans. However, Louis was faced with a political crisis when the Third Estate (made up of the rising middle class) withdrew to found a National Assembly and institute reform. Parisians feared an attack on the Assembly by Louis' forces and, on 14 July 1789, stormed the Bastille fortress, symbol of Bourbon tyranny. The rebellion spread rapidly .

In August 1789 the Assembly abolished the feudal system and issued its *Declaration of the Rights of Man*, which proclaimed freedom of conscience, property and speech, and established the principle that sovereign power resided in the nation rather than the king. After failing to escape from the country in 1791, Louis was compelled to approve a constitution that divested him of most of his power. By this stage, aristocrats who had managed to flee France had persuaded Prussia and the Habsburg

empire (Austria) to intervene on Louis' behalf. Opposition to revolutionary France soon crystallized into the First Coalition of European powers. The ensuing Revolutionary Wars (1792–1802) saw the French repulse an initial invasion and then go on the attack. The king and queen and many of their aristocratic supporters were executed, counter-revolutionary risings were suppressed, internecine struggles broke out among the revolutionaries (the "Terror"), and the French tried to export revolution to their hostile neighbors the Netherlands, Spain and Britain (where they fomented rebellion in Ireland).

The First Coalition was broken by a series of French victories in 1794–95, culminating in a

successful invasion of the Netherlands (ruled by France as the Batavian Republic until 1806). Prussia and Spain sued for peace, leaving Britain and the Habsburg empire isolated. Britain, though, maintained naval supremacy with victories over France, and latterly its Dutch and Spanish allies, from 1794–97. In 1798 a Second Coalition was formed.

Napoleon Bonaparte now began to emerge as the greatest of the French commanders through his brilliant campaigns in Italy and Austria. By late 1797, he had forced Austria to cede the Austrian Netherlands to France in exchange for Venice, in a peace treaty that also created French satellite states in northern Italy. As a prelude to his planned invasion

Legend

⎯⎯	borders, 1783
	border of Holy Roman empire, 1783
	Austrian Habsburg territory, 1783
	France, 1783
	Brandenburg-Prussia, 1783
	Great Britain & Hanover, 1783
	Ottoman empire, 1783
	Spanish Bourbon territory, 1783
	Russian empire, 1783
	Russian gains by 1795
	Brandenburg-Prussian gains by 1795
	Austrian Habsburg gains by 1797
	French gains by 1800
Roman Republic	state established by Revolutionary France
	extent of the "Great Fear" within France, 1789
	French counter-revolution, 1793
➜	French campaign, 1796–98
➜	Russian campaign, 1798–1800
🔥	town bombarded by Russian Black Sea fleet
⚓	Naval mutiny in Great Britain
✳	major revolt, riot or disorder

THE SANS-CULOTTE, "man without breeches", symbolized the radical republicans of France in 1790.

TIMELINE

Revolts

1784–87 Revolts occur in Dutch and Austrian Netherlands

1788 Louis XVI of France summons the Estates-General

1789 French Revolution begins; the Bastille is stormed

1793 Execution of Louis XVI; a royalist rebellion begins in the Vendée

1794 Tadeusz Kosciuszko leads a national rebellion in Poland

1797 Mutinies in the British Royal Navy at Spithead and the Nore

1798 United Irishmen rebel in a vain effort to win independence from Britain

Revolutionary wars

1792 The Prussians are checked at Valmy; Austrians are defeated at Jemappes

1793 France blocks Anglo-Hanoverians at Hondschoote; defeats Austrians at Wattignies

1794 Britain beats France at the Battle of the First of June

1798 The French defeat the Mamlukes at the Battle of the Pyramids but are defeated by British at Battle of the Nile

1799 Bonaparte returns to France and seizes power

1800 Bonaparte defeats the Austrians at Marengo

Alliances & treaties

1783 Britain recognizes the independence of the United States in the Treaty of Paris

1792 Austria and Prussia ally against France: start of the French revolutionary wars

1793 Second Partition of Poland; Spain, Holland, Britain and the empire join First Coalition against France

1795 Third Partition of Poland

1797 Treaty of Campo Formio follows the French defeat of Austria

1798 Second Coalition against France

1 In July and August 1789, a series of panics known as the "Great Fear" swept the French countryside, caused by rumors of brigands in the pay of aristocrats.

2 The Jacobin Maximilien Robespierre came to power in Paris in July 1793, initiating the revolutionary "Terror" and executing over a thousand people in the following twelve months.

3 The main counter-revolutionary revolt took place in the Vendée region of western France in 1793, and was brutally suppressed.

4 The Polish uprising against Russian rule in 1794 was led by Tadeusz Kosciuszko. Defeated and exiled, he refused to support subsequent attempts by France and Russia to grant Poland nominal independence.

5 Despite victories over France and its allies, harsh conditions in Britain's Royal Navy caused low morale, which led to two serious mutinies in 1797.

6 The French were persuaded by Wolfe Tone to support Irish risings against British rule. The rising of 1798 failed, and Tone committed suicide in prison.

---

of Britain, Bonaparte threatened Britain's trade route to India by attacking Egypt in 1798. Though victorious against Egypt's Mamluke rulers, his fleet was defeated by the British admiral Nelson at the Battle of the Nile. In response to reverses in Italy and on the Rhine, Bonaparte returned to France, overthrew the committee that had ruled France since 1795 (the "Directory") and installed himself as military dictator.

French military fortunes proceeded to rise; Napoleon's generals blocked an Anglo-Russian expedition to the Batavian Republic and defeated the Russians at Zürich, while he himself masterminded the defeat of the Austrians at Marengo (1800). Yet though his forces were all-powerful on land, his lack

of naval superiority meant that he could not prevent raids from the Russian Black Sea fleet in 1798–1800, or – more importantly – deliver a decisive blow against the Second Coalition.

In eastern Europe, Poland embarked on a course of constitutional reform modeled on Enlightenment ideas in the 1790s. Russia under Catherine II, which had annexed part of the country in 1772, responded by invading in 1792. Further regions were annexed by Russia and Prussia in the Second Partition (1793). A rebellion against the foreign overlords ended with the capitulation of Warsaw in 1794, and the Third Partition (1795) saw the disappearance of Poland as a sovereign country for over 120 years.

See also 5.08 (Napoleonic Europe)

French victories in 1800 virtually secured the defeat of Austria, but British naval power still frustrated Napoleon Bonaparte. His army in Egypt was forced out by the British in 1801, while the Danish fleet he hoped would keep Britain from the Baltic was destroyed at Copenhagen in the same year. A respite from war was confirmed by the Treaty of Amiens in 1802, enabling Britain to implement the Act of Union which incorporated Ireland into the United Kingdom, improving the islands' security.

War broke out again, however, in the spring of 1803. Napoleon revived his plan to invade Britain, which now stood alone against France, but he was unable to put it into action because of the undiminished strength of the Royal Navy. Britain's comprehensive naval victory at Trafalgar (1805), and the formation of the Third Coalition later that year, focussed Napoleon's attention back on the armies of Austria, overwhelming them at Ulm and Austerlitz. In 1806, Napoleon proclaimed the dissolution of the Holy Roman empire, united all the German states (apart from Austria and Prussia) into the Confederation of the Rhine, and then moved north to smash the Prussians at Jena–Auerstädt.

As in his earlier campaigns, Napoleon's generalship was unsurpassed and his army irresistible: the Treaty of Tilsit that followed his defeat of a Russian army at Friedland in 1807 broke the Third Coalition and placed Napoleon at the height of his power. He now turned to blockading all legitimate trade with Britain. The so-called "Continental System," established in Napoleon's Berlin and Milan decrees (1806, 1807), was designed to force the British to buy overpriced smuggled goods, thus depleting their gold reserves. Britain retaliated by prohibiting all French trade between one port and another.

Between 1804 (when he declared himself emperor) and 1814, Napoleon imposed his administrative and political ideas upon a conquered Europe while countering British attempts to probe the weak points in the continental blockade. In all his vassal states, he introduced the *Code Napoléon*, the French civil code that enshrined the revolutionary principles of equality and liberty, and provided the protection of private property.

A new phase of the Napoleonic wars opened in 1808, when a French army marched across the Iberian peninsula to force Portugal to adopt the Continental System. This sparked a uprising in Spain against the French, while the British under the command of Wellington established a base in Portugal. In a war of shifting fortunes, a number of hard-fought battles drained the reserves of both sides. At the same time, Napoleon was obliged to conduct another campaign against the Austrians, finally overcoming them at Wagram (1809) to reassert his position as master of Europe. Although this victory allowed Napoleon to concentrate his forces on Spain and temporarily reverse his setbacks suffered there, his decision to attack Russia in 1812 – again to enforce the Continental System – radically altered the situation. The campaign was a huge drain on men and supplies; after hunger, winter and Russian resistance forced a withdrawal from Moscow in late 1812, Napoleon's enemies seized the opportunity to create a Fourth Coalition. For the first time since 1795, a united Europe front opposed France.

Even the retreat from Russia did not break Napoleon's power; in 1813, his forces were still able to resist the new coalition at Lützen, Bautzen and Dresden but suffered heavy casualties in doing so. The loss of troops in Russia, combined with the huge international force ranged against him, finally proved decisive. At Leipzig – in the "Battle of the Nations"– Napoleon suffered his first major defeat and was forced to quit Germany. At the same time, Wellington managed to push north to Toulouse and conclude the Peninsular War. Allied armies pressed home their attack from Germany, and threatened Paris in 1814. Napoleon now abdicated and was sent into exile on the Mediterranean island of Elba.

While the victorious allies were redrawing the map of Europe at the Congress of Vienna, Napoleon escaped from exile and re-entered France in a final attempt to rebuild his empire. In his so-called "Hundred Days", he reformed his armies and challenged the combined British, Dutch and Prussian forces at Waterloo. The ensuing battle was closely contested, but ended in final defeat for Napoleon. He abdicated for a second time and was exiled to St Helena in the south Atlantic, where he died. Europe was finally at peace after twenty-three years of war.

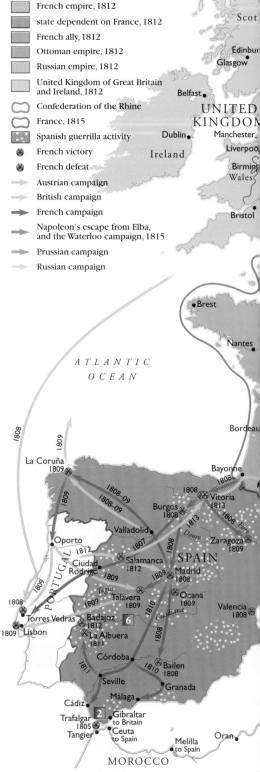

- borders, 1812
- French empire, 1812
- state dependent on France, 1812
- French ally, 1812
- Ottoman empire, 1812
- Russian empire, 1812
- United Kingdom of Great Britain and Ireland, 1812
- Confederation of the Rhine
- France, 1815
- Spanish guerrilla activity
- ⊗ French victory
- ⊗ French defeat
- → Austrian campaign
- → British campaign
- → French campaign
- → Napoleon's escape from Elba, and the Waterloo campaign, 1815
- → Prussian campaign
- → Russian campaign

TIMELINE

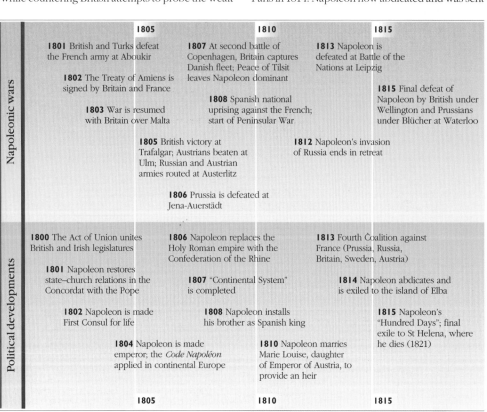

Napoleonic wars

	1805	1810	1815
	1801 British and Turks defeat the French army at Aboukir	**1807** At second battle of Copenhagen, Britain captures Danish fleet; Peace of Tilsit leaves Napoleon dominant	**1813** Napoleon is defeated at Battle of the Nations at Leipzig
	1802 The Treaty of Amiens is signed by Britain and France		
	1803 War is resumed with Britain over Malta	**1808** Spanish national uprising against the French; start of Peninsular War	**1815** Final defeat of Napoleon by British under Wellington and Prussians under Blücher at Waterloo
	1805 British victory at Trafalgar; Austrians beaten at Ulm; Russian and Austrian armies routed at Austerlitz	**1812** Napoleon's invasion of Russia ends in retreat	
	1806 Prussia is defeated at Jena-Auerstädt		

Political developments

	1805	1810	1815
	1800 The Act of Union unites British and Irish legislatures	**1806** Napoleon replaces the Holy Roman empire with the Confederation of the Rhine	**1813** Fourth Coalition against France (Prussia, Russia, Britain, Sweden, Austria)
	1801 Napoleon restores state–church relations in the Concordat with the Pope	**1807** "Continental System" is completed	**1814** Napoleon abdicates and is exiled to the island of Elba
	1802 Napoleon is made First Consul for life	**1808** Napoleon installs his brother as Spanish king	**1815** Napoleon's "Hundred Days"; final exile to St Helena, where he dies (1821)
	1804 Napoleon is made emperor; the *Code Napoléon* applied in continental Europe	**1810** Napoleon marries Marie Louise, daughter of Emperor of Austria, to provide an heir	
	1805	1810	1815

Map labels

North Sea

Helsinki
St Petersburg
Revel

Christiania

SWEDEN
1815 union with Norway

Göteborg

Stockholm

Vänern

Vättern

Gotland

Riga

Lake Peipus

Baltic Sea

Moscow 1812

Borodino 1812

Maloyaroslavets 1812

Smolensk 1812

Vitebsk 1812

Krasnoi 1812

Vilna

Berezina 1812

Minsk

Kovno

Tilsit

Königsberg

Friedland 1807

Danzig

Eylau 1807

East Prussia

Western Dvina

RUSSIAN EMPIRE

Kharkov

Kiev

Copenhagen 1801, 1807

Swedish Pomerania 1815 to Prussia

Heligoland 1807–14 to Britain

MECKLENBURG-SCHWERIN

Hamburg

Bremen

Pomerania

PRUSSIA 1807–13 allied to France

Stettin

Brandenburg

Berlin 1813

GRAND DUCHY OF WARSAW 1815 to Russia

Warsaw

Amsterdam

Holland

WESTPHALIA

HESSE

BERG

Frankfurt

Jena-Auerstädt 1806

Lützen 1813

SAXONY

Leipzig 1813

Dresden 1813

Bautzen 1813

Silesia

Oder

Elbe

Galicia and Lodomeria

Dniester

Vistula

Waterloo 1815

Brussels

Ligny 1815

Laon 1814

Reims 1814

Hanau 1813

Würzburg

Prague

Moravia

Austrian Silesia

Bessarabia 1812 to Russian empire

Château Thierry 1814

Paris 1814

Champaubert 1814

Mannheim

Bohemia

Austerlitz 1805

Montmirail & Vauchamps 1814

La Fère 1814

Champenoise 1814

WÜRTTEMBERG

Ratisbon 1809

Ulm 1805

Wagram 1809

AUSTRIAN EMPIRE 1809–13 allied to France

Bukovina

Jassy

Moldavia

Sebastopol

Orléans 1814

Montereau 1814

BADEN

Basel

Munich

BAVARIA

Ebersberg 1809

Salzburg

Vienna

Aspern 1809

Styria

Hungary

Transylvania

1806–12 under Russian occupation

Bucharest

Black Sea

FRANCE

Zürich

Berne

HELVETIA

Carinthia

Banat

Wallachia

Varna

Geneva

Lyon

Grenoble

Turin

Milan

Venice

Illyrian Provinces

Slavonia

Sava

Belgrade

Serbia

Danube

Bulgaria

Edirne

Genoa

ITALY

Bosnia

Herzegovina

MONTENEGRO

Constantinople

Toulouse 1814

Avignon

Marseille

Cannes

LUCCA

Florence

Tuscany

PIOMBINO

Papal States

Rome

NAPLES

BENEVENTO

Albania

Üsküb

Rumelia

ANATOLIA

OTTOMAN EMPIRE

Andorra

Corsica

Elba

Sardinia

Ajaccio

Catalonia 1812–13 to France

Barcelona 1808

Naples

Janina

Corfu to Russia, 1807 to France, 1815 to Britain

Balearic Islands

Palermo

Messina

SICILY

Ionian Islands to Russia, 1807 to France, 1809 to Britain

Morea

Athens

Rhodes

Tunis

Cythera to Russia, 1807 to France, 1809 to Britain

Crete

ALGIERS

Tunis

Malta to Britain

Mediterranean Sea

THE LÉGION D'HONNEUR, an award for all ranks for notable service to France, was created by Napoleon in 1802.

Cyrene

Cyrenaica

Aboukir 1799, 1801

Alexandria

EGYPT

Hull

ngland

ondon

ologne

Amiens

Numbered notes

1 By the Treaty of Amiens (March 1802), Britain and France both agreed to return most conquests made since 1793. Peace, though, lasted barely a year.

2 The Battle of Trafalgar, in which the French lost over half of their ships, ended Napoleon's plans to invade Britain. British commander Lord Nelson died of injuries sustained in the action.

3 Borodino was a costly victory for Napoleon, who lost a quarter of his men. Only 30,000 troops of an original French force of 600,000 survived the Russian campaign.

4 Napoleon planned to invade England from Boulogne in 1804, and assembled a fleet of 2,000 ships; he failed, however, to control the Channel.

5 Naval bombardment forced Denmark to surrender its fleet to Britain in 1807, further weakening French opposition to British sea power.

6 Napoleonic armies lived off the land in invaded countries, a strategy that brought disaster in the severe Russian winter of 1812–13. In contrast, British success in the Peninsular War was based on sustaining strong defensive positions with supplies from home.

0 ___ 600 km
0 ___ 400 mi

See also 5.07 (revolutionary Europe); 5.08 (mid-19th-century Europe); 5.10 (Industrial Revolution)

The decades after 1815 saw the emergence of nationalism in the aftermath of Napoleon's imperial rule. Liberals and democrats demanded nation-states embracing a common racial and linguistic identity and embodying constitutionally guaranteed rights for their citizens. Only a few nation-states were actually created in the early 19th century: Belgium, the Netherlands, Switzerland and Greece. More often, the monarchies restored after the fall of Napoleon (Prussia, Austria and Russia) stifled the nascent democracies. The strongest states to emerge – Italy and the German second empire – did so not through popular nationalist uprisings, but by coalescing around dynamic existing monarchies (Sardinia–Piedmont and Prussia respectively).

The Congress of Vienna (1814–15), convened at Napoleon's defeat, was intended to create a balance of power. Under the leadership of the conservative Austrian foreign minister Clemens Metternich, the Congress restored hereditary monarchies, created new enlarged kingdoms by unifying Norway with Sweden and Belgium with Holland, and established the "concert of Europe": congresses to deal with threats to political stability. A few concessions were made to nationalism: the Turkish sultan granted a measure of self-government to Serbia (1817) and to Moldavia and Wallachia (1829). However, when revolutions broke out in Naples, Spain and Portugal, the congresses at Troppau, Laibach and Verona authorized intervention; France sent troops to help conservatives suppress a liberal regime in Spain in 1823.

The Greek revolt against Ottoman rule broke out in 1821. The Greeks won control of the Peloponnese (Morea) by early 1822 when they declared Greece a sovereign state, but Turkish forces, bolstered by Egyptian troops, reinvaded in 1825. The conservative nature of the Greek rebellion, combined with strategic machinations against the crumbling Ottoman empire, led the European powers to approve

an autonomous Greek state. A British, French and Russian naval force destroyed the Turkish–Egyptian fleet at Navarino, and the Ottomans conceded Greek independence in 1832.

Revolutions in Modena, Parma, the Papal States, Poland and some areas of Germany broke out in 1830–31 but were all suppressed. The reactionary regime of Bourbon Charles X in France was ended by the July Revolution of 1830, though this lead not to a new republic but to the accession of the "citizen-king" Louis-Philippe. In the same year, Belgium began its struggle for independence from the Dutch.

The Congress of Vienna had replaced Napoleon's German state with an alliance of 39 states headed by Austria and Prussia, known as the German Confederation. Prussia gradually gained ascendancy, partly by forming the *Zollverein* free trade zone from 1819–44, isolating protectionist Austria.

The most serious challenge to Metternich came in 1848, the "Year of Revolutions". The catalyst was the fall of Louis-Philippe's regime to republicans in February. Unrest spread to Hungary, Croatia, and the Czech lands, where liberal governments were installed and democratic constitutions drafted. Metternich was forced to resign and flee abroad. Republics were proclaimed throughout Italy and a

Legend

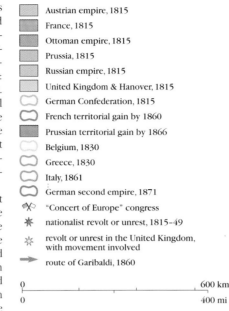

═══	borders, 1815
	Austrian empire, 1815
	France, 1815
	Ottoman empire, 1815
	Prussia, 1815
	Russian empire, 1815
	United Kingdom & Hanover, 1815
◯	German Confederation, 1815
◯	French territorial gain by 1860
	Prussian territorial gain by 1866
◯	Belgium, 1830
◯	Greece, 1830
◯	Italy, 1861
◯	German second empire, 1871
⚔	"Concert of Europe" congress
✳	nationalist revolt or unrest, 1815–49
✴	revolt or unrest in the United Kingdom, with movement involved
→	route of Garibaldi, 1860

```
0                    600 km
0                    400 mi
```

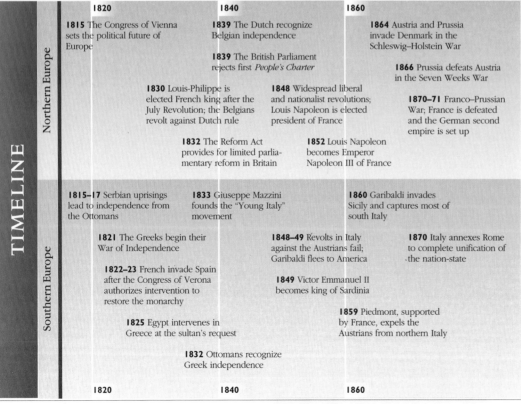

Map labels

Scotla
Edinbur
Glasgow
UNITED KINGDOM
Ireland
Dublin
Manches
1867 Fen
Liverpool
Wales
Birming
Tipperary 1848
Newport 1839 Chartists,
Bristol
Brest
ATLANTIC OCEAN
Nantes
Bordea
La Coruña 1820
Oviedo 1820
Pamplona 1820
Burgos
Oporto 1820, 1830
PORTUGAL
Valladolid
Zaragoza 1820
Doure
Salamanca
SPAIN
Madrid
Tagus
Lisbon 1820
Guadiana
Valencia 1820
Córdoba
Seville
Granada
Cádiz 1820
Málaga
Gibraltar to Britain
Tangier
Ceuta to Spain
Oran
Melilla to Spain
MOROCCO

NORWAY

SWEDEN
Union from 1815

Christiania

Stockholm

Vänern

Vättern

Göteborg

Gotland

*North
Sea*

Baltic Sea

Helsinki

Revel

St Petersburg
1825

Riga

*Lake
Peipus*

DENMARK
Copenhagen

Schleswig
1865 to Prussia

Holstein
1865 to Austria,
1866 to Prussia

Hamburg

Bremen

HANOVER
1866 to Prussia

Oldenburg

Amsterdam

BRUNSWICK

1830

1830

MECKLENBURG
SCHWERIN

Königsberg

Danzig

East Prussia

Pomerania

Stettin

PRUSSIA

Brandenburg

Berlin
1848

Poznan
1848

Warsaw
1830–31, 1848

Poland

Vistula

RUSSIAN
EMPIRE

NETHERLANDS

Westphalia

Brussels
1830, 1848

Belgium

Aix-la-Chapelle
1818

1830

HESSE

Frankfurt
1833, 1848

Dresden
1848

SAXONY

Prague
1848

Bohemia

Brünn
(Brno)
1848

Moravia

1815

Krakow
1846, 1848

1847 to Austrian empire

Troppau
1820

Oder

Silesia

1830

Lvov
(Lemberg)
1848

Galicia and Lodomeria

Dniester

Luxembourg

Palatinate
1815 to Bavaria

BADEN

BAVARIA
WÜRTTEMBERG

Hohenzollern

Munich
1848

Salzburg

1849

Rhine

Linz
1848

Vienna
1848

Austria

Pressburg
1848

Buda
1848

AUSTRIAN EMPIRE

Debrecen
1848

Koloszvar
1848

Transylvania

MOLDAVIA
1829 autonomous

Jassy
1848

Ochakov

FRANCE

Paris
1830, 1832,
1848

Alsace–Lorraine
1871 to German empire

Loire

Zürich

Berne

SWITZERLAND

Geneva

Lyon
1831, 1834, 1848

1860 to
France

Savoy
1815–30

Milan
1848

Brescia
1815–30

Magenta
1859

Turin
1815–30

Lombardy

Piedmont
to Sardinia

Avignon
1815–48 to Sardinia
1848 to France

Genoa
1834

Parma

Salzburg

Tyrol

Carinthia

Styria

Carniola

Venetia
1866 to Italy

Verona
1822

Solferino
1859

Venice
1848

Laibach
1821

MODENA

1831

Agram
1848

Belgrade

Sava

Danube

Slavonia

Bosnia

Herzegovina

Dalmatia

Temesvár
1849

Blaj
1848

Hungary

WALLACHIA
1829 autonomous

SERBIA
1817 autonomous

Bucharest
1848

Varna

*Black
Sea*

Sebastopol

MONACO
1861 independent

ANDORRA

Toulouse

Corsica

LUCCA

Tuscany

Florence
1849

Talamone

Macerata
1831

PAPAL STATES

Rome
1848

Volturno
1860

Naples
1820, 1848

Salerno
1815–30

BENEVENTO

Bari
1815–30

Reggio
1815–30

Milazzo
1860

KINGDOM OF THE TWO SICILIES

Palermo
1848–49

Catalfimi
1860

Sicily

Sardinia

Balearic Islands
to Spain

Barcelona
1820

Algiers

Tunis

ALGIERS
occupied by France from 1830
but not fully subjugated until 1848

*Malta
to Britain*

Tunis

*Mediterranean
Sea*

MONTENEGRO

Üsküb

OTTOMAN
EMPIRE

Macedonia

Albania

Janina

Ionian Islands
1815–63 to Britain
1863 to Greece

Missolonghi
1826

Athens

Morea

Navarino
1827

Bulgaria

*Cythera
1815–63 to Britain
1863 to Greece*

LORD BYRON, the British
Romantic poet, was inspired
by the cause of Greek
independence and died at
Missolonghi in 1824.

London
1867 Fenians

1. The reunification of the northern and southern
Netherlands in 1815 under the Protestant Dutch
monarchy caused resentment in Catholic Belgium.

2. Ferdinand VII, king of Spain (r.1808–33) brutally
suppressed liberal opposition after his return from
exile in 1814. In 1820, the army he had assembled to
reassert his rule in Latin America rose against him.

3. An early challenge to the rule of Louis-Philippe
occurred in Lyon in 1831, when 600 protestors were
killed in rioting.

4. A Roman republic was established by radicals
(including Garibaldi) in 1848–49, but was ended
when French troops restored Pope Pius IX to power

5. The head of the Bonaparte dynasty, Louis
Napoleon, was elected French president in 1848. He
became emperor Napoleon III after a coup (1851),
but was exiled after defeat by Prussia in 1871.

parliamentary assembly met in Frankfurt with the aim of uniting Germany. Yet internal divisions prevailed, and by late 1849 the Habsburgs regained control in Austria, Italy and Hungary (the latter with Russian help); the German assembly collapsed under pressure from Prussia, which consolidated its power by means of swift victories over Denmark, Austria and France.

In Italy, revolutionary movements from 1820 onward, such as the Carbonari, had failed to expel the Austrians or unite the country. In mid-century an unlikely champion arose of the unification movement (*Risorgimento* or "resurrection"): the rich industrial state of Sardinia–Piedmont. The Piedmontese king Victor Emmanuel II and his prime minister Camillo di Cavour instituted liberal domestic reforms and secured the help of Napoleon III's France to drive the Austrians from northern Italy in 1859. The liberal constitutional monarchy sought by Piedmont was threatened when the revolutionary Giuseppe Garibaldi and his "redshirts" took Sicily and overran much of the southern mainland. Yet Garibaldi passed his conquests to Victor Emmanuel II, who effectively became king of a united Italy.

Britain was less affected by nationalist agitation, though the Chartists – supporters of a "People's Charter" – sought universal manhood suffrage after limited parliamentary reform was conceded in 1832. Irish nationalism was given urgency by the famine of 1845–47, and the Irish Republican Brotherhood (Fenians), precursor of the movement that won Irish independence in 1921, was set up in 1858.

See also 5.08 (Napoleonic Europe); 5.11 (the rise
of Germany); 5.10 (Industrial Revolution)

From the last quarter of the 18th century to the outbreak of World War I, Europe was transformed from a series of traditional agrarian communities into a collection of modern industrial nations. Radical changes in the methods by which goods were produced – the widespread adoption of capitalism, mechanization and the factory system – gave rise to a period of unparalleled economic growth, though interrrupted by cyclical depressions. There was also a rapid increase in population and an influx of people from the countryside into the towns and cities that sprang up around the new workplaces.

The Industrial Revolution, as this transformation came to be known, had its origins in Britain. Its effects were first seen in the cotton and woollen industries in the north of the country. Mechanical innovations improved the speed and efficiency of weaving, and required new factories powered first by waterwheels and later by steam engines. These factories brought together the various operations involved in textile manufacture. Britain was ideally placed to pioneer and develop mass production, possessing abundant natural resources to power the new machinery, favorable terrain on which to construct extensive transport networks (canals in the late 18th and early 19th centuries, and rail from the 1830s onward), and a ready market for manufactured goods. By 1815, Britain's industrialists had already made it the "workshop of the world", with coal mining, textile production and pig-iron smelting exceeding the output of the rest of Europe combined. Industrialization had spread to mainland Europe at the end of the 18th century (for example, in the Belgian armaments industry or cotton weaving in Saxony and northern France), but Britain's embargo on the emigration of skilled artisans and the export of machinery during the Napoleonic period prevented a wider adoption of the new methods of production.

Beginning in the 1820s in Belgium, however, coal mining and the textile and metal industries took root in continental Europe. As in Britain, the new rail network played a prime role in promoting economic expansion; rail transport allowed rapid distribution of goods and its consumption

TIMELINE

Technological change

1783–84 A new purifying process makes iron smelting more efficient

1787 Edmund Cartwright (Br) invents the steam-operated weaving loom

1795 Joseph Bramah (Br) invents the hydraulic press

1800 Henry Maudslay (Br) invents the precision screw-cutting lathe

1825 The Stockton and Darlington Railway opens

1831 Michael Faraday (Br) builds the first electric motor and generator

1835 Germany's first railroad is opened (Bavaria)

1837 The first French railroad links Paris with Saint-Germain

1856 Henry Bessemer (Br) pioneers manfacture of steel from iron ore; first commercial synthetic dye is produced

1861 Siemens-Martin open-hearth steelmaking process (Ger)

1876 Nikolaus Otto (Ger) invents the internal-combustion engine

1878 The first electric street-lighting appears in London

1883 Orient Express brings rail travel between Paris and Constantinople

1885 Daimler and Benz develop the automobile (Ger)

1909 Bakelite, the first commercially viable plastic, is patented (Belgium)

Social change

1799–1800 Prohibition of trade unions in Britain

1833 Britain's Factory Act places restrictions on use of children in industry

1846 Corn Law repeal in Britain begins free trade era

1878 Dissolution of the German Social Democratic Party

1880–89 Bismarck introduces state social welfare system

1909–10 National strikes by rail and postal workers in France

border, 1914

heavy industrial or mining area

major textile manufacturing area

other large coal deposit

other large iron ore deposit

urban population, 1914

• under 100,000

■ 100,000–500,000

■ 500,000–1,000,000

◆ over 1,000,000

⚑ oilfield, 1914

⚓ port

⚑ center of socialism

Berlin research and development center for the chemical industry

19m national population (million) where known, 1914

railroad constructed by 1870

railroad constructed 1870–1914

0 ————— 600 km
0 ————— 400 mi

RUSSIAN EMPIRE
171m

AUSTRO-HUNGARIAN EMPIRE
51m

ROMANIA
7.1m

SERBIA
3.2m

BULGARIA
4.3m

MONTENEGRO
0.6m

GREECE

ANATOLIA

OTTOMAN EMPIRE

Black Sea

CHILD-LABOR was common in the mines of early 19th-century Britain, but was banned in 1842.

more hazardous. Employers exploited the large pool of child and female labor to depress wages. Living conditions deteriorated in the vastly expanding new cities, where sanitation failed to keep pace with population growth. Cholera and typhus epidemics were common. A second bout of industrialization after 1870, based on steel and the new power source of electricity, did little to alleviate these problems.

To challenge the effects of capital, both the industrial working classes and the rural peasantry (serfdom did not end in Russia until 1861) organized themselves into trade unions. These efforts met opposition from the state as well as the capitalists. Ideas for alternative ways of structuring society arose during this period. Socialist parties were formed to argue for a more equal distribution of wealth, becoming particularly strong in Germany and France. Karl Marx and Friedrich Engels published their *Communist Manifesto* in 1848, arguing for a class-based revolution in highly industrialized states such as Britain. Anarchists advocated the violent abolition of the state, while syndicalists sought worker-control of industry through general strikes. To forestall social upheaval, some governments enacted legislation to alleviate the worst effects of industrialization. Compulsory free state education was widely instituted; labor in factories and mines was gradually regulated; working hours were cut and wages rose (as did inflation); improved housing also became slowly available. The first decade of the 20th century was marked by widespread unrest, but the old problem of unemployment would be briefly answered by the demands of World War I.

For many people, the solution to poverty was to emigrate. Nearly half a million Poles moved west to find jobs in the industrialized Ruhr, and Italian farmers took harvest work in Germany, France and Austria. Yet far more people left Europe, emigrating in their millions to Australia and New Zealand, but above all to the Americas.

[1] The world's first railroad to use steam locomotive traction was opened for coal traffic in 1825 between Stockton and Darlington in northeast England.

[2] The new country of Belgium, flat and densely populated, was the first continental European state to complete its rail network, in the 1840s.

[3] A major early corporate investment bank was Crédit Mobilier, founded in Paris in 1852; ill-advised speculation led to the bank's collapse in 1867.

[4] In 1856, one of the world's first oil refineries opened in Ploisti. Foreign investment brought rapid expansion of the Romanian oilfields from 1895.

[5] The major iron-ore deposits in Lorraine were a serious loss to France's nascent steelmaking industry after the area was annexed by Germany in 1871.

[6] The German Social Democratic Party was the strongest prewar socialist party, despite laws banning it. The party claimed 1.5 million members in 1890.

[7] Barcelona and Bilbao were the two main industrial centers of 19th-century Spain; Barcelona's powerful anarcho-syndicalist movement was set up in 1910.

[8] A Luddite (machine-wrecker) revolt (1811–12) ended when its leaders were hanged in York 1813.

of materials stimulated further growth. By 1890 nearly all the main rail routes across Europe had been completed.

Private investment lay behind the success of many major industrial ventures, such as some early railroads, but spectacular bankruptcies showed the need for a new method of funding capital projects. Especially in continental Europe, joint-stock limited liability companies, supported by development banks, were founded to provide credit. Free trade (the abolition of import tariffs protecting local producers from competition) was another crucial factor in industrial expansion. Britain lifted its high import duties on corn in 1846; agreements with France, the Prussian *Zollverein* and Belgium in the 1860s further encouraged the reduction of tariffs. By 1870 most

European countries had expanded foreign trade and industrial production by lowering or abolishing their tariffs – though the position gradually reversed after the Franco-Prussian War (1870–71).

The social effects of the Industrial Revolution were as radical as its technological and financial consequences. The years of growth between 1840–70 also witnessed periodic financial crises and bouts of widespread unemployment. Harvests were critical, causing wild fluctuations in the price of food. Later, the import of cheap foodstuffs from Canada, the United States and Russia undercut agriculture in the industrializing states. New production methods threatened traditional skills, sometimes leading to machine-wrecking by disgruntled workers. As mechanization spread, working conditions became

See also 5.05 (migration); 5.06 (world trade)

In the north German states, the upheavals of 1848–49 largely took the form of political meetings and petitioning. A parliament was convened in Frankfurt by liberal forces to draft a national constitution, but it failed to reach consensus on the most suitable type of future government, and the assembly dissolved in disarray. One major rift was between the advocates of a "small Germany" (*Kleindeutschland*), excluding Austria, under Prussian leadership, and of a "big Germany" (*Grossdeutschland*) that included the huge Habsburg empire. For its part, Austria was anxious to protect its long predominance in central Europe. Thus, having restored internal order by 1850, Austria encouraged disunity among the small German principalities. In the meantime, Prussian influence temporarily declined.

In 1861 Wilhelm I of the Hohenzollern dynasty ascended the Prussian throne. A conservative militarist, Wilhelm had been instrumental in putting down an insurrection in Baden in 1849. On gaining power, he was immediately faced with demands for a constitutional monarchy by liberals in the Prussian *Diet* (parliament), who opposed his plans to expand the army and introduce three-year military conscription. Wilhelm sought a strong minister-president to impose his will on the parliament, and chose Otto Karl von Bismarck (1815–98), an anti-liberal and member of the rightwing *Junker* party. Bismarck's success on the king's behalf began a partnership that was to last until the king's death in 1888, and that became the prime mover of German unification.

Bismarck's policy of strengthening Prussia by asserting its preeminence in the German-speaking world was first seen when Prussian troops (in concert with Austrian forces) were sent to end Danish occupation of the northern duchies of Holstein (1863) and Schleswig (1864). Prussian military expertise prevailed; in the peace settlement, Prussia received Schleswig and Austria gained Holstein.

Tensions between Austria and Prussia over Schleswig–Holstein were soon to erupt. In preparation for conflict, Bismarck had forged a secret alliance, promising Venetia in Italy in return for support against Austria. In a lightning campaign against Austria and its allies in the German Confederation (the Seven Weeks War), the Prussian forces occupied Holstein, moved south by rail and overcame the Hanoverian army at Langensalza, and then invaded Austria. Although the Austrians were successful against Italy, they were overwhelmed by Prussia at the battle of Königgrätz (Sadowa), and sued for peace in the Treaty of Prague. Prussia's swift victory sent shock waves of alarm through Europe.

At a stroke, Bismarck had recast the map of Europe. Prussia gained Holstein, and Italy received Venetia. His new German Confederation of states north of the River Main united all of north Germany except Saxony under the Hohenzollerns; while the south German states were equally dependent upon Berlin through the *Zollverein* (customs union) and a web of mutual defense treaties. Austrian influence in German affairs was irrevocably ended, not by the revolutionary tactics favored in 1848 but through diplomacy and skillful deployment of the new Prussian army.

France was now faced with a new and powerful neighbor in the form of Prussia. Nevertheless, the French emperor Napoleon III (r.1852–70) had a general sympathy for the cause of strong national identity, which led him to intervene in a nationalist rising in Mexico (1863–67) and in Italy. The same impulse led him initially to support Prussian ambitions in northern Germany. Growing fears among his ministers of Prussian dominance of Europe seemed to be vindicated when the vacant Spanish throne was offered to a member of the Hohenzollern dynasty. Although acceptance of the crown was withdrawn, the French felt that national pride demanded an assurance from Wilhelm I that the candidature would never be renewed. Bismarck, who now saw an opportunity to unite the southern German states with Prussia in opposing a common French enemy, manipulated the conciliatory royal reply (the so-called "Ems Telegram") to make it appear a diplomatic insult. An enraged French court duly declared war on Prussia. Prussian commanders

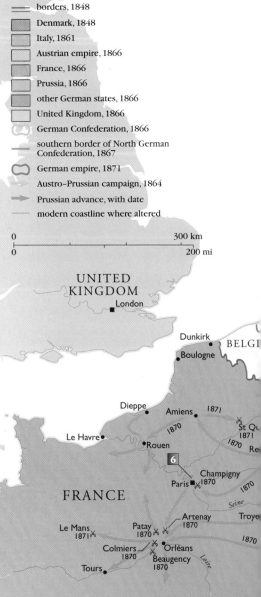

borders, 1848
Denmark, 1848
Italy, 1861
Austrian empire, 1866
France, 1866
Prussia, 1866
other German states, 1866
United Kingdom, 1866
German Confederation, 1866
southern border of North German Confederation, 1867
German empire, 1871
Austro-Prussian campaign, 1864
Prussian advance, with date
modern coastline where altered

0 — 300 km
0 — 200 mi

UNITED KINGDOM
London

Dunkirk
BELGI
Boulogne

Dieppe
Amiens 1871
1870
Le Havre
Rouen 1870
St Qu 1871
Re

6

Champigny
Paris 1870
1870

FRANCE

Seine

Artenay 1870
Troye
Le Mans 1871
Patay 1870
1870
Colmiers 1870
Orléans
Beaugency 1870
Tours
Loire

once again used the mobility of deployment by rail to surprise the enemy; within two weeks, 500,000 troops had invaded France from the Rhineland, pinning down a large French force in the fortress of Metz, and then routing an army sent to relieve it at the Battle of Sedan. Napoleon III was captured and Prussian forces advanced through France to besiege Paris, which eventually fell in January 1871. The Prussians finally conducted successful campaigns against French armies in the provinces.

As Prussia's heavy siege artillery bombarded Paris, at Versailles Wilhelm I was proclaimed *Kaiser*, emperor of a united Germany. The new German "second empire" was a federation of twenty-five states plus the *Reichsland* of Alsace–Lorraine, ceded by a defeated France. Crucially, because German unification had been effected by the centralizing dominance of Prussia, the new Germany was a unitary state, with none of the multinationalism that had so weakened its erstwhile rival, Austria.

Meanwhile Paris, which had suffered greatly in the siege, underwent a violent conflict when a municipal council or "commune" was set up in March 1871 with a radical program of decentralization. National troops retook the city in May, at the cost of many thousands dead and imprisoned.

TIMELINE

Political developments

1850	1860	1870
1848 Franz-Josef becomes emperor of Austria; Louis Napoleon president of France	**1861** Wilhelm I succeeds to the Prussian throne	**1870** The "Ems Telegram" arouses French national hostility towards Prussia
1849 The German National Assembly is dissolved	**1862** Conservative Otto von Bismarck is appointed Prussian minister-president and foreign minister	**1871** Wilhelm I of Prussia is proclaimed emperor of Germany at Versailles
1852 The accession of Emperor Napoleon III begins the French second empire		**1866–67** Prussia unilaterally ends the German Confederation and forms the North German Confederation
1853 Hanover and Oldenburg join the *Zollverein*		

Military developments

1848 Austrian troops crush a Czech revolt in Prague and suppress revolution in Vienna	**1857** Helmuth von Moltke is appointed chief of Prussian General Staff	**1866** Seven Weeks War: Austria, defeated by Prussia, loses Holstein and Venetia
	1859 Austrians defeated by France and Sardinia-Piedmont	**1870** Franco-Prussian War begins; emperor Napoleon III surrenders at Sedan; end of the second empire; siege of Paris
	1863–64 A Prussian–Austrian invasion of Schleswig-Holstein expels the Danes	**1871** The German military occupation of Alsace-Lorraine begins

| 1850 | 1860 | 1870 |

SWEDEN

Gotland

Öland

Baltic Sea

•Göteborg

•Königsberg

DENMARK

•Copenhagen
•Malmö

Bornholm

*North
Sea*

Fyn

Sjælland

•Danzig

Prussia

Dybböl• •Als

Lolland *Falster*

Schleswig
1863 autonomous,
1865 to Prussia

Heligoland
to Britain

•Kiel
Holstein
1865 to Austria,
1866 to Prussia
1865 to Prussia

•Lübeck

MECKLENBURG-
SCWERIN

Pomerania

RUSSIAN EMPIRE

•Stettin

Oder

Hamburg•

Lauenberg•

•Bremen

OLDENBURG

HANOVER
1866 to Prussia

•Poznan

Vistula

•Warsaw

•Amsterdam

•ETHERLANDS

SCHAUMBURG-
LIPPE

•Hanover

BRUNSWICK

Brandenburg

•Berlin

PRUSSIA

Posen

Poland

werp

LIPPE-DETMOLD

Westphalia

ANHALT

Elbe

•Breslau

s

WALDECK

Saxony

•Leipzig

•Dresden

1866

Silesia

HINE-
VINCE

NASSAU
1866 to
Prussia

HESSE-KASSEL
1866 to Prussia

Langensalza
1866

SAXONY

1866

Austrian Styria

an
0

•Ems

HESSE-
DARMSTADT

THURINGIAN
STATES

1866

•Prague

Königgrätz
1866

2

LUXEMBOURG

Frankfurt•

Main

Bohemia

HESSE-
DARMSTADT 1

•Würzburg

Moravia

otte
1870

Saarbrücken•

LICHTENBERG

•Nuremberg

1866

1866

s-la-
Tour
1870

•Metz

Spicheren
1870

Wissembourg
1870

BAVARIA

Stuttgart•

Wörth
1870

Danube

**AUSTRIAN
EMPIRE**

•Vienna

•Strasbourg

WÜRTTEMBERG

Upper
Austria

4

Lower Austria

•Pressburg

Danube

ALSACE-
LORRAINE
to German empire

BADEN

HOHENZOLLERN
1849 to Prussia

•Munich

5

1870

•Salzburg

•Buda

Pest

•Villersexel
1870

Rhine

Salzburg•

Styria

*Lake
Balaton*

Hungary

•Besançon

•Zürich

*Lake
Constance*

LIECHTENSTEIN

•Gastein

BISMARCK was known as the
Iron Chancellor, apparently
able to bend all Europe to his
vision of German strength.

Geneva

SWITZERLAND

*Lake
Geneva*

•Berne

Tyrol

Carinthia

Küstenland

Carniola

Sava

Savoy
1860 to
France

Venetia
1866 to Italy

•Trieste

Croatia

•Milan

Lombardy
1859 to Sardinia
then Italy

•Venice

Custozza
1848, 1866

Adige

•Turin
Italian capital
1860–65

Po

Parma
1860 to Italy

SARDINIA
1860 to Italy

Modena
1860 to Italy

•Genoa

•Bologna

Dalmatia

1848 to
France

SAN MARINO

MONACO
1861 independent

Florence
Italian capital
1865–70

*Adriatic
Sea*

3

rseille

•Siena

PAPAL
STATES
1860 to Italy

Lissa
1866

TUSCANY
1860 to Italy

Corsica

Patrimony of
St Peter
1870 to Italy

Tiber

KINGDOM OF THE
TWO SICILIES
1860 to Italy

•Rome
Italian capital
from 1870

*Mediterranean
Sea*

BENEVENTO
1870 to Italy

Sardinia

•Naples

---

1 The middle-class Frankfurt National Assembly
offered the German crown to Frederick William IV of
Prussia in 1849. He declined, claiming that only the
German princes were entitled to make such an offer.

2 In the Battle of Königgrätz (Sadowa), Prussian
breech-loading needle guns had the advantage over
Austrian slow muzzle-loading rifles.

3 The Battle of Lissa was fought between ironclad
steamships but the Austrian navy triumphed over an
Italian force using the ancient technique of ramming.

4 Austria's defeat in 1866 caused internal tensions to
resurface in the Habsburg empire; the solution was
the compromise (*Ausgleich*) of 1867, which created
the Dual Monarchy of Austria–Hungary.

5 Alsace and Lorraine, which had large German-
speaking populations, were annexed by Germany in
1871 to weaken France and to satisfy historic claims
to the region.

6 Conditions in Paris during the Prussian siege of
1870–71 became so desperate that its inhabitants
were compelled to eat the animals in the city's zoo.

See also 5.10 (the rise of nationalism);
5.13 (late 19th-century Europe)

The Russian empire, though ostensibly mighty, had structural weaknesses: above all, its sheer size made it difficult to govern and prevented ready exploitation of its abundant resources. As a result, corruption was rife and the country remained economically underdeveloped. Territorially, Russia continued to expand throughout the 18th and 19th centuries. Catherine the Great's energetic foreign policy added much of Poland and extended Russia's empire in the south. Czar Alexander I (r.1801–25) suffered Napoleon's invasion of 1812 but secured thereby a share of the spoils after the defeat of France. The Congress of Vienna ceded the remainder of Poland to Russia, thus augmenting its recent acquisitions in Finland and Bessarabia.

Territorial expansion left Russian rulers with a permanent fear of rebellion by conquered peoples. During the 1828–29 war with the Turks, Nicholas I (r.1825–55) was able to field barely 180,000 troops, as half a million frontline soldiers were committed to maintaining security in the Baltic provinces and the Caucasus. In 1830, a rising in Poland against Russian rule was only suppressed with difficulty. Internal dissent at autocratic rule began to grow; the "Decembrist" revolt of progressive army officers early in Nicholas I's reign was ruthlessly put down.

The principal aim of Nicholas' foreign policy was dominance over the Ottomans to ensure that Russia's grain exports had free passage across the Black Sea and through the Dardanelles to the Mediterranean. Russia endeavored to absorb Turkey's Balkan possessions and to encourage fellow Slavs to rebel against Ottoman rule in Europe. This policy brought Russia into conflict with the western powers. Britain saw its trade with India threatened by Russian expansion into the eastern Mediterranean, while France was concerned in its role as protector of the Catholic church within Turkish territories. Nicholas' decision to occupy the Ottoman

provinces of Moldavia and Wallachia in 1853 provoked Britain and France to invade the Crimea (1854). Once again, mustering sufficient manpower to resist the invaders proved a severe problem.

Russia's defeat in the Crimean War, its withdrawal from Moldavia and Wallachia and the requirement that it "neutralize" the Black Sea compelled Alexander II (r.1855–81) to review his power base. Russian autocracy had always depended on the conscription of serfs, yet such a force was no match for the modern armies of France and Britain. The nobility, whose wealth was grounded in serfdom, was reluctant to innovate or invest in modern industrial plant. To forestall revolution from below, Alexander reformed from above, emancipating the serfs and moving Russia toward a capitalist economy. Even so, millions of former serfs had to pay redemption fees for the lands they tilled. Massive discontent remained, held in check only by conscripts and the secret police; the czar was assassinated in 1881.

Alexander II had begun to tap the vast resources of Siberia, had extended the empire in central Asia and had secured a warm-water port in east Asia. The territory of Alaska was sold to the United States to concentrate development efforts on eastern Siberia and Vladivostok. Alexander's armies gradually sub-

TIMELINE

Domestic developments

1800	1850	1900
1796 Death of Catherine II; brief reign of her son Paul I ends in assassination	**1855** Alexander II becomes czar and institutes reform	**1894** Nicholas II, the last czar, ascends the throne
1801 Alexander I ascends the throne; kingdom of Georgia voluntarily unites with Russia	**1861** Russian serfs are emancipated by the "Czar Liberator" Alexander	**1905** Major uprisings sweep the country and lead to limited constitutional reform
1812 Napoleon invades Russia and occupies Moscow, but is forced to withdraw	**1881** Assassination of Alexander II in St Petersburg; Alexander III becomes czar and reasserts autocratic rule	**1911** Pyotr Stolypin, reforming prime minister under the first *dumas*, is assassinated
1825 Accession of Czar Nicholas I; Decembrist revolt of army officers fails	**1891** Trans-Siberian Railroad is begun; completed in 1916	

Foreign policy

1810–50 Russia extends its dominion in central Asia	**1860–70** Russian expansion into Turkestan	**1904–05** Russo-Japanese War; Russian forces are humiliated
1815 Congress Poland is united with Russian empire, but retains its government	**1867** Alaska is sold to the United States for US$7.2 million	**1914** Russia mobilizes its army against Germany; on the outbreak of war it suffers a major defeat at the Battle of Tannenberg
1830–31 Insurrection in Poland is brutally suppressed	**1877–78** Last of a series of Russo-Turkish wars; creation of the vassal state of Bulgaria	
	1849 Russian troops are sent to crush Hungarian liberals	
	1854–56 Crimean War; British and French halt Russian Black Sea expansion	

| 1800 | 1850 | 1900 |

CANADA

Russian
America
1867 to United States
and renamed Alaska

*Gulf of
Alaska*

[1] Catherine II annexed the Crimea in 1783 and ordered the construction of a huge naval facility at Sevastopol; this base was besieged by Anglo-French forces in 1854-56.

[2] Congress Poland, so-called because it was awarded to Russia by the Congress of Vienna in 1815, lost its constitution after the 1830 revolt, and was entirely absorbed by Russia after another rebellion in 1863.

[3] A strip of mountainous country known as Wakhan was appended to Afghanistan in 1905 to separate conflicting Russian and British interests in the region.

[4] The revolution of 1905 spread to the armed forces; sailors of the battleship *Potemkin* seized control of the ship in Odessa and sought asylum in Romania.

[5] Count Sergei Witte, Minister of Finance 1892-1903, was the driving force behind the Russian rail network and industrial expansion.

[6] The loop of the Trans-Siberian railroad around Lake Baykal was completed in 1915, and the eastern Siberian link in 1916.

[7] Thousands of political dissidents were sent to Siberian labor camps by the czarist regime, including the Bolsheviks Lenin (Shushenskoye), Stalin (Kureika), and Trotsky (Verkholensk).

Wrangel Island
1867 to Russian
empire

*Bering
Sea*

RUSSIAN EMPIRE

Surgut

Turukhansk
Kureika

Narym

Ob

Yenisey

Tomsk

Novosibirsk

Krasnoyarsk

Shushenskoye

Lake
Baykal

Irkutsk

Kyakhta

Viluisk

Yakutsk

Lena

Verkholensk

Barguzin

Chita

Kara

Amur
1858 to Russian empire

Nikolayevsk

1853 to Russian
empire

*Sea of
Okhotsk*

Sakhalin

1875 to Russian
empire, 1905
to Japan

Aleutian Islands

*PACIFIC
OCEAN*

Hami

MONGOLIA
1900-14 under Russian influence

Gobi Desert

Khabarovsk

Ussuri
1860 to Russian empire

Manchuria
1900-05 Russian
occupation

Harbin

Kuril Islands
Northern islands to Japan 1875

Yellow

Mukden
(Shenyang)

Beijing

Vladivostok

*Sea of
Japan*

JAPAN

Lanzhou

Port Arthur
(Lushun)

KOREA

Seoul

Edo
(Tokyo)

Tsushima
Strait
1905

Russian empire, 1802

Russian territorial gains, 1809-55

Russian territorial gains, 1855-1914

Russian sphere of influence, 1907

Austro-Hungarian empire, 1853

Ottoman empire, 1853

"Big Bulgaria", 1878

territory under Japanese control by 1910

Manchu empire, 1912

British India, 1914

British sphere of influence, 1907

border, 1914

Russian urban population, 1914

■ under 100,000

▣ 100,000-500,000

◆ over 500,000

area of heavy grain export

area of heavy industry, 1914

coal mining, 1914

gold mining, 1914

iron ore mining, 1914

oilfield, 1914

port

Tula mutiny or strike, 1905

czarist prison/labor camp

railroad by 1917

trade route

Russian campaign, 1853

Anglo-French campaign, 1854

Jewish Pale of Settlement, subject to pogroms, 1881-1907

MANCHU EMPIRE

Yangtze

Chongqing

*Yellow
Sea*

dued the khanates in Bukhara, Khiva and Tashkent south of Lake Balkhash and the Aral Sea. However, a new war against Turkey and the creation of a client state in Bulgaria so alarmed the other great powers that Alexander let the Berlin Congress of 1878 put a brake on his Balkan ambitions.

Under his successor, Alexander III (r. 1881–94), Russia was poised to exploit trade routes in east Asia. The Trans-Siberian Railroad was begun, giving greater access to the mineral wealth of Siberia and central Asia and helping Russian entrepreneurs to penetrate Manchuria and Korea. This expansion brought Russia into collision with Britain and Japan. When antagonism eruped over the Russian occupation of Port Arthur, Japan humiliated the forces of czar Nicholas II (r.1894–1917) in 1904–05. Russia lost

south Sakhalin, the lease of Port Arthur and control of the railroads in southern Manchuria.

Discontent grew in European Russia with news of the defeats in the east. In January 1905, a peaceful demonstration in St Petersburg was fired upon by troops. The authorities eventually acceded to liberal demands and allowed an elected national assembly (*duma*) with limited powers. In its foreign relations, Russia agreed "spheres of influence" in Persia with Britain in 1907. However, Russian interest revived in seeking access to the Mediterranean through the Balkans. Pan-Slavic Russian involvement with militant Serb groups opposing Austrian domination fueled the Balkan crisis of 1914 that sparked World War I. Within three years, Russia was beaten and the empire of the Russian czars had collapsed.

See also 5.20 (Russo-Japanese war)

Bismarck, who initiated the complex web of alliances that developed after the Franco–Prussian War, now had as his ultimate objective the preservation of peace on the continent. He aimed to prevent France from launching a war of revenge by isolating it from any potential ally.

Bismarck's first step was to form the league of Three Emperors (*Dreikaiserbund*) between Germany, Austria–Hungary and Russia in 1873. In doing so, he had to reconcile a number of conflicting interests. Since the Crimean War, Russia had tried to reassert its position in Europe by championing the cause of Slav freedom from Austrian and Turkish rule. This brought Austria and Russia into conflict, as both empires cherished ambitions to secure the Balkan lands of the moribund Ottoman empire. The loose alliance that Bismarck forged was designed to stabilize southeast Europe, as its signatories agreed to act in concert against subversive movements in the region. In 1878, however, the Congress of Berlin forced Russia to renounce some of the excessive Balkan gains it had wrested from Turkey in 1877–78.

The chief beneficiary of the Berlin Congress was Austria, which negotiated a secret, defensive Dual Alliance with Germany (who, in World War I, were known as the Central powers). This relationship was to be the main focus of Bismarck's subsequent diplomacy; he publicly renewed the *Dreikaiserbund* in 1881 and distracted France by encouraging its colonial ambitions in north Africa, but secretly created a Triple Alliance between Germany, Austria and Italy.

When the *Dreikaiserbund* expired in 1887, Bismarck replaced it with a bilateral Reinsurance Treaty, which recognized the Balkans as a Russian sphere of influence and confirmed that Russia and Germany would stay neutral unless Germany attacked France, or Russia attacked Austria. This represented the pinnacle of Bismarck's diplomacy, which

sought to secure German predominance in central Europe and avoid dangerous adventurism.

In 1890, a sea-change occurred in the politics of European alliances, when growing antagonism between the headstrong new emperor Wilhelm II and Bismarck brought the latter's resignation. The Reinsurance Treaty was allowed to lapse without renewal and the Russian harvest failed the same year. France offered aid to Russia, so laying the groundwork for a military alliance. This was duly signed in 1894, with the critical provision that if a Triple Alliance country mobilized its armies then Russia and France would do likewise. Mobilization of any armed forces was thus likely to lead to war.

— border proposed by the Treaty of San Stefano, 1878
═ borders, 1912
▮ Allied powers, Aug 1914
▯ Central powers, Aug 1914

Schlieffen plan, 1905
▲ German army position
➡ route of German attack

⬚ fortress of the Central powers
⬚ fortress of the Allied powers
⬚ Belgian fortress
⚓ major naval base
⚒ major armaments center
◯ league of Three Emperors, 1873–87
◯ Triple Alliance, 1882–1915
● *Entente Cordiale*, 1904
● Triple Entente, 1907
— key railroad line for transferring German troops to Russian front
➡ anticipated Russian attack
▦ Slavic language in central Europe

EUROPEAN royalty in the early 20th century had close family ties; Britain's King George V (shown here with Queen Mary) was cousin to Wilhelm II.

Britain had stood aloof from these alliances but after the death of Queen Victoria in 1901 the new king Edward VII made overtures to France that culminated in the *Entente Cordiale* of 1904. A similar agreement was made with Russia in 1907, forming a Triple Entente (of what became known as the "Allied powers" in 1914) to balance the Triple Alliance.

Several international incidents occurred that tested the commitment of the European powers to peace. Germany's claims to Morocco ran into opposition from both Britain and France, and resulted in the Tangier crisis (1905), settled at the Algeciras conference, and the Agadir crisis of 1911, which resulted in German recognition of France's claim to Morocco. The Balkans, too, continued to provide a highly charged arena. The Balkan peoples tried to organize

TIMELINE

Alliances and ententes

1890		1910

1873 Bismarck negotiates the League of the Three Emperors (*Dreikaiserbund*)

1890 Bismarck resigns over differences with Kaiser Wilhelm II

1904 *Entente Cordiale* signed between Britian and France

1879 Dual Alliance: Germany and Austria-Hungary

1894 Franco-Russian military alliance is announced after France aids Russian famine

1907 Agreement between Britain and Russia results in a Triple Entente in Europe

1882 Italy joins the Dual Alliance, thus creating the Triple Alliance

1902 The Anglo-Japanese Naval Alliance guarantees naval security in east Asia

1914 Germany pledges total support ("Blank Check") for Austrian actions in Balkans

1887 German Reinsurance Treaty with Russia

Crises and rearmament

1875–78 Eastern crisis begins when Bosnia and Herzegovina rebel against Turks

1898 Fashoda crisis: a clash between French and British military missions in Sudan causes mutual hostility

1911 The visit of a German gunboat to Agadir causes the second Morocco crisis

1877–78 Russo-Turkish War ends; Russia gains much from the Treaty of San Stefano

1900 Second German Naval Law (First 1898) confirms growth of the Imperial Navy

1914 The Sarajevo crisis leads to Austrian bombardment of Belgrade, Russian mobilization and war

1878 The Congress of Berlin compels Russia to reduce its recent gains in the Balkans

1905–06 German colonial ambitions spark the first Morocco crisis

1885–86 Tension between Austria and Russia over Bulgaria destroys the *Dreikaiserbund*

1906 HMS *Dreadnought* revolutionizes warship design

1908 Austria–Hungary annexes Bosnia–Herzegovina

1889 Britain guarantees dominance of the Royal Navy

1890		1910

Map Labels

NORWAY
Bergen
Christiania
SWEDEN
Stockholm
Göteborg
Vänern
Vättern
Gotland
North Sea
Baltic Sea
Helsinki
Revel
St Petersburg
Lake Ladoga
Lake Peipus
Riga
Western Dvina
DENMARK
Copenhagen
Memel
Kovno
Vilna
Minsk
5
Heligoland 1890 to Germany
Kiel Canal
Kiel
Hamburg
Wilhelmshaven
Bremerhaven
Bremen
Königsberg
Danzig
Grodno
RUSSIAN EMPIRE
Stettin
Amsterdam
arwich
Chatham
NETHERLANDS
Antwerp
Wesel
Essen
Thorn
Poznan
Warsaw
Brest-Litovsk
Ivangorod
Hanover
Berlin
Oder
Elbe
GERMAN EMPIRE
BELGIUM
Brussels
Liège
Namur
oulogne
Leipzig
Cologne
Dresden
Breslau
Glatz
Vistula
Przemsyl
Lemberg
Frankfurt
Prague
Krakow
LUXEMBOURG
Diedenhofen
Neuenburg
4
Pilsen
La Fère
en Laon
Reims
Verdun
Toul
2
Nancy
Strasbourg
Neuf-Brisach
Ingolstadt
AUSTRO-HUNGARIAN EMPIRE
Danube
Munich
Vienna
Salzburg
Komorn
Budapest
rléans
Epinal
Le Creusot
Belfort
Basel
Zürich
LIECHTENSTEIN
Odessa
RANCE
SWITZERLAND
Geneva
Trent
Karlsburg
Sevastopol
Lyon
Turin
Milan
Venice
Trieste
Peterwardein
ROMANIA independent 1878
Bucharest
Black Sea
Grenoble
Briançon
Pola
Sava
Belgrade
Danube
Genoa
Bologna
1878 occupied by Austria–Hungary, 1908 annexed by Austria–Hungary
Bosnia-Herzegovina
Sarajevo
SERBIA independent 1878
Aleksinac 1876
BULGARIA independent 1908
Varna
Nice
MONACO
SAN MARINO
MONTENEGRO
Mostar
1913 to Montenegro
Pleven 1877
Sofia
East Rumelia 1885 to Bulgaria
Kirk Kilisse 1912
Marseille
Toulon
ITALY
Florence
Trebinje
Cattaro
Kumanovo 1912
Edirne
1913 to Bulgaria
Constantinople
1
San Stefano
Corsica
Rome
Albania independent 1913
1913 to Serbia
1913 to Greece
Lüleburgaz 1912
ANATOLIA
Naples
Taranto
Thessalonica
OTTOMAN EMPIRE
Balearic Islands
Sardinia
Ionian Islands
GREECE
Palermo
Messina
Athens
Sicily
Rhodes
Dodecanese 1912 to Italy
Cyprus 1878 to Britain
arcelona
Tunis
Malta to Britain
Mediterranean Sea
Crete 1898 autonomous, 1908 to Greece
lgiers
Algeria
Tunisia 1871 autonomous, 1881 French protectorate

Numbered Notes

1 The Treaty of San Stefano concluded between Russia and Turkey in 1878 envisaged the creation of a large new Bulgarian state beholden to Russia.

2 In France in 1886–89, a vociferous *revanche* ("revenge") movement arose over Alsace-Lorraine, headed by war minister Georges Boulanger.

3 From 1887–89, British prime minister Lord Salisbury resisted Bismarck's requests for an Anglo-German alliance. Salisbury described Britain's disdain for alliances as "splendid isolation."

4 One of the greatest European industrial complexes was the Skoda Works in Pilsen, built to produce a new machine-gun for the Austrian army in 1890.

5 Britain transferred sovereignty of the North Sea island of Heligoland (Helgoland) to Germany in return for Zanzibar in 1890. Germany developed Helgoland into a major naval base.

6 The *Entente Cordiale* was tested in 1905, when Wilhelm II spoke in Tangier in favor of Moroccan independence. The Algeçiras conference in 1906 upheld French claims to the territory.

into nation-states and the Balkan Wars of 1912 and 1913 radically transformed the map of southeast Europe, arousing the hostility of Austria–Hungary.

Throughout this period, plans were made for war. The most ambitious was devised by the German chief of staff, Alfred von Schlieffen, for a war on two fronts. The Schlieffen plan required a surprise push through neutral Holland, Belgium and Luxembourg to isolate Paris from the coast and encircle the French armies. Troops would then be transferred by rail to reinforce the eastern front against Russia, which was expected to attack near Königsberg.

Rapid developments were also made in armaments. Germany produced medium and heavy artillery of high quality, France excelled in rapid-fire field guns, while all countries were perfecting the machine-gun. At sea, the British *Dreadnought* class of battleship, begun in 1906, inaugurated a new era of naval design. Heavily armored, equipped entirely with big guns and driven by steam turbines, these ships started a race to build ever more powerful fleets. Wilhelm II was especially keen to develop the navy to challenge the might of Britain's Royal Navy.

Conscription swelled the size of the continent's armies. Most German youth served for three years in the army corps; French conscripts served for two. Both these countries (and Italy) could mobilize a million men within days. Austria and Russia could call on three times this number, though more slowly. The threat of war had loomed for so long over Europe that by 1914 all countries had arsenals and forces of unparalleled size and efficiency.

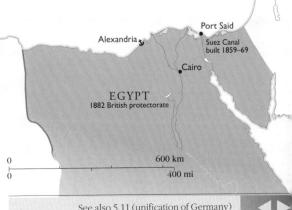

Port Said
Alexandria
Suez Canal built 1859–69
Cairo
EGYPT
1882 British protectorate

0   600 km
0   400 mi

See also 5.11 (unification of Germany)

In the late 18th century the Europeans continued to encroach on the Ottoman empire. In a second war against the Turks (1787–92), Catherine II of Russia failed to partition the Ottoman empire, but still extended Russian control of the northern Black Sea coast. Further losses were incurred in 1806–12, when Russia gained Bessarabia. Insurrections also broke out in Serbia in 1804 and 1817. Later attempts by the Ottomans to regain control of Serbia and the Principalities (Wallachia and Moldavia) resulted in the Russo-Turkish war of 1828–29, and the concession of Serbian autonomy.

Yet the most serious threat to the empire's survival during this period came from its vassal state of Egypt. Napoleon's invasion of 1798 profoundly altered Egypt's internal politics: Mehmet Ali, an Albanian officer of the force sent by Sultan Selim III to expel the French, seized control of the moribund state, becoming viceroy in 1805. At first, this dynamic modernizing ruler aided the Ottomans, ending the occupation of the Muslim holy sites of Arabia by the fanatical Wahhabi sect and acceding to Sultan Mahmud II's request in 1825 for help in the Greek War of Independence. However, in 1831 Mehmet Ali and his son Ibrahim Pasha (commander of the Egyptian force in Greece) invaded Syria to assert their authority against the sultan. Ottoman power was almost broken by defeats in 1832 at Konya in Anatolia, and in 1839 at Nezib (northern Syria), but the empire was saved by the Austrians and the British, who feared that a power vacuum in the region would threaten their links with India.

Further western support for the Ottomans appeared during the Crimean War. This arose from a Russian claim to protect Orthodox Christians in Ottoman European territories, and was fueled by disagreements between Russia and France over the administration of holy sites in Jerusalem. Russia invaded Moldavia and Wallachia, and in response

Turkey (supported by Britain and France) declared war. Turkey's naval defeat at Sinope was followed by British and French assaults on the Crimea. The outcome of the war was a united Romania (in 1861) and a great power agreement to preserve the diminishing Ottoman empire.

French influence in the Levant grew after France sent an expedition to Syria in 1860 to halt a massacre of Maronite Christians. France had also gained the concession to build the Suez Canal in 1854 (completed in 1869). However, the debt-ridden *khedive* (the Ottoman viceroy of Egypt's new title) sold his canal shares to Britain in 1875. Arab nationalists led by Urabi Pasha now began to agitate against European influence in Egyptian affairs. France and Britain gradually adopted a more interventionist approach toward Ottoman survival. France established a protectorate in Tunisia in 1881, and Egypt, nominally still an autonomous viceroyalty of the Ottoman empire, was occupied by Britain.

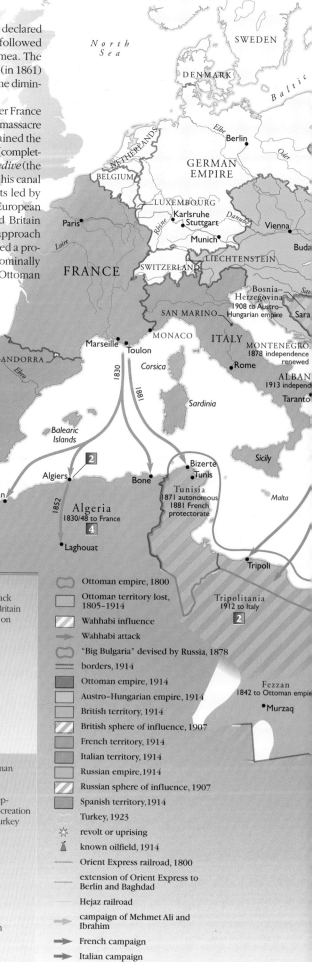

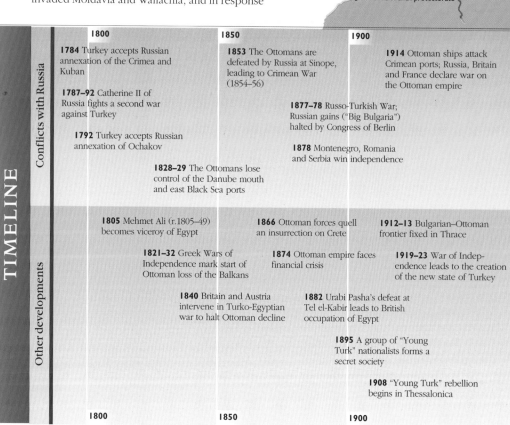

Ottoman empire, 1800
Ottoman territory lost, 1805–1914
Wahhabi influence
Wahhabi attack
"Big Bulgaria" devised by Russia, 1878
borders, 1914
Ottoman empire, 1914
Austro–Hungarian empire, 1914
British territory, 1914
British sphere of influence, 1907
French territory, 1914
Italian territory, 1914
Russian empire, 1914
Russian sphere of influence, 1907
Spanish territory, 1914
Turkey, 1923
revolt or uprising
known oilfield, 1914
Orient Express railroad, 1800
extension of Orient Express to Berlin and Baghdad
Hejaz railroad
campaign of Mehmet Ali and Ibrahim
French campaign
Italian campaign
Russian campaign, 1877–78

Nationalist rebellions in Bosnia–Herzegovina, Serbia, Bulgaria and Montenegro provoked yet another Russian invasion of the Ottoman empire (1877); the ensuing Peace of San Stefano created a pro-Russian "Big Bulgaria". Yet a Congress of European powers at Berlin in 1878 revised these frontiers to check Russian expansion. The Ottomans' last foothold in Bulgaria – eastern Rumelia – was lost when this province rebelled and merged with Bulgaria in 1885–88

In 1898, a surprise visit to Constantinople by Kaiser Wilhelm II consolidated a growing Ottoman association with Germany. Turkey and Germany agreed to extend the Orient Express railroad across Asia Minor to Baghdad. Subsequently Sultan Abdul Hamid II raised Muslim subscriptions to build the Hejaz railroad between Damascus and Medina.

Fears for the continuing demise of the Ottoman empire led disaffected army officers under Enver Pasha – the "Young Turks" – to overthrow Abdul Hamid in 1909. The reformers promoted westernization, but foreign encroachment began again. Austria annexed Bosnia–Herzegovina in 1908, Italy took Tripolitania in 1912, and two Balkan wars (1912–13) were precipitated, further reducing the Ottoman empire. Apart from eastern Thrace, all the European and north African provinces had now vanished.

In 1914 Turkey's new rulers staked its future on a secret alliance with Germany. The Treaty of Sèvres (1920), signed upon the defeat of the Central powers, stripped the Ottoman empire of all its non-Turkish regions. After capitulation, a war of independence was waged by nationalists under Kemal Atatürk from 1919–23, which drove foreign forces from Anatolia. In 1923 the Ottoman empire ceased to exist, after more than six hundred years.

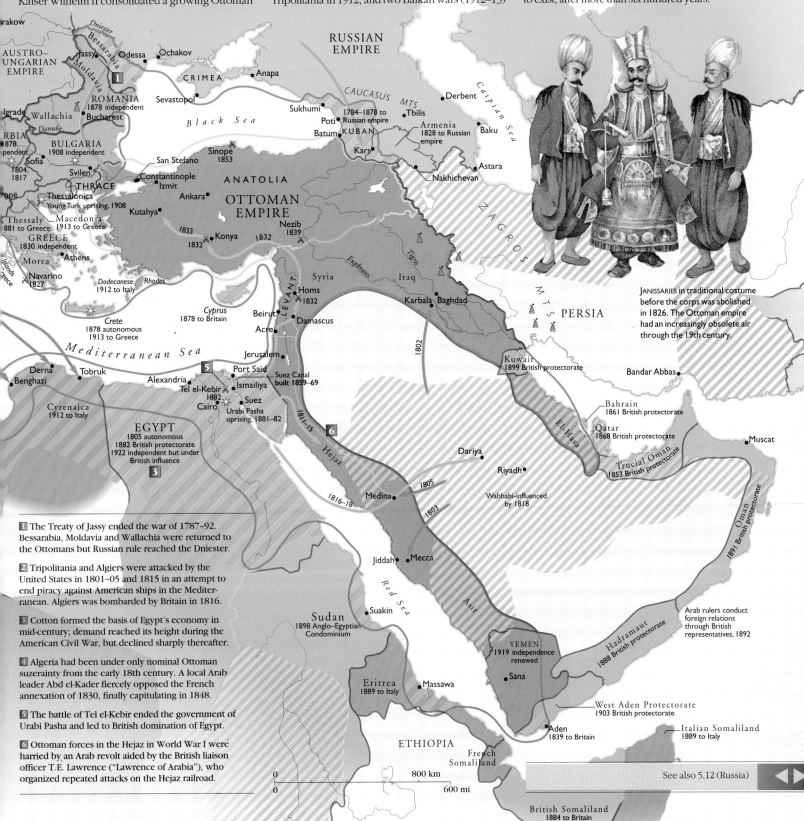

JANISSARIES in traditional costume before the corps was abolished in 1826. The Ottoman empire had an increasingly obsolete air through the 19th century.

1 The Treaty of Jassy ended the war of 1787–92. Bessarabia, Moldavia and Wallachia were returned to the Ottomans but Russian rule reached the Dniester.

2 Tripolitania and Algiers were attacked by the United States in 1801–05 and 1815 in an attempt to end piracy against American ships in the Mediterranean. Algiers was bombarded by Britain in 1816.

3 Cotton formed the basis of Egypt's economy in mid-century; demand reached its height during the American Civil War, but declined sharply thereafter.

4 Algeria had been under only nominal Ottoman suzerainty from the early 18th century. A local Arab leader Abd el-Kader fiercely opposed the French annexation of 1830, finally capitulating in 1848.

5 The battle of Tel el-Kebir ended the government of Urabi Pasha and led to British domination of Egypt.

6 Ottoman forces in the Hejaz in World War I were harried by an Arab revolt aided by the British liaison officer T.E. Lawrence ("Lawrence of Arabia"), who organized repeated attacks on the Hejaz railroad.

See also 5.12 (Russia)

Before the late 19th century European settlement of Africa was mostly confined to French colonization of Algeria, a few Spanish settlements, British and French trading stations in west Africa and Portuguese trade along the coast. Native peoples offered stern resistance, notably the Asante of west Africa. The largest European presence was formed by Afrikaner and British settlers in southern Africa, first in Cape Colony and (after the Great Trek, which began in 1835–36) in the Orange Free State and Transvaal. Disruption was caused by population movements, expansion by indigenous states such as Egypt, holy wars (*jihads*), the continuing slave trade and the emergence of new empires in east, central and west Africa.

Zulu expansion led to an extensive migration of warriors known as the *mfecane*, a condition of almost perpetual conflict. Shaka, who formed the Zulu kingdom from 1816, initiated a period of expansion in southern Africa. Zulu victories caused a chain-reaction among other nations, which surrendered to the Zulu confederacy or came into conflict with other nations as they fled. New states emerged, including Moshoeshoe's Lesotho, Mswati's Swazi kingdom and Mzilikazi's kingdom of Ndebele.

In west Africa, Usman dan Fodio (1754–1816) proclaimed himself the harbinger of the *Mahdi*, the Islamic Messiah, and aimed to create a unified Muslim state in Hausaland. He established the Sokoto caliphate which his successors built into a well-administered empire that survived until the 20th century. To the west, Sheikh Ahmad Lobbo led the Masina *jihad*, with its capital at Hamdallahi; his rival Al Hajj Umar created the Tukulor caliphate with the aid of followers from Futa Toro and Futa Jalon. Another military leader, Samori Toure, brought order, prosperity and Islamic law to a diverse set of peoples torn by commercial and religious conflict where he created the First Samori empire.

The trade in slaves was abolished by Denmark, Britain, France and the United States in the early 19th century, but Portugal allowed it to continue until 1882. Over 50,000 slaves a year were taken from Angola and Madagascar to South America and (up to 1865) illegally into the United States. The trans-Saharan and east African slave trades also flourished.

1 Sierra Leone was established by philanthropists as a home for freed British slaves in 1787. It became a British colony in 1808.

2 The conquests of the Zulu king Shaka (r.1816–28) were based on his of effective tactics of encirclement and on the new *assegai*, a deadly stabbing spear.

3 Kazembe was envied for its prosperity and subjected to constant attacks by Utetera, Yeke Katanga and Bemba.

4 In 1820, an army under the formidable Egyptian commander Ismail Pasha conquered Nilotic Sudan in search of gold and slaves.

5 The American explorer-journalist H.M. Stanley created the direct link between exploration and colonization. In 1874, he journeyed into central Africa to discover suitable colonies for Leopold II of Belgium.

A permanent settlement of the Omani Arabs in Zanzibar guaranteed a demand for African slaves in the Middle East and Asia. Not until 1873 did Britain manage to persuade the sultan of Zanzibar to close the slave market. Many African peoples became closely involved in the slave trade; the Yao and Nyamwezi, for example, depopulated much of east Africa in search of slaves for their plantations.

The presence of Muslim slave traders – Swahilis, Arabs, Egyptians and Sudanese – led to a spate of African state-building. Commercial empires such as Tippu Tip's Sultanate of Utetera emerged. This was at its peak by 1880, dealing in slaves and ivory throughout east central Africa. The Nyamwezi formed the trading empires of Urambo, Ukimbu and Unyanyembe. One outstanding leader, Mirambo (or Mbulya Mtelala), expanded Urambo and commanded a professional army of 50,000 riflemen. On the floodplain of the upper Zambezi was the rich, centralized Lozi empire, while to the northeast lay Kazembe, a prosperous agricultural state. In Angola Cokwe hunters successfully expanded their ivory exports and developed rubber plantations.

African leaders who had abandoned the slave trade now depended on export of commodities. In west Africa exports of timber, gum, gold, beeswax, ivory and hides doubled 1808–80. There was also a growing interior trade in kola nuts. Everywhere,

Africans and Europeans were in conflict over trade and access to raw materials; the ensuing rivalries created the conditions for partition. The Africans' confidence that they could stop Europeans from advancing inland, though, proved to be misplaced.

European explorers increased in number and ambition. In 1827–28, the Frenchman René-Auguste Caillé traveled through west Africa, an area also charted by the German Heinrich Barth on behalf of the British in the 1850s. The greatest explorer was the Scottish missionary David Livingstone, who journeyed extensively in central and southern Africa from 1840 and fought to destroy the slave trade. With the discovery of mineral wealth in southern Africa in the 1870s there began the "scramble" for Africa, a more systematic encroachment; the continent was almost totally colonized by 1900.

DAVID LIVINGSTONE combined geographical, religious, commercial, and humanitarian goals in his exploration journeys.

Cape Verde Islands

Idjil

Arguin

Ouadar

1854 French protectorate

Senegal

St Louis

Kaédi

TUKULOR CALIPHATE

KAAR

Gorée

FUTA TORO

Gambia
1843 British colony

Fort James

Cacheo

FUTA JALON

Senegal

Portuguese Guinea
1879 Portuguese colony

Sierra Leone
1808 British colony

FIRS SAMO EMPI

Freetown

LIBERIA

Monrovia

TIMELINE

	1800	1825	1850	1875
West Africa	1783 France recovers Senegal at the end of the American War of Independence	1821 Hamdallahi becomes capital of a new Masina state	1841 The Ibadan empire begins its expansion in quest of slaves and tribute	1861 Britain annexes Lagos and begins to suppress the Sokoto caliphate
	1787 400 freed slaves are settled in Sierra Leone	1822 Liberia is founded for freed US slaves	1849 France founds Libreville for freed slaves	1865 Samori Toure (1830–90) founds his first Madinka empire
	1804 Usman dan Fodio begins a *jihad*	1826 The Asante are defeated by British in the first of four wars (to 1896)		
N. & E. Africa	1806 Sayyid Said rebuilds Omani power in east Africa	1830 The French conquest of Algeria begins	1850 Tippu Tip introduces large trading caravans in east Africa	1873–76 Britain persuades the sultan Barghash of Zanzibar to suppress slavery
	1820 Ismail Pasha begins his invasion of Sudan	1840 Death of Kazembe IV, with his empire at its peak	1855 Emperor Tewedros revives Ethiopian empire	1875 Egypt moves into the Horn of Africa
South Africa	1810 The kingdom of Merina gains control of Madagascar	1835–36 The Great Trek begins to leave Cape Colony		1868 French commercial treaty with Madagascar signed
	1816 Shaka is made *Inkosi*, king of the Zulus	1840 Mzilikazi founds the Ndebele kingdom		1879 Britain defeats the Zulu kingdom
	1800	1825	1850	1875

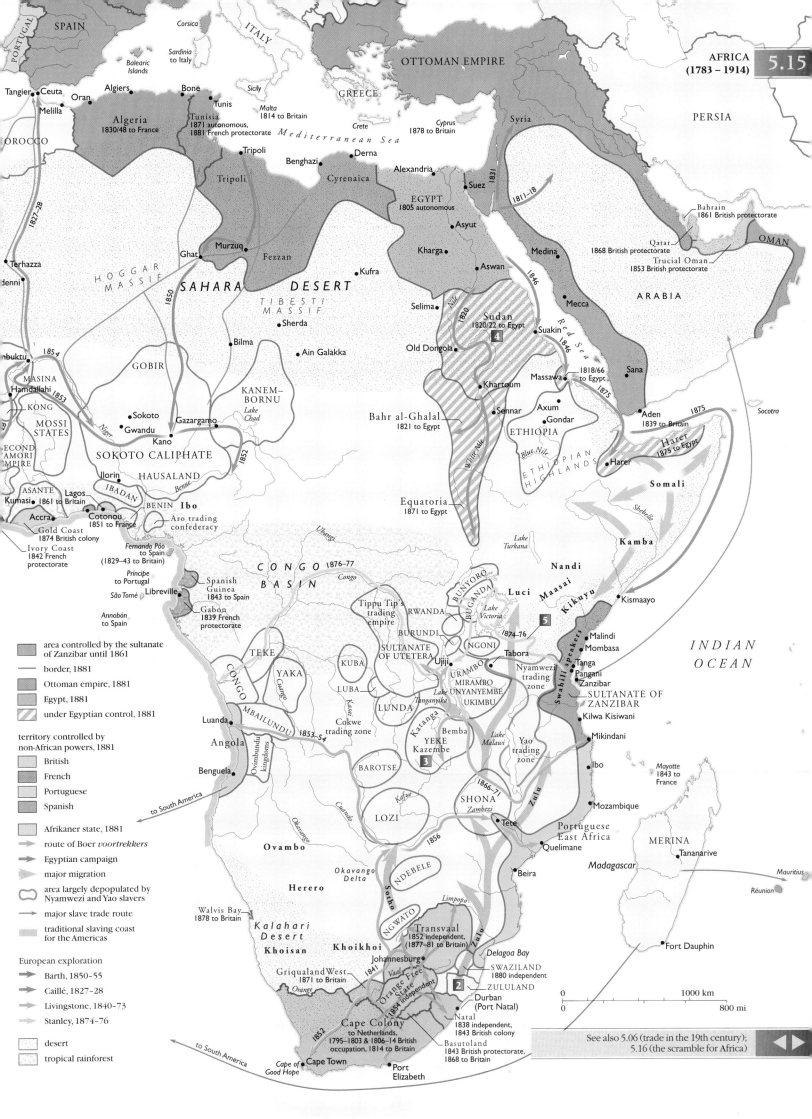

In 1884–85 representatives of fifteen European nations met in Berlin to settle rival claims to Africa. The Berlin Conference did not designate specific regions as colonies; rather it established the broad principles of the "scramble for Africa". The hinterland of a coast occupied by a European power was defined as a sphere of influence. To claim it, a power had to show itself capable of protecting "existing rights" and "freedom of trade and transit". This doctrine of "effective occupation" meant the process of colonization was conducted violently. Although the partition of Africa occurred quickly, it was the climax of years of activity by traders, administrators, soldiers and missionaries.

Africans were confronted with sudden piecemeal colonization. Some European governments worked through commercial ventures such as the Portuguese Niassa Company, the German South West and East Africa Companies, the Imperial East Africa Company, the Royal Niger Company and the British South Africa Company. By crudely imposing western practices – abolishing existing currencies, introducing hut taxes and removing middlemen from established trade patterns – these companies sowed the seeds of confrontation and armed resistance. In other cases companies conquered territory without reference to their governments. Sometimes, though, Africans invited the Europeans in, then found them impossible to remove.

The Europeans brought changes in modes of life and work. To pay the new taxes, Africans had to undertake wage labor. Imperial enterprises created a vast demand for unskilled labor: railroads, rubber, sugar and cocoa estates, and mining operations in central and southern Africa were all highly labor-intensive. By forcing Africans into these jobs, Europeans took away their culture and independence.

The response was varied. Some – such as the Bugandans who helped the British take over the states between the Great Lakes and form Uganda in 1903 – collaborated with the invaders. Others put their faith in religion: in the Sudan, Muhammad Ahmed (the *Mahdi*) rebelled against Anglo-Egyptian rule and founded a strict Islamic state. Yet apart from

1 The British general Charles Gordon, appointed governor of the Sudan by Khedive Ismail Pasha in 1873, was killed when Mahdist forces overran Khartoum in 1885.

2 In an uprising in 1905-07, Kinkjikitele Ngwale promised his followers that magic water (*maji-maji*) would protect them against machine-guns.

3 The Uganda railroad was built from 1896-1901, and was the most important factor in opening up the landlocked but fertile area north of Lake Victoria.

4 German colonization of Africa was characterized by foreign minister Bernard von Bülow in 1897 as the country claiming its right to "a place in the sun".

5 In 1898, at Fashoda on the White Nile, a confrontation between a French expeditionary force sent from west Africa and British troops almost led to war. The French ultimately withdrew.

the Mahdist revolt and the defiance of the west African Asante, most African resistance was short-lived. Artillery and rapid-fire maxim guns brought many uprisings to a swift end: the Ijebu surrendered in 1892, the Matabele in 1896, the Mandinka (under Samori Toure) in 1898 and the Zulu in 1908.

The Swazi branch of the Zulu nation was never defeated in battle; their state was guaranteed independence by the Transvaal and the British, before becoming a British protectorate in 1905. Only one state successfully defied the Europeans: Ethiopia, led by a modernizing Emperor Menelik II, crushed the Italian army at the Battle of Adowa in 1896. The freed-slave state of Liberia also survived despite losing parts of its territory to Britain and France.

By 1914, virtually the whole continent had come under European control. African raw materials and human resources were exploited for the benefit of European industry and commerce. Portugal shipped thousands of indentured laborers to the cocoa plantations on São Tomé and Príncipe, where they lived and died in appalling conditions. Leopold II of Belgium, who took the Congo Free State as his personal possession in 1885, amassed a fortune in revenues from rubber and ivory. By 1908 when the

Belgian state annexed the Congo, its population was half what it had been in 1891. Conditions then improved only marginally: thousands of people were moved forcibly to work the copper mines.

With footholds in the west, south and north of Africa, Britain was well placed to acquire half of the new colonies and protectorates during the "scramble". Its Gold Coast colony was the world's top rubber producer by 1895. Threatened by competitors in southeast Asia, the colony switched to cocoa and became world leader in this crop by 1914.

Germany came late to colonization. Among its African possessions was Togoland, where medical reforms, support for missionary schools, new roads and rail links brought some benefits of modern life.

QUEEN VICTORIA of Britain, as visualized by a Yoruba craftsman in Nigeria in the late 19th century.

Madeira

Ifni
1912 Spanish protectorate

Canary Islands
1912 Spanish protectorate

Spanish Saha

Rio de Oro
1884 Spanish protectorate

Mauritan

Cape Verde Islands

St Louis
Dakar
Kaédi
1881
1891
Senegal
Gambia
Kayes
1883
Fort James
Cacheo
Bamak
Portuguese Guinea
Bai Bureh's war
French Guinea
Conakry
Samori's resistance 1881–92
Sierra Leone
Freetown

Monrovia
LIBERIA

TIMELINE

European colonial policy

	1890		1900		1910
1881 Bey of Tunis accepts a French protectorate	**1889** Italy establishes its first colony in Eritrea		**1898** Britain creates the West African Frontier Force	**1906** Control of Morocco split between Spain and France	
	1883 French culture is imposed on African colonies	**1890** Britain gives Germany Heligoland in exchange for Pemba and Zanzibar		**1904** *Entente Cordiale* settles the Anglo-French disputes over Morocco, Egypt, the Suez Canal and Madagascar	**1912** Italy annexes Tripolitania and Cyrenaica
	1883 France begins its conquest of Madagascar		**1894** Britain occupies Uganda		**1914** Amalgamation of Northern and Southern provinces into Nigeria
	1884 The Berlin Conference on Africa opens			**1904** France creates a federal structure for its African empire, based at Dakar	

Wars and conflicts

	1884 Samori Toure proclaims his Islamic theocracy	**1892** France destroys the Tukulor empire (Mali)		**1900** Death of Samori Toure, two years after his capture	**1911** German gunboat *Panther* creates international incident at Agadir
	1885 British relieve Khartoum from Mahdist attack	**1893** French suppress the Fon warriors of Dahomey		**1900** Britain finally subjugates the Asante of west Africa	
					1914 European warfare transfers to all the German colonies in Africa
	1889 Chief Abushiri, leader of the Swahili peoples, is executed	**1896** Ndebele massacre whites and their African supporters in Matabeleland		**1905–07** Maji-Maji rebellion in German East Africa leads to an estimated 75,000 deaths	
	1890 Hendrik Witbooi leads the first Nama rebellion against Germans in South-West Africa	**1898** Kitchener defeats the Mahdists at Omdurman and defuses the Fashoda incident		**1906–08** Chief Bambata leads the last Zulu revolt	
	1890		1900		1910

By 1800 there were 15,000 Afrikaner (Dutch-origin) colonists at the Cape. British influence then began to grow; a brief occupation of the Cape to secure Britain's trade routes during the French Revolutionary Wars was followed by the construction of a naval base in 1806 and formal annexation of the area in 1814. Tension rose with the original settlers a decade later as unpopular land reforms were introduced. In response, Cape Boers (Afrikaners) embarked on the Great Trek, a migration into the interior to escape British administration. Some of these *voortrekkers* (pioneers) went north, others east into Natal. Violent clashes sometimes occurred with the native peoples they encountered.

Britain annexed Natal in 1843 and the Boers moved on again, crossing the Drakensberg mountains and heading into the high veld, where they founded the republics of Orange Free State and Transvaal. Britain recognized the independence of the Boer republics in the early 1850s. Their economies developed without staple crops or plantations as vast estates were rented out to African farmers who paid their dues in kind or labor. House slaves were commonly held by Boer families, who based their prestige on land ownership, superior weapons and a belief in racial supremacy.

Diamonds were discovered at Kimberley in Griqualand in 1871, revolutionizing the history of southern Africa and beginning a flood of European immigration. By 1880 diamond exports from here, increasingly in the hands of Cecil Rhodes' De Beers Mining Company Ltd, were worth over US$20 million annually. Then a gold boom started in 1886

in Witwatersrand, and was even more spectacular; *Uitlanders* (mainly British immigrants) poured into the Transvaal to make their fortunes. Rhodes financed settler expeditions traveling north into Bechuanaland and Zambesia, where they encountered Lobengula's Ndebele armies in Matabeleland, Lewanika's Lozi kingdom and the declining Kazembe kingdom northwest of Lake Malawi.

New roads and railroads transformed the countryside. Migrants from Mozambique and India came to work in the deep extractive mines. Soon the Witwatersrand was the world's biggest goldfield, attracting foreign investment and expertise, and transforming the Transvaal into a modern nation-state. To assert their predominance in the region and forestall German and Portuguese expansion, the

Legend:

- African kingdom
- independent Afrikaner state, 1795
- independent Afrikaner state, 1881
- British territory, 1806
- British territory, 1854
- British territory, 1914
- Belgian territory, 1914
- German territory, 1914
- Portuguese territory, 1914
- gold field
- diamond field
- Great Trek, 1835-46
- British expansion
- German expansion

Anglo-Boer War, 1899–1902
- territory captured by Afrikaners, 1899
- Afrikaner campaign
- British campaign
- Afrikaner victory
- British victory
- under siege by Afrikaners, 1899–1900
- railroad by 1914
- borders, 1914

0   300 km
0   400 mi

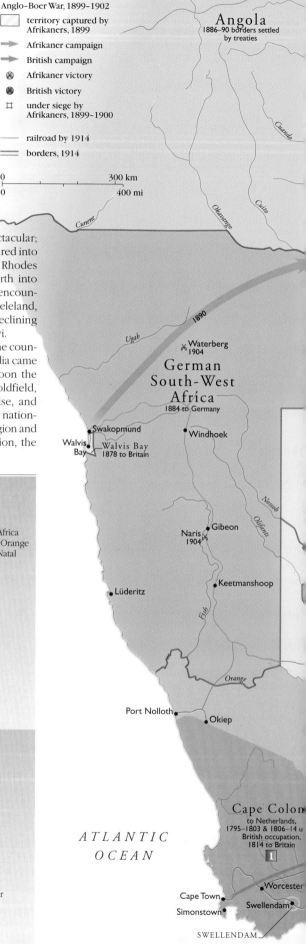

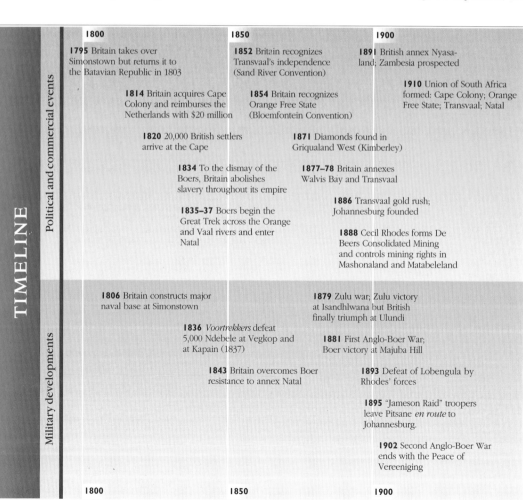

TIMELINE

Political and commercial events

1800	1850	1900
1795 Britain takes over Simonstown but returns it to the Batavian Republic in 1803	**1852** Britain recognizes Transvaal's independence (Sand River Convention)	**1891** British annex Nyasaland; Zambesia prospected
1814 Britain acquires Cape Colony and reimburses the Netherlands with $20 million	**1854** Britain recognizes Orange Free State (Bloemfontein Convention)	**1910** Union of South Africa formed: Cape Colony; Orange Free State; Transvaal; Natal
1820 20,000 British settlers arrive at the Cape	**1871** Diamonds found in Griqualand West (Kimberley)	
1834 To the dismay of the Boers, Britain abolishes slavery throughout its empire	**1877–78** Britain annexes Walvis Bay and Transvaal	
1835–37 Boers begin the Great Trek across the Orange and Vaal rivers and enter Natal	**1886** Transvaal gold rush; Johannesburg founded	
	1888 Cecil Rhodes forms De Beers Consolidated Mining and controls mining rights in Mashonaland and Matabeleland	

Military developments

1800	1850	1900
1806 Britain constructs major naval base at Simonstown	**1879** Zulu war; Zulu victory at Isandhlwana but British finally triumph at Ulundi	
1836 *Voortrekkers* defeat 5,000 Ndebele at Vegkop and at Kapain (1837)	**1881** First Anglo-Boer War; Boer victory at Majuba Hill	
1843 Britain overcomes Boer resistance to annex Natal	**1893** Defeat of Lobengula by Rhodes' forces	
	1895 "Jameson Raid" troopers leave Pitsane *en route* to Johannesburg.	
	1902 Second Anglo-Boer War ends with the Peace of Vereeniging	

1800	1850	1900

Belgian Congo
(Congo Free State)
1885 to Leopold II,
1908 to Belgium as Belgian Congo

Lake Mweru

KAZEMBE

German East Africa
1885 to Germany

Elisabethville

K A T A N G A

Lake Bangweulu

Ndola

ZAMBESIA

Kabompo

Lake Malawi

Nyasaland
1891 British protectorate

Northern Rhodesia
1911 to Britain

Luangwa

Lusaka

Kafue

Zambezi

Blantyre

Zambezi

LOZI

BAROTSELAND

Tete

CAPRIVI STRIP

Livingstone

MASHONALAND

Salisbury

Shona

Mozambique
1891–94 borders determined by treaties

Okavango Delta

Shangani Patrol 1893

Southern Rhodesia
1888 British protectorate

NDEBELE

Gwelo
Shangani River 1893

Mbembezi River 1893

Beira

Bulawayo
Mangwe

Fort Victoria

MATABELELAND

Save

Shona

Kalahari Desert

Bechuanaland
1885 British protectorate

Tuli

Motloutse

Shoshong Ngwato

Messina

Venda

Rhodes' Pioneers, 1890

Limpopo

Pietersburg

Transvaal
(South African Republic)
1852 independent, 1877 to Britain,
1881 independent
1900 to Britain

Limpopo

Pitsane

Kapain 1837

Pretoria 1900

Koomati Poort

Mafeking

Doornkop 1896

Johannesburg

Belfast

Mbabane

Delagoa Bay
Lourenço Marques

WITWATERSRAND

Vryburg

Vereeniging

Zulu

Swaziland
1880 independent,
1895 to Transvaal,
1905 British protectorate

Vaal

Vegkop 1836

Majuba Hill 1881

Hollkrans 1899

Rorke's Drift 1879

Isandhlwana 1879

Ulundi 1879

Molopo

IQUALAND WEST

Kimberley 1899

Magersfontein 1899

Elandslaagte 1899
Spion Kop 1900

Ladysmith

Zulu

ZULULAND
1897 to Natal

Modder River 1899

Paardeberg 1900

Caledon

Colenso 1899, 1900

Bloemfontein

Maseru

Natal
1838 independent,
1843 British protectorate,
1868 to Britain

UNION OF SOUTH AFRICA
1910 British dominion

Orange Free State
1848 to Britain, 1854 independent
1900 to Britain

Boomplaats 1848

Basutoland
1868 to Britain

Pietermaritzburg

Durban

Orange

Springfontein

Colesberg

De Aar

DRAKENSBERG MOUNTAINS

Middelburg

Stormberg 1899

Graaff Reinet

GRAAFF REINET

Sondags

East London

Port Elizabeth

AFRIKANERS defended their homeland stubbornly against the British, using guerrilla tactics in 1899–1902.

British annexed the Transvaal and invaded Zululand. The Zulu War of 1879 began with a crushing defeat for the British at Isandhlwana but victory at Ulundi was followed with the capture of the Zulu leader Cetshwayo. The following year, the Transvaal Boers rebelled; they defeated the British at Majuba Hill in the first Anglo-Boer War and regained independent status as the South African Republic.

Cecil Rhodes ultimately hoped to extend British rule from the Cape to Cairo. To gain control of the strategically and economically vital Transvaal, he sent an armed party commanded by Leander Starr Jameson to overthrow its government in 1895–96. The "Jameson Raid" was a fiasco, souring Anglo-Boer relations. Three years later, the Second Anglo-Boer War broke out. Initially Boer forces besieged Ladysmith, Mafeking and Kimberley and won victories at Magersfontein, Colenso and Stormberg during December 1899. Led by generals Roberts and Kitchener, the British relieved the besieged towns and invaded the two Boer republics. The Boers switched to guerrilla warfare and Kitchener resorted to armored trains to counter the Boer commandos. Boer farms were destroyed and displaced families interned in hastily built concentration camps. This, together with the British use of African troops and a steady flow of British reinforcements (to 300,000 by 1901) forced the Boers to surrender in 1901.

The Peace of Vereeniging (1902) incorporated the Boer republics within the British empire. Britain granted US$12 million to rebuild the Afrikaner homesteads and introduced responsible government to the Transvaal (1906) and to the Orange Free State (1907). The Union of South Africa was formed in 1910; Louis Botha, the Afrikaner leader, became prime minister of the new state, in which Afrikaners formed the predominant white minority.

In the struggle between Boers and British, the Africans were the real losers. Zulus and many other indigenous peoples were deprived of their lands, forced to live in segregated territories and to become migrant workers in mining and industrial centers. The new South African state immediately enacted systematic racial discrimination. The Natives' Land Act (1913) decreed that no African might own land except in prescribed and often unproductive areas.

1 The humane treatment of the native population by British missionaries who had arrived at the Cape in 1816, followed by abolition of slavery throughout the British empire, was strongly opposed by the Boers.

2 The first Indians in Africa were indentured laborers imported to work on Natal sugar plantations in 1860.

3 At Rorke's Drift (23 January 1879), a British garrison of around 100 troops held off an assault by thousands of Zulu *impi*. After losing 350 men, the Zulus withdrew out of respect for British bravery.

4 Lobengula of the Ndebele (or Matabele) granted mining concessions to Cecil Rhodes. When the British aimed to annex the kingdom, Lobengula vainly resisted in 1893 and committed suicide.

5 After the defeat of the Jameson Raid at Krugersdorp (1 January 1896), a congratulatory telegram sent by Kaiser Wilhelm II to president Kruger of the Transvaal created a crisis in Anglo-German relations.

See also 5.16, 5.17 (19th-century Africa)

European settlement in Australia began when the British government, faced with severe overcrowding in its jails, resolved in 1786 to found a penal colony there. The first convict transports arrived at Botany Bay in 1788; prisoners were subsequently transferred to settlements at Sydney (Port Jackson) and on Norfolk Island. The young colony began to expand as discharged soldiers and freed convicts cultivated their own parcels of land. Conflict arose with the Aboriginal inhabitants whose raids on settlements brought reprisals culminating in the massacre of Myall Creek (1838). In the 1830s settlers on Van Diemen's Land (Tasmania) attempted a wholesale expulsion of Aboriginals to Flinders Island; those who resisted were massacred.

The free Swan River colony established at Perth and Fremantle in the west attracted over a thousand people by 1831; again, hostilities developed with local peoples. The British government helped sustain the western Australian colony with convict labor until the practice was discontinued in 1868. By then, some 160,000 prisoners had been transported.

The inhospitable interior meant that the continent was not fully charted for eighty years. Matthew Flinders sailed around Australia in 1802–03; Edward Eyre, with the help of guides, crossed South Australia in 1839–41; Ludwig Leichhardt struck north from Moreton Bay; Burke and Wills crossed from south to north, followed by Stuart on a different route 1861–62; Warburton explored north of Adelaide and reached Port Hedland; Giles traversed the Gibson Desert and Macdonnell Ranges via Perth.

The non-convict populace of Australia rose after 1851, when gold was found at Bathurst, Ballarat, Bendigo and Kalgoorlie. In ten years the population exceeded one million; it doubled during the next decade with a huge influx of Chinese and Asian indentured labor. Racial violence led to strict immigration laws (later emulated in New Zealand). Gold mining played a role in Australian political history: in 1854, the pro-democratic Eureka uprising by Ballarat miners was put down by troops. All the states enjoyed self-government by 1890, and the following year, Australia's population topped three million, nearly a third of them first-generation immigrants.

European settlers first arrived in New Zealand's Bay of Islands during 1792, exchanging muskets with the indigenous Maoris for land. This trade caused "musket wars" between Maori tribes from 1818. Australian whalers also established coastal settlements on South Island. Disputes between the Maoris and the settlers led to the Treaty of Waitangi, which confirmed the Maoris' right to their land. However, settlers soon violated its terms, and the First Maori War (1843–48) saw fierce fighting at Ohaeawai *pa* (fortified site). Maori unity appeared in the "King Movement" of 1858 and then in the "Fire in

pastoral use within Australia

- by 1845
- by 1860
- by 1880
- by 1900
- since 1900
- unsuitable

- borders, 1914
- ■ state capital
- penal colony, with date of operation
- area of Aboriginal or Maori resistance
- goldfield
- area of sealing or whaling before 1840
- **Ngai Tahu** Maori tribe, 19th century

route of explorer

- Flinders, 1802–03
- Eyre, 1839–41
- Leichhardt, 1844–45
- Burke and Wills, 1860–61
- Stuart, 1861–62
- Warburton, 1872–75
- Giles, 1875–76

- —— railroad by 1914
- ----- seasonal river or lake

Timor Sea

Wyndham

Kimberley Plateau

Broome

Fitzroy

Port Hedland
Roebourne

Great Sandy Desert

Ashburton

Gibson Desert

Western Australia
founded 1829
1890 self-governing

Murchison

Mount Magnet

Geraldton

Menzies

Kalgoorlie

Nullarbor Plain

Perth Northam
Fremantle
Bunbury

Pinjara
1834

Esperance

Great Australian Bight

Albany

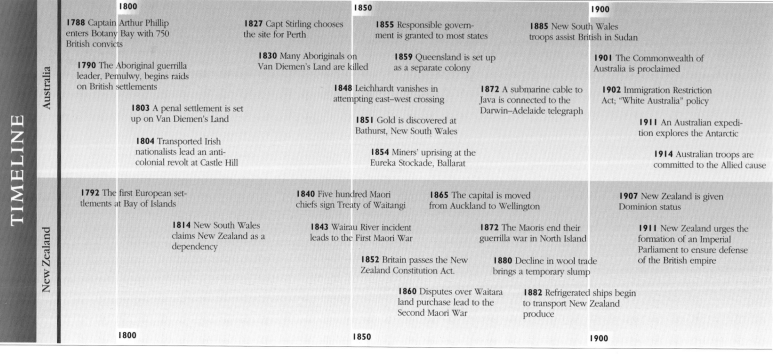

Australia

1800

1788 Captain Arthur Phillip enters Botany Bay with 750 British convicts

1790 The Aboriginal guerrilla leader, Pemulwy, begins raids on British settlements

1803 A penal settlement is set up on Van Diemen's Land

1804 Transported Irish nationalists lead an anti-colonial revolt at Castle Hill

1827 Capt Stirling chooses the site for Perth

1830 Many Aboriginals on Van Diemen's Land are killed

1850

1855 Responsible government is granted to most states

1859 Queensland is set up as a separate colony

1848 Leichhardt vanishes in attempting east–west crossing

1851 Gold is discovered at Bathurst, New South Wales

1854 Miners' uprising at the Eureka Stockade, Ballarat

1900

1885 New South Wales troops assist British in Sudan

1872 A submarine cable to Java is connected to the Darwin–Adelaide telegraph

1901 The Commonwealth of Australia is proclaimed

1902 Immigration Restriction Act; "White Australia" policy

1911 An Australian expedition explores the Antarctic

1914 Australian troops are committed to the Allied cause

New Zealand

1792 The first European settlements at Bay of Islands

1814 New South Wales claims New Zealand as a dependency

1840 Five hundred Maori chiefs sign Treaty of Waitangi

1843 Wairau River incident leads to the First Maori War

1852 Britain passes the New Zealand Constitution Act.

1860 Disputes over Waitara land purchase lead to the Second Maori War

1865 The capital is moved from Auckland to Wellington

1872 The Maoris end their guerrilla war in North Island

1880 Decline in wool trade brings a temporary slump

1882 Refrigerated ships begin to transport New Zealand produce

1907 New Zealand is given Dominion status

1911 New Zealand urges the formation of an Imperial Parliament to ensure defense of the British empire

1800

1850

1900

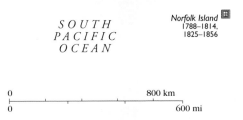

the Fern", a guerrilla war that began in 1860. Resistance to European settlers died out in 1870–72, but peace was not formally concluded until 1881.

Discovery of gold in Otago in 1861 stimulated immigration to New Zealand. Yet the main incentives to emigrate to Australia or New Zealand were cheap fares offered by shipping lines and unusually high standards of living. Both countries were enriched by the export of wool and foodstuffs; the introduction of refrigerated holds on steamships in 1882 enabled the bulk transportation of meat and dairy products. A minimum wage and generous welfare benefits attracted migrants, whose adopted countries gained self-government when Australia became a Commonwealth in 1901 and New Zealand a Dominion in 1907. Both retained emotional ties with Britain, and committed large forces to aid the "mother country" in 1914.

A transcontinental telegraph system was quickly established in Australia, though deserts and mountain ranges presented obstacles to a railroad system and different gauges were adopted by different states. The Trans-Australia railroad was completed in 1912–17, with the Kalgoorlie–Port Augusta link across the Nullarbor Plain. New Zealand's railroads were also slow to develop. Christchurch and Invercargill were linked in 1880, and the regular services began between Wellington and Auckland in 1908.

---

1 The Dutch explorer Abel Tasman was the first European to visit New Zealand, in 1642–63.

2 In 1794, John Macarthur began farming Merino sheep (a breed noted for its wool) in New South Wales, thus establishing Australia's future prosperity.

3 Aboriginals numbered c.300,000 when European colonization began. This figure declined drastically with exposure to disease and settler violence.

4 Irish political prisoners, transported after the anti-British rising of 1798, staged the Castle Hill uprising (1804). It was ruthlessly suppressed.

5 Burke and Wills' expedition of 1860–61 ended tragically; they narrowly missed a relief party and starved.

6 One form of Maori opposition to European settlement from 1865 onward was the Hau-hau movement, a blend of Christianity and native mythology.

7 Canberra was the site selected for the Australian Commonwealth capital in 1908. Its Parliament building was opened in 1927.

See also 5.04 (the world 1914)

Under the expansionist Manchu (Qing) dynasty, China enjoyed unrivaled power in east Asia. By 1783, emperor Qianlong (r.1736–96) had settled colonists in Xinjiang and imposed tributary status on Burma and Annam. He restricted foreign merchants to Guangzhou and shunned the industrial innovations offered by western "barbarian" traders. After his abdication, however, imports of opium from British India increased steadily, and eventually led to two "Opium Wars" with China (1839–42; 1856–60). The outcome of the first was the 1842 Treaty of Nanjing, which confirmed Britain's gain of Hong Kong and right to trade through five "treaty ports"; the second resulted in two agreements (in 1858 and 1860) for more western commercial footholds.

Russian ambitions focussed on acquiring strategically important Chinese territory. Russian forces annexed the valuable Ili region and advanced into Xinjiang, from which they withdrew in return for cash compensation in 1881. Russia also annexed eastern Siberia (1858–60) to secure ice-free waters in the Sea of Japan. A similar policy of territorial acquisition was adopted by Britain, France and Japan, which began to encroach on the tributary states beyond the Manchu borders. Britain moved into Lower Burma in 1852 and annexed the entire country in 1886. France, entrenched in southern Indo-China, was anxious to open trade with the southern Chinese province of Yunnan; it therefore fought a brief war with China to establish a protectorate over Tongking by 1885. Between 1875 and 1880, Japan annexed the Chinese tributary of the Ryukyu islands and began to weaken Chinese influence in another tributary, Korea. Taiwan and the Pescadores were also lost by China in 1894–95. These concessions and defeats represented unprecedented humiliation for the Qing dynasty.

While foreign powers eroded its frontiers, China faced even greater dangers from within. Official corruption, high taxation and continuing internal migration caused local uprisings. Many were caused by secret societies with political aspirations. The White Lotus sect vowed to overthrow the Qing and restore the Ming dynasty. Their rebellion raged through central China 1796–1804, though some unrest continued to 1813. After 1850 these revolts became so serious as to threaten the survival of the Qing. Hong Xiuquan led the Taiping rebellion, proclaiming the end of Manchu rule and the advent of the "Heavenly Kingdom of the Great Peace". This insurrection and its suppression by Qing forces cost up to 20 million lives. Disaffection with Manchu rule also brought rebellion in Taiwan, Muslim revolts in Xinjiang and Yunnan, Nian peasant risings in Henan and Miao tribal unrest in Guizhou.

The short-lived "self-strengthening movement" instigated by the statesman Li Hongzhang in the 1860s attempted to construct a modern military and industrial state. Yet his plan to purchase foreign armaments and build arsenals and factories met with little support from the dowager empress Cixi (r.1862–1908) and her court at Beijing. Meanwhile, the western clamor for land concessions, mining rights, railroad, building and trade facilities continued. In Cixi's reign, anti-western sentiment took on a republican flavor, and crystallized into the nationalist movement led by Sun Yixian (Sun Yat-sen).

The shame of further territory losses in 1898 led to the Boxer Uprising of 1900–01. This major revolt engulfed several provinces but concentrated chiefly on attacking the foreign legations in Beijing. The outcome of this rebellion, which was supported by the dowager empress, was the International Protocol of 1901, which gave the powers yet more trade concessions and a huge indemnity payment from the Qing. Western soldiers guarded the civilian settlements, while gunboats patrolled the rivers. Merchant and missionary activity increased. Foreign

RUSSIAN EMPIRE

Lake Balkhash

Ili
1854 annexed by Russia
DZUNGARIA

Ili
1871–81
to Russia

TIEN SHAN

Tarim

Xinjiang 1

KUNLUN MTS

TIBET
1912 independent

TRADITIONAL ways of life, including the use of head stocks (known since Han times) for criminals, survived throughout the Manchu era.

1 With acquisitions of new territories such as Xinjiang by the Manchu, the Chinese population rose to over 400 million by the mid-19th century.

2 Opium was imported to China not as a narcotic, but as a pharmaceutical. Its addictive properties led to imperial decrees against its import and cultivation from 1800 onward.

3 Hong Kong was ceded to Britain by China in 1841 (confirmed in 1842); in 1898, the British signed a 99-year lease on the territory.

4 Shanghai was one of the first treaty ports, opened to western trade in 1842. In these ports, westerners were free from all aspects of Chinese jurisdiction, including taxation.

5 The Taiping rebellion of 1850–64 took its egalitarianism from Christianity brought by western missionaries. Its leader Hong Xiuquan claimed to be the younger brother of Jesus Christ.

6 The Boxers – or "League of Righteous Harmonious Fists" – were an anti-foreigner, anti-Christian secret society originating in the Shandong peninsula.

7 Germany sent a force to occupy the port of Qingdao in 1897. Thereafter the site was heavily industrialized; with the outbreak of war in 1914, Japan (an Allied country) captured the city.

TIMELINE

Trade and politics

1800	1850	1900
1793 Emperor Qianlong snubs a British trade mission under Lord Macartney	**1839** Imperial commissioner Lin Zexu sent to Guangzhou to stop opium trade	**1885** Chinese troops defeat a French force at Langson
1796 Qianlong abdicates in order not to rule longer than his grandfather	**1839–42** First Anglo-Chinese War opens up "treaty ports"	**1886** Britain completes its annexation of Burma
1816 Expulsion of British Lord Amherst's trade mission	**1844** France and the United States sign trade agreements with China	**1894–95** Sino-Japanese War: China is defeated and loses Taiwan and the Pescadores
1830 Anglo-American illicit supply of opium increases	**1856–60** Second Anglo-Chinese War	**1896** China, through Li Hongzhang, permits Russia to build a railroad across Manchuria
	1860 An Anglo-French force destroys the imperial palace at Beijing	**1901** An International Protocol is imposed on China

Rebellions

1800	1850	1900
1796–1804 The White Lotus rebellion disrupts most of central China	**1850** The Taiping rebellion (*Taiping*: "heavenly kingdom") begins in Jintian; it is crushed by 1864	**1895** Sun Yixian's attempt at revolution in Guangzhou fails
	1855–57 The Miao rebellion against Manchu in Guizhou	**1900** Boxer Uprising against foreign influence
	1855–57 The Christian, nationalist Hakka rebel against their Manchu overlords	**1908** Death of the dowager empress Cixi
		1911 Chinese revolution begins
	1863–73 Muslim rebellion in Gansu, Qinghai and Shanxi	**1912** Yuan Shikai president of the new Chinese Republic

| 1800 | 1850 | 1900 |

banks virtually ran China's economy, funding such projects as the rail link across Manchuria between the Trans-Siberian railroad and Vladivostok.

In 1911, an army mutiny in the industrial conurbation of Wuhan was exploited by Sun Yixian's Revolutionary Alliance Party, or Guomindang (KMT), which proceeded to seize power in central and southern China and overthrow the Qing dynasty. Sun Yixian returned from overseas exile to Shanghai, proclaimed the Three Principles of the republican revolution – nationalism, democracy and people's livelihood – and was duly appointed provisional president of China. On 1 January 1912 the Chinese Republic was founded. However, when the Manchu boy-emperor Pu Yi abdicated on 13 February, General Yuan Shikai was named as president. For the sake of national unity, Sun Yixian voluntarily relinquished the presidency. Yet Yuan Shikai's desire to found a new imperial dynasty led to suppression of the Guomindang. In 1913, Sun Yixian established the first of a series of provisional governments at Guangzhou.

See also 5.12 (19th-century Russia)

The military bureaucracy (*bakufu*) that had been established at Edo by Tokugawa Ieyasu at the beginning of the 17th century held sway over Japan until the mid-19th century. Under this system, the governor (*shogun*) exercised absolute power and kept close control of the provincial barons (*daimyo*) and the increasingly poverty-stricken *samurai* warrior class. The emperor remained a remote, divine figurehead, residing at Kyoto some 480 kilometers (280 miles) from Edo.

Contact with foreigners was abhorred by this closed society. Russian and American ships that attempted to trade with Japan in 1791–92 were repelled. However, the opening up of California and the 1849 gold rush made the United States conscious that the Pacific offered unexplored commercial opportunities. The arrival at Uraga in 1853 of US Commodore Matthew Perry's "black ships" – a naval expedition to open trade with Japan – brought the question of contact with the outside world to the fore. Perry's return to Edo Bay the following year with a squadron of warships and 4,000 marines forced the *bakufu*'s hand, and the first limited concessions were granted to westerners to trade through the small ports of Shimoda and Hakodate.

The years following Perry's expedition saw resistance to foreign influence, organized by young samurai. Attacks on shipping caused a multinational naval force to bombard the forts at Kagoshima and Shimonoseki in 1863–64. Anti-foreign sentiment grew into concerted opposition to the shogunate. During 1867–68 civil war led to the the shogun being replaced with the emperor, in a development known as the Meiji ("enlightened rule") restoration. The emperor moved to Edo, now renamed Tokyo.

Under the new imperial regime, Japan resolved to compete with the west by industrializing, building a modern army and navy and adopting an aggressive foreign policy. In this way, it was intended that Japan should become the dominant power in east Asia. A pragmatic line was now taken toward foreign influence; western expertise was harnessed to build Japan's first light industrial enterprise, a silk-reeling factory. The growth of heavy industry also required the import of western plant and materials – steel, steam engines, and railroad rolling stock were all purchased from overseas. Through the offices of a samurai financier, Masayoshi Matsukata, the Japanese government borrowed money from the four giant *zaibatsu*, (financial organizations) that dominated banking, industry and commerce – Mitsui, Mitsubishi, Sumitomo and Yasuda.

Between 1871 and 1914 Japan achieved dominance in east Asia; the country acquired the Ryukyu Islands, the Bonin Islands (Ogasawara), southern Sakhalin and the Kuril Islands. In 1894 the Tonghak revolt in Korea reflected a growing socio-economic crisis at home but this provoked Chinese and Japanese intervention, with war erupting between the two powers the same year. Japanese ships destroyed the Chinese navy at the Battle of the Yellow Sea, while its army crushed the Chinese in Manchuria. The Japanese took Taiwan and the Pescadores; Korea became briefly independent. Yet intervention by the great powers subsequently deprived Japan of Port Arthur and the Liaodong Peninsula. When Russia was granted a lease of Port Arthur by China and attempted to expand its influence in Korea, Japanese fears grew stronger. Japan negotiated an alliance with Britain in 1902 that effectively neutralized Russia's ally, France, in the event of war, and then resolved to confront and overcome its chief rival in the region.

In 1904 Japanese troops landed in Korea and moved north toward the Yalu. Japanese warships attacked and then blockaded the Russian fleet at Port Arthur. On 1 January 1905 the Russian base surrendered. At Mukden Japan defeated the Russian army. Meanwhile the Russian Baltic Fleet, having sailed halfway around the world, arrived in Tsushima Straits too late to relieve Port Arthur. In one of the most important sea victories in history, Admiral Togo annihilated the obsolescent Russian fleet. In 1905 by the Treaty of Portsmouth (USA), Russia surrendered south Sakhalin and leases on Port Arthur and the South Manchurian railway (completed in 1904). In 1910 Japan annexed independent Korea. By 1914 Japan had a major sphere of influence in east Asia.

Irkutsk

Lake Baykal

Chi

Trans-Siberian railroad

RUSSIAN EMPIRE

Mongolia
1912 independent

— border, c.1850
Japanese territory, c.1850
Japanese territorial gain by 1914
Japanese sphere of influence by 1914
Manchu empire, c.1850
Republic of China, 1914
Russian empire, c.1850
Russian territorial gain by 1914
Russian sphere of influence by 1914
Russian occupation, 1897–1905
area allied against *Bakufu*, 1868
area leased by China to a foreign power
→ Commodore Perry's visits to Japan, 1853 and 1854
→ Japanese campaign, Sino-Japanese war, 1894–95
→ Japanese campaign, Russo-Japanese war, 1904–05
→ Russian campaign, 1904–05
☆ Japanese trading port by 1860
bombardment by western powers, 1863–64
battle, 1894–95
battle, 1904–05
peasant protest or riot, 1780–1850
Tonghak revolt, 1894
Japanese industrial area by 1914
— railroad, c.1914

0 _____ 400 km
0 _____ 400 mi

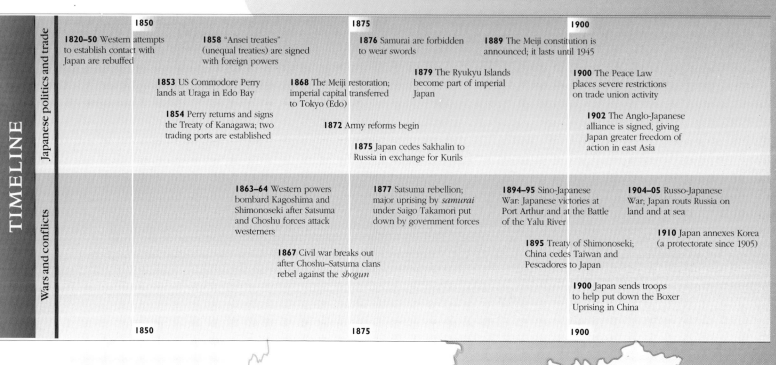

TIMELINE

	1850		1875		1900	

Japanese politics and trade

1820–50 Western attempts to establish contact with Japan are rebuffed

1858 "Ansei treaties" (unequal treaties) are signed with foreign powers

1876 Samurai are forbidden to wear swords

1889 The Meiji constitution is announced; it lasts until 1945

1853 US Commodore Perry lands at Uraga in Edo Bay

1868 The Meiji restoration; imperial capital transferred to Tokyo (Edo)

1879 The Ryukyu Islands become part of imperial Japan

1900 The Peace Law places severe restrictions on trade union activity

1854 Perry returns and signs the Treaty of Kanagawa; two trading ports are established

1872 Army reforms begin

1902 The Anglo-Japanese alliance is signed, giving Japan greater freedom of action in east Asia

1875 Japan cedes Sakhalin to Russia in exchange for Kurils

Wars and conflicts

1863–64 Western powers bombard Kagoshima and Shimonoseki after Satsuma and Choshu forces attack westerners

1877 Satsuma rebellion; major uprising by *samurai* under Saigo Takamori put down by government forces

1894–95 Sino-Japanese War: Japanese victories at Port Arthur and at the Battle of the Yalu River

1904–05 Russo-Japanese War; Japan routs Russia on land and at sea

1910 Japan annexes Korea (a protectorate since 1905)

1867 Civil war breaks out after Choshu-Satsuma clans rebel against the *shogun*

1895 Treaty of Shimonoseki; China cedes Taiwan and Pescadores to Japan

1900 Japan sends troops to help put down the Boxer Uprising in China

1850 .... 1875 1900

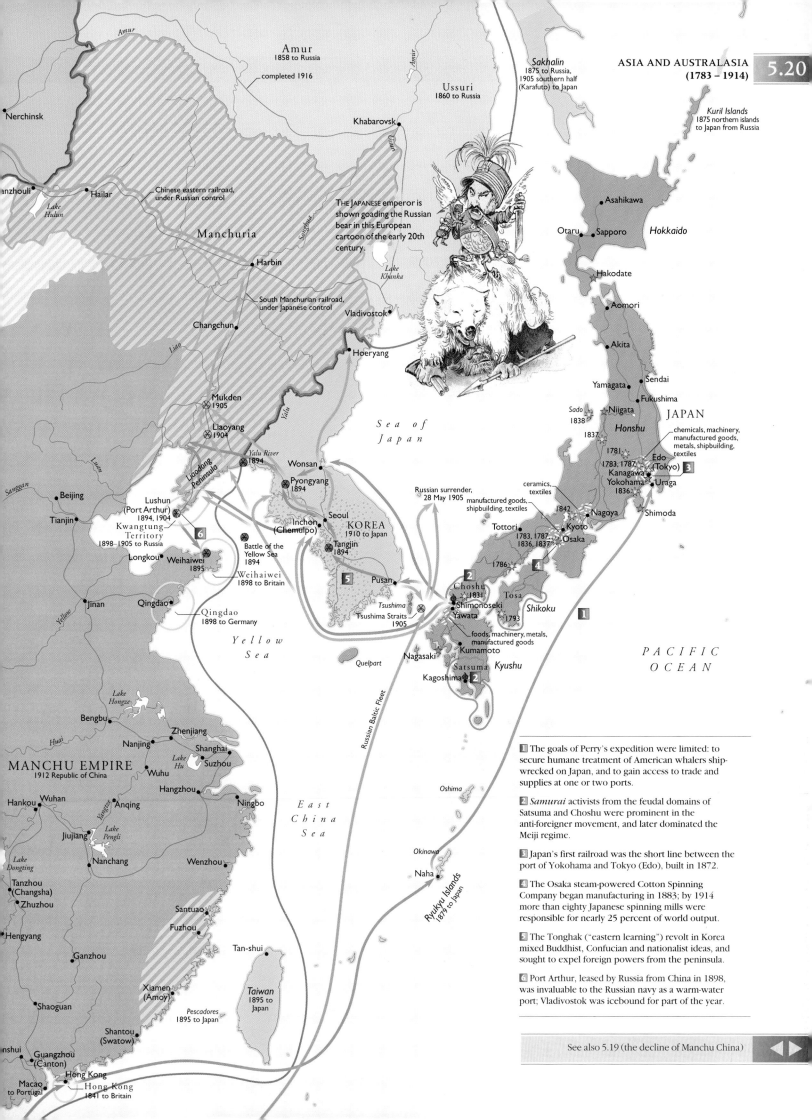

Amur
1858 to Russia

completed 1916

Nerchinsk

Khabarovsk

Ussuri
1860 to Russia

Amur

anzhouli

Lake
Hulun

Hailar

Chinese eastern railroad,
under Russian control

Manchuria

Songhua

Harbin

Changchun

Liao

Hoeryang

South Manchurian railroad,
under Japanese control

Vladivostok

Lake
Khanka

THE JAPANESE emperor is
shown goading the Russian
bear in this European
cartoon of the early 20th
century.

Mukden
1905

Liaoyang
1904

Yalu River
1894

Wonsan

Pyongyang
1894

Sea of
Japan

Russian surrender,
28 May 1905

Beijing

Lushun
(Port Arthur)
1894, 1904

Kwangtung
Territory
1898–1905 to Russia

Liaodong
Peninsula

Inchon
(Chemulpo)

Seoul

KOREA
1910 to Japan

Tangjin
1894

Tianjin

Longkou

Weihaiwei
1895

Weihaiwei
1898 to Britain

Battle of the
Yellow Sea
1894

5

Pusan

Jinan

Qingdao

Qingdao
1898 to Germany

Yellow
Sea

Tsushima

Tsushima Straits
1905

Choshu
1831

Tosa

Shikoku

Russian Baltic Fleet

Quelpart

Nagasaki

Shimonoseki
Yawata

foods, machinery, metals,
manufactured goods

Kumamoto

Satsuma

Kagoshima

Kyushu

East
China
Sea

Oshima

Okinawa

Naha

Ryukyu Islands
1879 to Japan

Sakhalin
1875 to Russia,
1905 southern half
(Karafuto) to Japan

Kuril Islands
1875 northern islands
to Japan from Russia

Asahikawa

Otaru   Sapporo

Hokkaido

Hakodate

Aomori

Akita

Yamagata   Sendai

Fukushima

Sado
1838   Niigata

1837

JAPAN

Honshu

chemicals, machinery,
manufactured goods,
metals, shipbuilding,
textiles

1781

1783, 1787   Edo
(Tokyo)   3

Kanagawa

Yokohama
1836   Uraga

ceramics,
textiles

1842   Nagoya

Shimoda

Tottori

Kyoto

1783, 1787,
1836, 1837   Osaka

manufactured goods,
shipbuilding, textiles

1786

PACIFIC
OCEAN

MANCHU EMPIRE
1912 Republic of China

Lake
Hongze

Bengbu

Zhenjiang

Huai

Nanjing

Lake
Hu

Shanghai

Suzhou

Wuhu

Hankou   Wuhan

Yangtze

Anqing

Hangzhou

Ningbo

Lake
Pengli

Jiujiang

Nanchang

Lake
Dongting

Tanzhou
(Changsha)

Zhuzhou

Wenzhou

Santuao

Hengyang

Fuzhou

Ganzhou

Tan-shui

Shaoguan

Xiamen
(Amoy)

Pescadores
1895 to Japan

Taiwan
1895 to
Japan

shui

Guangzhou
(Canton)

Macao
to Portugal

Hong Kong

Hong Kong
1841 to Britain

1 The goals of Perry's expedition were limited: to
secure humane treatment of American whalers shipwrecked on Japan, and to gain access to trade and
supplies at one or two ports.

2 Samurai activists from the feudal domains of
Satsuma and Choshu were prominent in the
anti-foreigner movement, and later dominated the
Meiji regime.

3 Japan's first railroad was the short line between the
port of Yokohama and Tokyo (Edo), built in 1872.

4 The Osaka steam-powered Cotton Spinning
Company began manufacturing in 1883; by 1914
more than eighty Japanese spinning mills were
responsible for nearly 25 percent of world output.

5 The Tonghak ("eastern learning") revolt in Korea
mixed Buddhist, Confucian and nationalist ideas, and
sought to expel foreign powers from the peninsula.

6 Port Arthur, leased by Russia from China in 1898,
was invaluable to the Russian navy as a warm-water
port; Vladivostok was icebound for part of the year.

See also 5.19 (the decline of Manchu China)

Despite its territorial acquisitions toward the end of the 18th century, the British East India Company still saw its role in the subcontinent as primarily commercial. This was enshrined in the India Act passed by the British Parliament in 1784, which forbade further annexation. Nevertheless, British rule (*raj*) in India continued to grow, as successive governors-general felt obliged to occupy hostile territory or form protectorates to prevent disruption to trade. Thus, when Tipu Sultan of Mysore attacked Travancore in 1789, he saw half his dominions annexed by Lord Cornwallis (governor-general 1786–93) in the ensuing war. Warfare was resumed against the Marathas of central India in 1803.

The fear of an assault on India by Napoleon radically altered British policy. A far more aggressive approach was adopted, in which independent principalities such as Hyderabad were reduced to dependencies by the stationing of British troops there. After the French threat had passed, Company interest turned toward countering Burmese aggression in the east and guarding against Russian incursions from the north. Assam, Arakan, and Tenasserim were acquired from Burma in 1824–26. On the northwest frontier, the First Afghan War (1839–42) was begun against Dost Muhammed; in both this and a later conflict (1878–80), the British occupied Kabul but failed to dominate the country. An attack on Sind secured the Bolan Pass in 1843, while two bloody wars against the Sikhs brought control of the Punjab. Lord Dalhousie (governor-general 1848–56) now evolved the doctrine of "lapse" (when a Hindu prince had no natural heirs his lands passed to the Company) and, on the pretext of ineffective government, annexed Muslim Oudh in 1856.

The East India Company also instituted administrative reforms. These began with revision of land revenue collection (the principal source of public finance) and a reorganization of the judicial system along British lines. Despite a Parliamentary directive urging respect for the people's rights and customs, the Company often disregarded religious and cultural sensitivities – particularly under governor-general Lord Bentinck (1828–35) who tried to ban *suttee* (the immolation of Hindu widows), *thuggee* (ritual robbery and murder) and infanticide. Continuing Christian conversion, plans to extend roads and railroads and an insistence on English as the language of education and commerce all threatened the traditional ways of life of both Hindus and Muslims.

Opposition to British rule was not, however, anticipated among the Company's *sepoy* (native) armies. Three such armies had been raised in India; those based at Madras and Bombay were largely untroubled by questions of caste and religion, but the Bengal *sepoys* – high-caste Hindus and Shi'ite Muslims – were offended by a rumor that new rifle cartridges (which had to be bitten before use) were greased with pork and beef fat. This violated the dietary proscriptions of their religions. Thus began the most serious challenge to British rule in India.

The Indian mutiny (also known as the First War of Independence) arose in January 1857 among troops stationed at Meerut and rapidly spread through north central India. The army revolt acted as a catalyst to a number of other grievances, and the mutineers were supported by peasant uprisings and some isolated *jihads*. The capture of Delhi and the besieging of the cities of Kanpur and Lucknow were serious blows to British authority. However, the Bombay and Madras armies remained largely loyal, and there was no strategy for a national revolt.

Though brief, the mutiny changed the face of British India; suspicion was now widespread on both sides. The 1858 Government of India Act transferred sovereignty from the East India Company to the British monarch and ended the doctrine of lapse, but other reforms were never instituted. Theoretically, racial impartiality operated in recruitment to the Indian civil service; in practice few Indians were admitted. The insular community of Anglo-Indians shunned contact with the indigenous population and became ever more prosperous, partly through investment in plantations in southeast Asia and Africa. Gurkha and Sikh troops from the northwest of India now formed the backbone of the army.

The British policy in frontier regions continued to be determined by fear of Russian expansion; this led to the Second Afghan War of 1878–80, which ended with the recognition that Afghanistan could not be incorporated within the Indian empire. Similarly, in 1903 the British under Colonel Younghusband invaded Tibet. After a year's conflict Tibet agreed not to concede territory to a foreign power.

Excluded from the administration of their country, educated Indians turned increasingly toward nationalism. The Indian National Congress was founded in 1885 and Gopal Gokhale, its president in 1905, worked for peaceful constitutional progress towards responsible government. The All-India Muslim League, a similarly constitutional organization, was founded in 1906. The Morley–Minto constitutional reforms (1909) brought in a measure of representative government, but Indians were still denied true legislative and financial power.

Map legend

- territory under direct Maratha rule, 1785
- British territory, 1805
- British territorial gains by 1838
- British territorial gains by 1857
- British territorial gains by 1914
- British sphere of influence, 1914
- princely state or protectorate, 1914
- border of princely state or protectorate
- border, 1914
- battle in the second Maratha War, 1803-05
- disruption to British administration during the Indian mutiny, 1857-59
- *Sepoy* army base remaining loyal to Britain, 1857
- center of rebellion
- naval station
- *coal* source of commodity
- British campaign
- railroad by 1914

AFGHANISTAN
Kandahar
Quetta
PERSIA
1893 to Britain
Bolan Pass
Baluchistan
1876 British protectorate

TIMELINE

Political & social change

1800	1850	1900
1784 The India Act declares that "territorial expansion" is repugnant to the nation	**1836** Major road-building program begins	**1905** Bengal is partitioned into Bengal, East Bengal and Assam
1798 Ceylon becomes a Crown Colony	**1853** The first railroad in India is opened in Bombay	**1906** The All-India Muslim League is founded in Dhaka
1813 Christian missionaries are licensed to preach	**1857** The first Indian doctors graduate in Agra	**1877** Queen Victoria is proclaimed Empress of India in Delhi
	1858 Queen Victoria assumes sovereignty of India as East India Company is wound up	**1909** The Morley–Minto reforms give India a first taste of representative government
	1835 English language made the medium of instruction	**1885** The Indian National Congress is formed in Bombay
		1911 King George V attends coronation *Durbar* in Delhi

Military developments

1800	1850	1900
1799 Tipu Sultan is defeated by Cornwallis and killed	**1839–42** Disastrous Afghan War is fought to counter a perceived Russian threat	**1878–80** Second Afghan War; Britain fails to subdue Afghanistan
1803 Second Maratha War begins (lasts until 1818)	**1843–49** Forcible annexation of Sind and the Punjab	**1903–04** British military expedition to Tibet forces trade agreement
1816 The Nepalese end their war with the British	**1857** Mutiny begins with the capture of Delhi and sieges of Lucknow and Kanpur	**1886** Upper Burma is annexed by the British
		1912 Viceroy of India is wounded by terrorist bomb
		1897 A Pathan uprising on the northwest frontier is put down with difficulty

1800 1850 1900

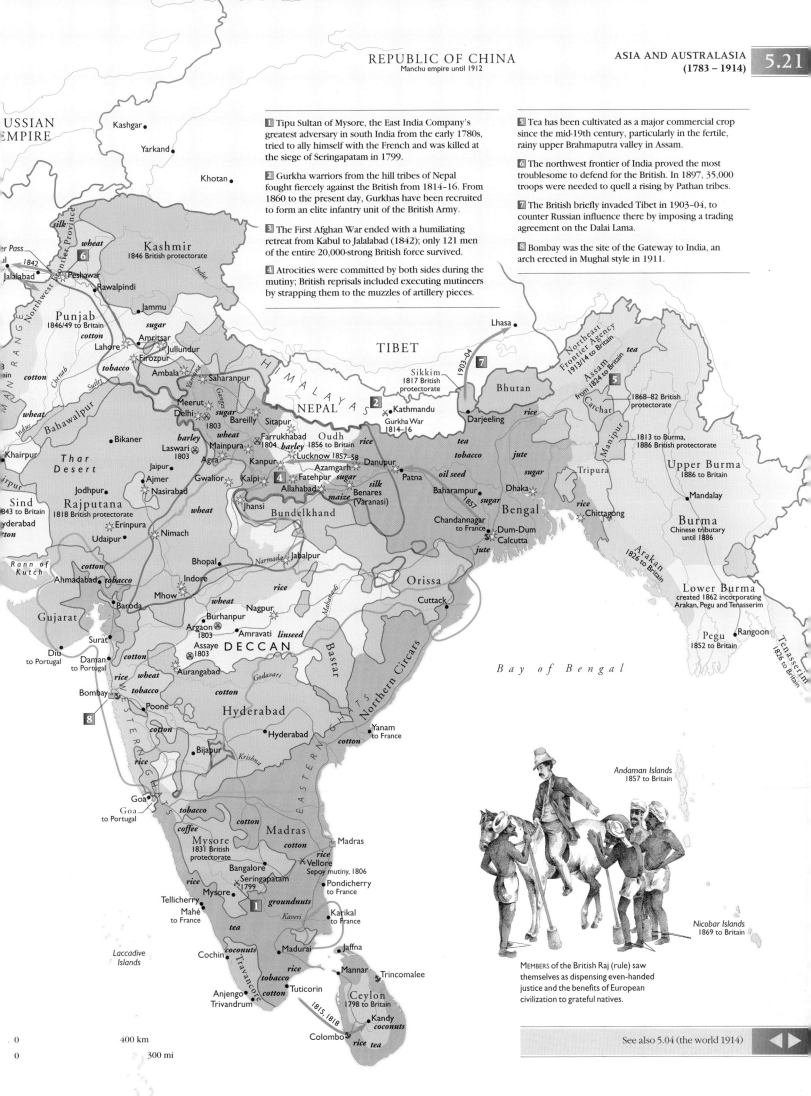

1 Tipu Sultan of Mysore, the East India Company's greatest adversary in south India from the early 1780s, tried to ally himself with the French and was killed at the siege of Seringapatam in 1799.

2 Gurkha warriors from the hill tribes of Nepal fought fiercely against the British from 1814–16. From 1860 to the present day, Gurkhas have been recruited to form an elite infantry unit of the British Army.

3 The First Afghan War ended with a humiliating retreat from Kabul to Jalalabad (1842); only 121 men of the entire 20,000-strong British force survived.

4 Atrocities were committed by both sides during the mutiny; British reprisals included executing mutineers by strapping them to the muzzles of artillery pieces.

5 Tea has been cultivated as a major commercial crop since the mid-19th century, particularly in the fertile, rainy upper Brahmaputra valley in Assam.

6 The northwest frontier of India proved the most troublesome to defend for the British. In 1897, 35,000 troops were needed to quell a rising by Pathan tribes.

7 The British briefly invaded Tibet in 1903–04, to counter Russian influence there by imposing a trading agreement on the Dalai Lama.

8 Bombay was the site of the Gateway to India, an arch erected in Mughal style in 1911.

RUSSIAN EMPIRE

Kashgar
Yarkand
Khotan

silk
wheat
6
1842
Jalalabad
Peshawar
Rawalpindi
Jammu
Kashmir
1846 British protectorate

Punjab
1846/49 to Britain
sugar
cotton
Amritsar
Lahore
Jullundur
Firozpur
Ambala
tobacco
Saharanpur
cotton
wheat

HIMALAYAS

TIBET

Lhasa
1903–04
7

Sikkim
1817 British protectorate

Bhutan

Northeast Frontier Agency 1913/14 to Britain
tea
Assam from 1824 to Britain
5
Cachar
1868–82 British protectorate

Meerut
Delhi
1803
Bareilly
Sitapur
Nepal
2 Kathmandu
Gurkha War 1814–16
Darjeeling
tea
tobacco
jute
Manipur
1813 to Burma, 1886 British protectorate

Bikaner
barley
Laswari 1803
Mainpura
wheat
Farrukhabad 1804
barley
Oudh 1856 to Britain
Lucknow 1857–58
rice
sugar
Tripura
Upper Burma 1886 to Britain

Thar Desert
Jaipur
Ajmer
Nasirabad
Agra
Kanpur
Azamgarh
Danupur
Patna
oil seed
Baharampur
1857
sugar
Dhaka
Bengal
Mandalay

Jodhpur
Gwalior
Kalpi
4 Fatehpur
Allahabad
sugar
maize
silk
Benares (Varanasi)
Bengal

Rajputana
1818 British protectorate
Erinpura
Nimach
wheat
Jhansi
Bundelkhand
Chandannagar to France
Dum-Dum
Calcutta
rice
Chittagong
Burma
Chinese tributary until 1886

Sind
1843 to Britain
Hyderabad
cotton
Udaipur
Bhopal
Narmada
Jabalpur
jute
Arakan 1826 to Britain

Rann of Kutch
cotton
Ahmadabad
tobacco
Indore
rice
Orissa
Lower Burma
created 1862 incorporating Arakan, Pegu and Tenasserim

Gujarat
Baroda
Mhow
wheat
Nagpur
Cuttack
Pegu 1852 to Britain
Rangoon

Surat
Diu to Portugal
Daman to Portugal
cotton
rice *wheat*
Argaon 1803
Amravati
linseed
Assaye ⊗ 1803
DECCAN
Aurangabad
Burhanpur
cotton
Godavari
Bastar
Northern Circars
Tenasserim 1826 to Britain

Bombay
8
tobacco
Poone
cotton
Hyderabad
Hyderabad
Krishna
Yanam to France
cotton
Bay of Bengal

rice
Bijapur

Goa
Goa to Portugal
tobacco
cotton
Madras
Andaman Islands
1857 to Britain

coffee
Mysore
1831 British protectorate
cotton
Madras
Bangalore
Vellore
Sepoy mutiny, 1806
rice

Tellicherry
rice
Mysore
Seringapatam 1799
Pondicherry to France
1
groundnuts
Mahé to France
Kaveri
Karikal to France

tea
Madurai
Jaffna
Cochin
coconuts
Trincomalee
Nicobar Islands
1869 to Britain

Laccadive Islands
tobacco
cotton
Tuticorin
Mannar

Anjengo
Trivandrum
Travancore
rice
Ceylon
1798 to Britain
1815–1818
Kandy
coconuts
Colombo
rice *tea*

MEMBERS of the British Raj (rule) saw themselves as dispensing even-handed justice and the benefits of European civilization to grateful natives.

0   400 km
0   300 mi

See also 5.04 (the world 1914)

Southeast Asia had suffered extensive foreign intervention by the end of the 18th century. While the Dutch seaborne empire in island southeast Asia remained the major European presence, British entrepreneurs had also set up bases for trade with China. French missionaries and traders, interested in Vietnam since the 17th century, were given more leeway through a 1787 treaty. However, the first major French expedition did not occur until 1858–59, when the empire-building aspirations of Napoleon III resulted in the capture of Saigon. Despite resistance in the Mekong delta area, the French made further gains, establishing a protectorate over the Buddhist state of Cambodia and opening Hanoi and Tourane (Da Nang) as treaty ports. In an undeclared war with China (1883–85), France tried to win control of the whole of Indo-China, a goal achieved in 1887 with the merging of Cochin China, Cambodia, Annam and Tongking as the Indo-Chinese Union (French Indo-China). In 1893 it was extended to include Laos.

At first the French in Indo-China concentrated on modernizing and maximizing profits. Peasants were urged to sell land to boost rice production, so undermining traditional large viable villages. Landless peasants took jobs in salt and opium factories or worked for landlords.

British involvement in mainland southeast Asia began with the purchase of the island of Penang from the sultan of Kedah in 1786. During the Napoleonic Wars (when the Netherlands was under French control), Britain attacked Batavia to win control of Java and safeguard its trade routes to China through the island channels. The administrator Sir Stamford Raffles founded the free port of Singapore in 1819, which rapidly became the commercial center of the region, stimulating demand for British cotton manufactures in southeast Asia and China. In 1824 Britain ceded Benkulen and its claims to Sumatra in exchange for Dutch recognition of British sovereignty over Penang, Port Wellesley, Singapore and Malacca (collectively known as the Straits Settlements). Britain became involved in combating piracy and slavery, and settling disputes among the Malay princely states and sultanates on

sultanate of Aceh, 1873
Federated Malay States, 1896
Unfederated Malay States, 1909
borders, 1914
British territory, 1914
British sphere of influence
Dutch East Indies, 1914
French Indochina, 1914
German territory, 1914
Portuguese territory, 1914
United States territory, 1914
area of piracy
area of resistance by indigenous peoples
British campaign
French campaign
United States campaign
gold source of commodity
trade route through Malacca Straits

0   600 km
0   400 mi

TIMELINE

Indo-China

1800

1782–1809 Rama I founds Bangkok and increases Siam's influence in Chiangmai, the Lao states and Cambodia

1786 Britain acquires Penang from Sultan of Kedah

1795 Britain takes Malacca from the Dutch

1802 Nguyen Anh unifies Vietnam and rules from Hue as the first Nguyen emperor

1819 Founding of Singapore by Sir Stamford Raffles

1820–42 Vietnamese emperor Minh-Manh revives Confucianism and persecutes Christians

1824 The Anglo-Dutch Treaty confirms British dominance in Malaya (and Singapore)

1824–25 The British take Rangoon in First Burmese War

1850

1852–53 Second Burmese War; British gains reduce Burma to an inland state

1855 King Mongkut (r.1851–68) opens Siam to British trade

1858–59 French and Spanish naval force bombards Tourane and occupies Saigon

1873 France begins the occupation of Tongking

1900

1883 The Treaty of Hué leads to the creation of French protectorates in Annam and Tongking

1886 Britain annexes Upper Burma in Third Burmese War

1887 The Indo-Chinese Union is created by France

1896 Malay states of Perak, Selangor, Negri Sembilan and Pahang are federated

1909 Anglo-Siamese Treaty; Britain controls Kedah, Perlis, Kelantan and Trengganu

1914 100,000 Vietnamese go to France to serve in labor battalions in World War I

Island southeast Asia

1811 The Dutch surrender Java to a British invasion force

1814–16 The Netherlands regains Sumatra and Java

1841 The sultan of Brunei cedes Sarawak to Brooke

1859 The Dutch and Portuguese agree to partition island of Timor

1873 The Dutch attack the Aceh sultanate (to 1907)

1884 Germany annexes northern New Guinea and the Bismarck Archipelago

1898–99 US takes Philippines in the Spanish-American War

1901 Filipino leader Emileo Aguinaldo is captured

1800   **1850**   **1900**

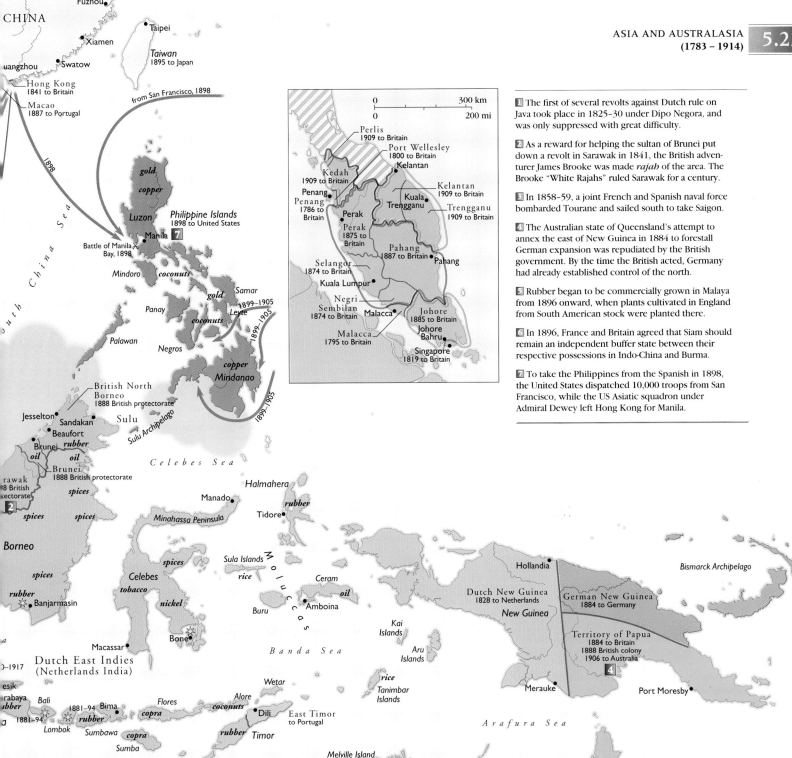

CHINA

Fuzhou

Taipei

Xiamen

uangzhou Swatow

Taiwan
1895 to Japan

Hong Kong
1841 to Britain

from San Francisco, 1898

Macao
1887 to Portugal

1898

gold

copper

Luzon

Philippine Islands
1898 to United States

Manila **7**

Battle of Manila
Bay, 1898

Mindoro *coconuts*

gold

Panay Samar

1899–1905

Leyte 1899–1905

coconuts

Palawan

Negros

copper
Mindanao

British North
Borneo
1888 British protectorate

Jesselton Sulu

Sandakan

Beaufort

Brunei *rubber*

oil

Brunei *oil*
1888 British protectorate

Celebes Sea

rawak
8 British
ectorate

2

spices *spices*

spices

Borneo

spices

rubber

Banjarmasin

South China Sea

Halmahera

Manado

rubber
Tidore

Minahassa Peninsula

Celebes *spices*

tobacco

nickel

Bone

Macassar

Sula Islands

rice

Ceram

oil
Amboina

Buru

M o l u c c a s

Kai
Islands

Aru
Islands

Banda Sea

Hollandia

Dutch New Guinea
1828 to Netherlands

German New Guinea
1884 to Germany

New Guinea

Bismarck Archipelago

Territory of Papua
1884 to Britain
1888 British colony
1906 to Australia

4

Dutch East Indies
(Netherlands India)

0–1917

esik

rabaya
bber

Bali 1881–94 Bima *copra*

rubber 1881–94 *rubber*

Lombok Sumbawa *copra*

Sumba

Flores

Wetar

Alore

coconuts

Dili

East Timor
to Portugal

rice

Tanimbar
Islands

Merauke

Port Moresby

A r a f u r a   S e a

rubber Timor

Melville Island

0 300 km
0 200 mi

Perlis
1909 to Britain

Port Wellesley
1800 to Britain

Kelantan

Kedah
1909 to Britain

Penang

Kelantan
1909 to Britain

Penang
1786 to
Britain

Perak

Kuala
Trengganu

Trengganu
1909 to Britain

Perak
1875 to
Britain

Pahang
1887 to Britain Pahang

Selangor
1874 to Britain

Kuala Lumpur

Negri
Sembilan
1874 to Britain

Malacca

Johore
1885 to Britain

Johore
Bahru

Malacca
1795 to Britain

Singapore
1819 to Britain

1 The first of several revolts against Dutch rule on Java took place in 1825–30 under Dipo Negora, and was only suppressed with great difficulty.

2 As a reward for helping the sultan of Brunei put down a revolt in Sarawak in 1841, the British adventurer James Brooke was made *rajah* of the area. The Brooke "White Rajahs" ruled Sarawak for a century.

3 In 1858–59, a joint French and Spanish naval force bombarded Tourane and sailed south to take Saigon.

4 The Australian state of Queensland's attempt to annex the east of New Guinea in 1884 to forestall German expansion was repudiated by the British government. By the time the British acted, Germany had already established control of the north.

5 Rubber began to be commercially grown in Malaya from 1896 onward, when plants cultivated in England from South American stock were planted there.

6 In 1896, France and Britain agreed that Siam should remain an independent buffer state between their respective possessions in Indo-China and Burma.

7 To take the Philippines from the Spanish in 1898, the United States dispatched 10,000 troops from San Francisco, while the US Asiatic squadron under Admiral Dewey left Hong Kong for Manila.

the peninsula. In 1896 Federated Malay States was set up under a British resident-general. Thirteen years later other states were acquired from Siam; these formed the Unfederated Malay States. Tin exports increased after mining was mechanized in the early 1900s. Rubber also became a major export; by 1911 nearly half a million hectares of rubber was being grown, mainly on large, European-owned estates. The 1824 treaty had also provided a case for the "white rajah" James Brooke to gain British protection for the state he created in Sarawak in 1841. In North Borneo commercial competition for concessions from Brunei and Sulu led eventually to an 1881 royal charter for a British North Borneo Company, which undertook the exploitation of the territory.

To protect India's borders, Britain also annexed Burma in the course of three brief wars. The first (1824–26) was in response to a Burmese invasion of Bengal, and resulted in Burma surrendering large

tracts of territory. Lower Burma was secured by the British in the second war (1852–53), and Upper Burma in the third (1885–86). The British administered the country as part of India.

Germany and the United States were late beginning their colonial ventures in southeast Asia. Rival claims to the eastern part of New Guinea eventually saw Germany occupy the northeast and the adjacent islands (renamed the Bismarck Archipelago), and a British protectorate over the southeast of the island. A crown colony in 1888, British New Guinea became a territory of the Australian Commonwealth in 1906. The United States acquired its first and most important southeast Asian colony in 1898, when Admiral Dewey destroyed a Spanish fleet in Manila Bay to secure the Philippines. Filipino nationalists, who had been encouraged by the United States to fight for their independence against Spanish rule, now felt betrayed by US actions and fierce fighting

ensued on Mindanao during 1902–05. The conflict wrecked the fragile economy and, in addition to military casualties, 100,000 people died from famine.

After the withdrawal of the British from Sumatra, the Dutch faced opposition from indigenous people in the East Indies. Prince Dipo Negoro's rebellion led to the Java War of 1825–29; Tuanku Imam, Minangkabau's militant leader, fought the Dutch 1830–39; and persistent attacks on merchant shipping by the state of Aceh led the Dutch to declare war in 1873. Thirty years of conflict drained the Dutch reserves so that effective occupation of the islands was still incomplete by 1914, although the governor-general J.B. Van Heutsz (1904–09) strove relentlessly to govern the East Indies as a single state from Batavia.

See also 5.04 (the world 1914)

Napoleon's invasion of the Iberian peninsula in 1808–09 was the catalyst to the independence movements in the American colonies of Spain and Portugal. In the Spanish territories, wars of liberation broke out when Napoleon's brother Joseph Bonaparte took the Spanish throne. Brazil played host to Portugal's prince regent, later JoãoVI, who fled there in 1807 after the French occupied Portugal. When he returned home in 1822, his son Pedro became emperor of an independent Brazil. The new state was recognized by Portugal in 1825.

Mexico's war of independence, led by the priest Miguel Hidalgo, began in 1810. Hidalgo was executed, but his conservative successor Agustín Iturbide united Mexican society and in 1822–23 formed the Mexican empire with himself as emperor. At the same time, the Spanish colonies in Central America proclaimed a Confederation of the United Provinces, which lasted until 1838, when its constituent parts became individual sovereign states.

The principal figure of South American independence, Simón Bolívar (the "Liberator"), began his fight to free his native Venezuela and adjoining territories from Spanish rule in 1811. Bolívar's victory at Boyacá in 1819 heralded the proclamation of the Republic of Gran Colombia, and his defeat of the royalists at Carabobo in 1821 led to the fall of Caracas and to Venezuelan independence. In Argentina, revolutionary forces were led by José de San Martín, a veteran of the Peninsular War. San Martín trained an army and led it across the Andes in 1817 to take Lima in 1821. He proclaimed Peru's independence, then gave up control to Bolívar who established a revolutionary government at Lima. With the final battle of the wars of liberation at Ayacucho in 1824, all Spanish possessions in the Americas were independent, except Cuba and Puerto Rico.

The new states not only inherited the frontiers of the former Spanish and Portuguese administrative regions; social divisions also remained intact. There was no tradition of pluralistic government, and color was still decisive. Spanish-born whites or *peninsulares* (and *reinóis*, the Portuguese equivalent in Brazil) were dominant. The majority of the people (*mestizos* or Indian–Europeans) had limited power

Portuguese colony c.1800

Spanish colony c.1800

Republic of Gran Colombia, 1819–30

united with Mexico 1821–23, independent as United Provinces of Central America 1823–38

Confederation of Peru & Bolivia 1836–39

1838 date of independence as a nation-state

territory gained by former Spanish colony since independence, with date

territory gained by the United States from Mexico, with date

→ campaign by Simón Bolívar 1819–24

→ campaign by José de San Martín 1817–22

→ campaign by United States forces, 1846–48

⊗ battle fought by José de San Martín

⊗ battle fought by Bolívar or de Sucre

⊗ battle during the Mexican–American War, 1846–48

⊗ battle during the Paraguayan War (War of the Triple Alliance), 1864–70

⊗ battle during the War of the Pacific 1879–83

— border c.1840

- - - other border

— railroad within Latin America by 1914

oil trade commodity

➤ movement of peoples

SIMON BOLIVAR was a remarkable military leader, and is the only individual to have a state named for him today.

Galapagos Islands 1832 to Ecuador

TIMELINE

Wars and revolutions

1810–11 Miguel Hidalgo leads an unsuccessful popular revolt in Mexico

1810–14 An attempted revolution in Chile is defeated

1819 Simón Bolívar routs the Spanish at Boyacá and founds Republic of Gran Colombia

1821 Battle of Carabobo; independence of Venezuela

1836 Texas gains its independence from Mexico at the Battle of San Jacinto

1836–39 Bolivia and Peru form a brief confederation

1846–48 Mexican–American War following US annexation of Texas (1845); Mexico loses all its northern territories

1863 Ill-fated attempt by Mexican conservatives and French to install emperor (Maximilian I; executed 1867)

1864–70 War of the Triple Alliance is fought by Paraguay against Argentina, Uruguay and Brazil.

1879–83 War of the Pacific between Chile and Bolivia and Peru

1903 A revolution in Panama brings independence from Colombia

1910 The Mexican Revolution begins; forces under Francisco Madero oppose dictatorship of Porfirio Diaz (1876–1911)

1914 United States Marines occupy Veracruz to safeguard US interests

Social and political change

1807 The Braganzas (Portuguese royal family) flee to Brazil under British escort

1823 US recognizes newly independent states and proclaims the "Monroe Doctrine"

1829–52 Dictatorship of Juan Manuel Rosas in Argentina

1831 Emperor Pedro I of Brazil abdicates and his son Pedro II succeeds

1853 Mexico sells the Mesilla Valley to the United States in the "Gadsden Purchase"

1870–88 Liberal Guzman Blanco is president in Venezuela; many social and political reforms are instituted

1879 French company under Ferdinand de Lesseps is set up to build the Panama Canal

1889 The Brazilian empire is succeeded by Republic of the United States of Brazil

1904 US engineers begin cutting the Panama Canal (completed 1914)

while the *mulattoes* (African–Europeans), *zambos* (Indian–Africans), blacks and Indians all suffered discrimination. Sectional interests, such as the military, the church, industrialists, bankers and landlords were often in conflict, and power was frequently seized by *caudillos*, dictators who ruled through patronage and private armies.

The *caudillo* José Francia helped lead Paraguay's struggle for independence and was "el supremo" 1814–40. Bernardo O'Higgins was prominent in Chile's revolution and became "supreme director" 1817–23. The Mexican Antonio de Santa Anna, after a period as an elected president (1833–36), intermittently took dictatorial powers. During his rule

Mexico fought, largely unsuccessfully, against the United States, and ceded large tracts of land by 1850.

Intervention by European powers in Latin American affairs was effectively preempted by the Monroe doctrine of 1823, which signaled US hostility toward any attempt to colonize the region. Most territorial changes that occurred did so as a result of wars between the new sovereign states. Major conflicts of the period were the War of the Pacific, in which Chile defeated Peru and Bolivia, and the War of the Triple Alliance), involving Paraguay, Brazil, Argentina and Uruguay. The 1910–11 Mexican revolution led to chaos, mass slaughter and eventual US intervention, as US president Wilson supported General Huerta who exterminated the nationalist Zapata rebels while Pancho Villa's bandits ran riot in the north. Wilson sent warships to Tampico and troops to Veracruz in 1914.

Economic change came swiftly to Latin America. Foreign capital funded railroad and harbor construction; the Panama Canal was completed by US engineers in 1914 after an earlier French venture had failed. British firms exploited the natural phosphates and nitrates of Peru and northern Chile, for use in fertilizers and explosives. US investment turned coffee exports into a vital element in Brazil's economy. In Argentina, revenue from wool, leather and beef exports brought a sharp rise in the standard of living; meat exports grew after refrigerated sea transport was introduced in the 1880s; but a decline in world trade in the 1890s ended the boom years. Immigrants were among the region's greatest assets. Initially they entered Chile and Argentina (which saw a huge influx of Italian immigrants from the 1850s), but Brazil became the preferred destination after slavery was abolished there in 1888. Over one million Europeans arrived in Brazil by 1898; they were favored over the original inhabitants for educational and work opportunities. Chinese and Japanese laborers were also imported in large numbers to work on the railroads and in the mines.

[1] Peruvian *guano* (seabird droppings used as fertilizer) was a major source of foreign revenue after independence, but deposits were exhausted in 20 years.

[2] At the Alamo in 1836, during the Texan War of Independence from Mexico, 180 defenders resisted Mexican forces but were eventually overcome.

[3] The War of the Triple Alliance was the bloodiest conflict in Latin American history. Paraguay lost over 60 percent (300,000) of its population.

[4] Costa Rica was the first Central American republic to export coffee beans. The United Fruit Company developed the country, building its railroad and port facilities. The first elections were held there in 1885.

[5] Manaus, in the Amazon basin, saw great prosperity in the rubber boom of 1890-1920; the town's lavishly appointed opera house was built in 1896.

[6] Mechanization (railroads, steam excavators) and medical provision against malaria were crucial in the success of the US Panama Canal project (1904-14).

See also 5.26 (expansion of the United States)

Map labels:

Bermuda Islands to Britain

ATLANTIC OCEAN

HAITI to France, **1804**
sugar
Santo Domingo
Puerto Rico 1898 to US
Guadeloupe to France
Dominica to France
Martinique to France
Barbados to Britain
Port-au-Prince
DOMINICAN REPUBLIC 1822–44 to Haiti, **1844**

Caribbean Sea
Margarita
Trinidad to Britain
British Guiana (Berbice, Demerara, Essequibo) to the Netherlands, 1814 to Britain
Dutch Guiana to the Netherlands
French Guiana to France

over 3 million immigrants from southern Europe from the mid 1830s

Carabobo 1821
Caracas
Ciudad Bolivar (Angostura)
San Carlos
coffee
coffee
cattle
1904 from Venezuela
VENEZUELA 1821 to Colombia, **1830**
sheep
1905 from Venezuela
Orinoco
Guiana Highlands
timber
Belém
cocoa
Fortaleza (Ceará)

Panama Canal Zone 1903 to United States
ama City
Boyacá 1819
cattle
Bogotá
cattle
COLOMBIA **1819**
1904-05 from Colombia
Negro
Amazon
Manaus
rubber
rubber
rubber
cotton
sugar
Recife (Pernambuco)
coffee

Bombona 1822
hincha 1822
Quito
cattle
1880 from Colombia
Japura
Putumayo
Amazon Basin
Madera
Tapajós
Xingu
BRAZIL **1822**
coffee
tobacco
Salvador (Bahia)

bananas
ECUADOR 1822 to Colombia, **1830**
aquil
1880 from Peru
timber
Purus
Ucayali
rubber
rubber
rubber
São Francisco

sugar
ANDES
copper
1903 from Bolivia
1867 from Peru
rubber
Brazilian Highlands
coffee

Junín 1824
silver
Callao 1880
Lima
Chorrillos 1881
Pisco
Ayacucho 1824
PERU **1821**
nitrates
Tacna 1880
Arica
Iquique 1879
La Paz
BOLIVIA **1825**
copper, silver, tin
Potosí
Matto Grosso Plateau
Corumbá
rubber
coffee
Rio de Janeiro
cattle
Jundiaí
São Paulo
Santos
coffee

guano
1880 to Bolivia
1870 from Paraguay
Curupayty 1866
PARAGUAY **1811**
Asunción
1874 from Paraguay
cattle

1883 from Peru
Antofagasta 1879
1884 from Bolivia
Paso de Patria 1866
Riachuelo 1865
1874 from Paraguay
Porto Alegre
cattle
Pelotas
Rio Grande

copper, manganese, silver, tin
timber
Paraná
ARGENTINA **1816**
URUGUAY **1828**
cattle
Montevideo
Campana
Buenos Aires

La Serena
Chacabuco 1817
Rosario
San Luis
cattle, cereals, sheep
Mar del Plata

Valparaiso
Santiago
Maipo River 1818
CHILE **1818**
Bahia Blanca
Punta Alta
sheep

Valdivia
ANDES
PATAGONIA
1902 to Chile
1881 to Argentina

PACIFIC OCEAN

Falkland Islands (Malvinas) 1820 to Argentina, 1833 to Britain

0   1200 km
0   800 mi

In the late 18th century, British and French Caribbean cane sugar plantations became extremely lucrative ventures. Profits were particularly high on the French islands: St Domingue (Haiti), where 37,000 white planters and 450,000 slaves farmed some of the richest and most extensive estates in the Caribbean, provided 85 percent of France's foreign trade. Yet the heart of the French Caribbean empire was destroyed by the slave insurrection that began on St Domingue in 1791. Under the leadership of Toussaint L'Ouverture and Jean-Jacques Dessalines, the slaves established the independent state of Haiti and repelled French attempts to retake the island. Rebellions among maroons (escaped slaves) in Jamaica and slaves in Guadeloupe, Grenada, St Vincent, Dominica and Barbados failed to repeat the success of the Haitian rebellion.

After the Napoleonic Wars, Britain emerged as the dominant power in the Caribbean. Britain secured St Lucia and Tobago from France; Trinidad from Spain; and Demerara, Essequibo and Berbice from Holland (forming British Guiana). West Indian cane sugar remained the most valuable element of British overseas commerce until the early 1820s.

The prosperity of British Caribbean plantations faced both internal and external threats as the 19th century progressed. The growing presence of Christian missions (first established on Jamaica in 1783) was opposed by planters as contributing to the cause of slave emancipation. Moreover, British West Indian cane sugar faced competition from Mauritius and India, French and German beet sugar and (most serious of all) the huge plantations being developed in Spanish Cuba, independent Brazil and Louisiana, all of which relied heavily on slave labor. In 1834 the abolition of slavery throughout the British empire

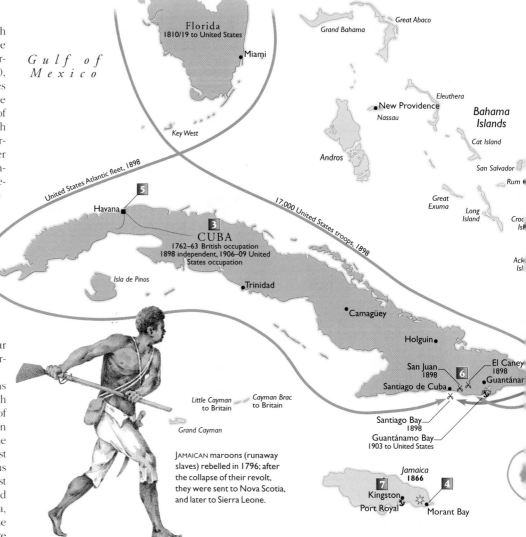

CUBA
1762–63 British occupation
1898 independent, 1906–09 United States occupation

JAMAICAN maroons (runaway slaves) rebelled in 1796; after the collapse of their revolt, they were sent to Nova Scotia, and later to Sierra Leone.

realized the planters' worst fears. The government paid compensation and set a transitional period during which freed slaves would work the land for wages until 1838, but the industry declined steadily.

On the slave plantations of other countries, industrialization brought increased production. Spanish Cuba constructed the first railroad in the region and invested in new refineries. Brazil was equally progressive. No longer able to compete in the sugar trade, some Caribbean islands began to diversify. Jamaica exported its first bananas to New York in 1870, thus inaugurating a thriving trade. As well as new products, many colonies needed fresh labor to remain viable. Although the remaining French islands did not emancipate their slaves until 1848, they had to attract indentured workers from the Congo. The Dutch imported Javanese laborers, while Cuba and Puerto Rico brought in 125,000 Chinese. Over 430,000 Indians arrived before 1914, adding a new Asian element to the Guianas, Trinidad, Guadeloupe, Martinique and Jamaica.

A rebellion that broke out in 1865 among smallholders at Morant Bay on Jamaica profoundly changed the way the British colonies were governed. The brutal suppression of the uprising by the island's governor persuaded Britain to introduce direct crown colony government to most of its Caribbean possessions, in an effort to improve colonial government, modernize sugar production and promote social welfare. The remaining sugar

TIMELINE

Wars and uprisings

1800	1850	1900
1791 Slave revolt begins in Saint Domingue, led by Toussaint L'Ouverture	1844 Santo Domingo wins its independence through revolution	1895–98 Renewed revolt against Spanish rule in Cuba
1795 Slave uprisings begin in the Windward Islands	1865 Morant Bay rebellion brings constitutional change in most British colonies	1898 The Spanish–American War establishes the United States as an imperial power
1822 Haitian forces overrun and occupy Santo Domingo for over twenty years	1868–78 "Ten Years War" in Cuba; anti-Spanish rebels revolt against government	1906–17 Several revolts on Cuba are suppressed by US intervention

Social and political change

1800	1850	1900
1804 Jean-Jacques Dessalines makes himself emperor of Haiti (assassinated 1806)	1871 The Federation of Leeward Islands is set up	
1814 The last exchange of possessions between Britain and France takes place	1873 30,000 slaves are emancipated in Puerto Rico	
1818–43 Jean-Pierre Boyer rules Haiti and unites the island of Hispaniola	1882 British colonies are urged to diversify	
	1885 The first company is founded to export bananas from the Caribbean	
1834 663,600 slaves are emancipated in the British Caribbean colonies		1905 Substantial oil deposits are found on Trinidad
1837 The first railroad in the Caribbean is built in Cuba		1906 Stevedores strike in Georgetown, British Guiana
1845 The first British colonial railroad opens in Jamaica		1907 The Jamaican Trades and Labor Union is set up
1800	1850	1900

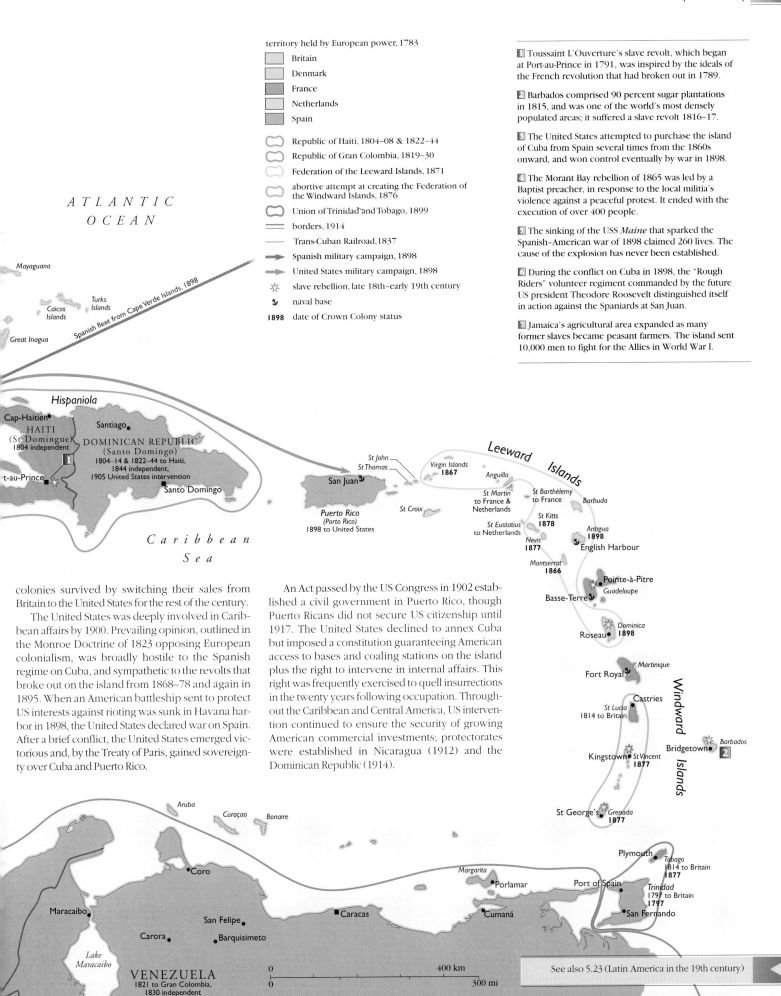

territory held by European power, 1783

Britain

Denmark

France

Netherlands

Spain

Republic of Haiti, 1804-08 & 1822-44

Republic of Gran Colombia, 1819-30

Federation of the Leeward Islands, 1871

abortive attempt at creating the Federation of the Windward Islands, 1876

Union of Trinidad and Tobago, 1899

borders, 1914

Trans-Cuban Railroad, 1837

Spanish military campaign, 1898

United States military campaign, 1898

slave rebellion, late 18th-early 19th century

naval base

1898 date of Crown Colony status

1 Toussaint L'Ouverture's slave revolt, which began at Port-au-Prince in 1791, was inspired by the ideals of the French revolution that had broken out in 1789.

2 Barbados comprised 90 percent sugar plantations in 1815, and was one of the world's most densely populated areas; it suffered a slave revolt 1816–17.

3 The United States attempted to purchase the island of Cuba from Spain several times from the 1860s onward, and won control eventually by war in 1898.

4 The Morant Bay rebellion of 1865 was led by a Baptist preacher, in response to the local militia's violence against a peaceful protest. It ended with the execution of over 400 people.

5 The sinking of the USS *Maine* that sparked the Spanish–American war of 1898 claimed 260 lives. The cause of the explosion has never been established.

6 During the conflict on Cuba in 1898, the "Rough Riders" volunteer regiment commanded by the future US president Theodore Roosevelt distinguished itself in action against the Spaniards at San Juan.

7 Jamaica's agricultural area expanded as many former slaves became peasant farmers. The island sent 10,000 men to fight for the Allies in World War I.

ATLANTIC
OCEAN

Mayaguana

Turks Islands

Caicos Islands

Spanish fleet from Cape Verde Islands, 1898

Great Inagua

Hispaniola

Cap-Haitien•

HAITI (St Domingue)
1804 independent

Santiago•

DOMINICAN REPUBLIC
(Santo Domingo)
1804–14 & 1822–44 to Haiti,
1844 independent,
1905 United States intervention

t-au-Prince•

Santo Domingo•

St John
St Thomas

Virgin Islands
1867

Leeward Islands

Anguilla

San Juan

St Martin
to France & Netherlands

St Barthélemy
to France

Barbuda

Puerto Rico
(Porto Rico)
1898 to United States

St Croix

St Kitts
1878

St Eustatius
to Netherlands

Antigua
1898

English Harbour

Nevis
1877

*Caribbean
Sea*

Montserrat
1866

Pointe-à-Pitre

Guadeloupe

Basse-Terre•

Dominica
1898

Roseau•

colonies survived by switching their sales from Britain to the United States for the rest of the century.

The United States was deeply involved in Caribbean affairs by 1900. Prevailing opinion, outlined in the Monroe Doctrine of 1823 opposing European colonialism, was broadly hostile to the Spanish regime on Cuba, and sympathetic to the revolts that broke out on the island from 1868–78 and again in 1895. When an American battleship sent to protect US interests against rioting was sunk in Havana harbor in 1898, the United States declared war on Spain. After a brief conflict, the United States emerged victorious and, by the Treaty of Paris, gained sovereignty over Cuba and Puerto Rico.

An Act passed by the US Congress in 1902 established a civil government in Puerto Rico, though Puerto Ricans did not secure US citizenship until 1917. The United States declined to annex Cuba but imposed a constitution guaranteeing American access to bases and coaling stations on the island plus the right to intervene in internal affairs. This right was frequently exercised to quell insurrections in the twenty years following occupation. Throughout the Caribbean and Central America, US intervention continued to ensure the security of growing American commercial investments; protectorates were established in Nicaragua (1912) and the Dominican Republic (1914).

Martinique

Fort Royal

Castries

St Lucia
1814 to Britain

Windward Islands

Kingstown• *St Vincent*
1877

Bridgetown• *Barbados*
2

St George's• *Grenada*
1877

Aruba

Curaçao

Bonaire

Plymouth

Tobago
1814 to Britain
1877

•Coro

Margarita

•Porlamar

Port of Spain

Trinidad
1797 to Britain
1797

Maracaibo•

San Felipe•

■Caracas

Cumaná•

•San Fernando

Carora•

•Barquisimeto

*Lake
Maracaibo*

VENEZUELA
1821 to Gran Colombia,
1830 independent

0   400 km

0   300 mi

See also 5.23 (Latin America in the 19th century)

The demographic composition of Canada changed markedly with Britain's loss of its thirteen American colonies in the late 18th century. After this conflict loyal colonists, having no wish to be citizens of the new United States, migrated northward. Thousands of white loyalists from New York and South Carolina, together with the Mohawks who had fought alongside the British, settled in Nova Scotia, New Brunswick, Cape Breton and Prince Edward Island. Ontario (Upper Canada) saw an influx of new arrivals. In addition, the numbers of immigrants from Britain, especially Scotland, continued to rise. French settlers, most of whom had remained in Canada after Britain gained control in 1763 (and whose rights and customs had been enshrined in the 1774 Quebec Act), now found themselves overwhelmed. To reflect this change, in 1791 the Canada Act provided for a governor and two deputies to oversee the interests of Quebec (Lower Canada) and Ontario. Expansion westward began in 1812, when the Red River Colony, the nucleus of what later became Manitoba, was founded by Thomas Douglas, Easl of Selkirk. Yet further growth in this direction was hampered by the rocky terrain of the Canadian Shield.

Trouble between British North America and the United States flared up in the 1812 Anglo-American War. A United States invasion of Canada was followed by a British attack on Washington (1814) and the Battle of New Orleans (1815). The major effect of this brief war was to foster a new Canadian patriotism, founded on fear of American encroachment. Thereafter, border issues were settled peacefully: the 1818 agreement on the 49th Parallel created an undefended US–Canadian frontier from the Lake of the Woods to the Rockies, which the 1846 Oregon Treaty then extended to Vancouver.

Two rebellions in 1837 – Papineau's attempt to

1 Loyalist settlers in Upper Canada in the years following the American War of Independence were given US$30 million by the British government.

2 William Mackenzie's unsuccessful Toronto rebellion of 1837 was directed against the "Family Compact", a system of patronage that benefited the privileged classes.

3 In 1866–70, the Fenian Brotherhood, an American arm of the Irish Republican Brotherhood, carried out raids in Canada, trying to change British policy on Irish independence. The first attack was at Fort Erie.

4 British Columbia joined the Dominion of Canada in 1871, on the condition that the Canadian Pacific Railway would be built across its territory in ten years.

5 The gold rush that began in 1896 on the Klondike river in Canada's Yukon territory lasted five years and Dawson, established to cater for the influx of prospectors, had a population of 30,000 by 1900.

6 Hardy new wheat strains boosted grain production on the prairies so that by 1914 Canada was one of the world's greatest wheat-exporting nations.

break Quebec's links with the British empire and Mackenzie's protest in Toronto against elitist government – resulted in the drafting of a report that recommended unifying Upper and Lower Canada and introducing responsible government. Though this was duly awarded in 1840–47, the American Civil War (1861–65) proved to be the decisive factor in Canadian unification. The Federal victory in 1865, attacks by the Fenian Brotherhood on Canadian territory (1866–70) and the inexorable westward expansion of the United States together caused Canada to press for a coast-to-coast union to ensure national security. The British North America Act of 1867 united Nova Scotia, New Brunswick, Quebec and Ontario in the Dominion of Canada. Manitoba

PROSPECTORS panning for gold flooded to the Canadian west in the later 19th century.

joined in 1870, British Columbia in 1871 and Prince Edward Island in 1873. The first government of the new dominion promoted a "national policy" aimed at peopling the Canadian Shield and the Far West, building a transcontinental railroad and introducing tariffs to protect farm prices.

The rights and claims of indigenous peoples were largely ignored by the new Canadian state. Many Iroquois, Crees and Algonquins entered reservations, and were joined by refugees from the American Indian wars. Some Ojibwa, on the other hand, took the option of moving into uncharted territories. The Métis of Manitoba (Franco–Indians of

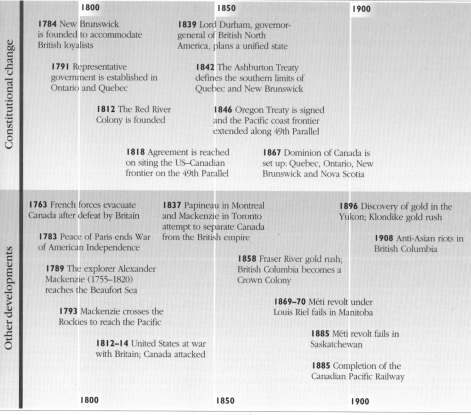

TIMELINE

Constitutional change

1784 New Brunswick is founded to accommodate British loyalists

1791 Representative government is established in Ontario and Quebec

1812 The Red River Colony is founded

1818 Agreement is reached on siting the US–Canadian frontier on the 49th Parallel

1839 Lord Durham, governor-general of British North America, plans a unified state

1842 The Ashburton Treaty defines the southern limits of Quebec and New Brunswick

1846 Oregon Treaty is signed and the Pacific coast frontier extended along 49th Parallel

1867 Dominion of Canada is set up: Quebec, Ontario, New Brunswick and Nova Scotia

Other developments

1763 French forces evacuate Canada after defeat by Britain

1783 Peace of Paris ends War of American Independence

1789 The explorer Alexander Mackenzie (1755–1820) reaches the Beaufort Sea

1793 Mackenzie crosses the Rockies to reach the Pacific

1812–14 United States at war with Britain; Canada attacked

1837 Papineau in Montreal and Mackenzie in Toronto attempt to separate Canada from the British empire

1858 Fraser River gold rush; British Columbia becomes a Crown Colony

1896 Discovery of gold in the Yukon; Klondike gold rush

1908 Anti-Asian riots in British Columbia

1869–70 Méti revolt under Louis Riel fails in Manitoba

1885 Méti revolt fails in Saskatchewan

1885 Completion of the Canadian Pacific Railway

Cree Native American nation

exploration route
→ Hearne, 1770-71
→ Mackenzie, 1789-93
→ Thompson, 1789-1811

expansion of Canada
Canadian provinces, 1867
territory added 1870
province added by 1873
territory added 1880
British crown colony
Canadian territorial claim surrendered to the United States, with date
1867 date of achieving provincial status

Métis' rebellion under Louis Riel
✳ Red River, 1869-70
✳ Northwest (Saskatchewan), 1885
✳ other rebellion, 1837
⬭ goldfield
◇ other metal deposit
△ oil or gas field
fertile belt of the Canadian prairies
Canadian Pacific Railway, 1881-85
other railroad by 1914
migration of Mohawk and colonists loyal to Britain, 1783
other migration of peoples
borders, 1914
▣ state capital
■ provincial capital

0 ____ 1000 km
0 ____ 700 mi

mixed-blood) saw their buffalo-hunting culture threatened by immigrants, a process exacerbated by the surrender of the province to the Crown by the Hudson's Bay Company in 1869. The ensuing Red River Rebellion (1869–70) and the Northwest Rebellion in Saskatchewan (1885) – both led by Louis Riel – were vain attempts to preserve the traditional way of life of the Métis.

The long-promised Canadian Pacific Railway was completed in 1885 and the first transcontinental services began in 1886. This was a crucial element in the unification of Canada; the railroad consolidated the western frontier, created new towns along its route and provided a tangible link between British Columbia and the east.

Canada's frontiers continued to expand to the north. In 1912 Manitoba advanced to the 60th Parallel (to match Saskatchewan and Alberta). In the same year Quebec and Ontario were extended to the Hudson Bay and the Arctic. Another frontier developed as Canada's northernmost territories, home to the Inuit, were encroached upon first by fur-trappers and then thousands of gold prospectors (notably at the Yukon in the far northwest in 1896). Petroleum companies arrived in Alberta when oil reserves were found there in 1912–14.

The first French-Canadian and Catholic prime minister of Canada was the Liberal Wilfred Laurier (1896–1911). Laurier maintained the policy of expansion by encouraging American and eastern European immigrants to settle the prairies. During his premiership, the annual immigration figure rose to almost 400,000. Among them were Japanese and Chinese who worked in railroad construction, timber industries and in mining for coal and gold.

See also 5.26 (expansion of the United States)
◀▶

Two decisions made by the Congress of the embryonic United States of America set up the conflict between white settlers and native Americans that characterized the country's expansion. In 1787 the indigenous peoples were promised that their lands and property could only be ceded with their consent. Yet four years later, George Washington authorized expansion westward along the Ohio. Initially the growth of the United States was limited by Spain's (from 1800, France's) possession of lands beyond the Mississippi. However, even at this stage, strong trade links existed between the thirteen eastern states of the Union and the Pacific; in time, these would spur westward expansion.

Expeditions into native territories began in the late 18th century. The Shawnee and Piankashaw succeeded in repelling a group led by General St Clair in 1791. Yet by 1795, in the Treaty of Greenville, the pattern of substantial territorial gains by the whites and displacement of native Americans to vacant lands in the west was set. The process was hastened by Thomas Jefferson's purchase of Louisiana from France in 1803, when, at a stroke, the territory of the United States was doubled.

In the ensuing decades further territories were gained by the United States, through purchase or conflict: Florida, Texas, Oregon, the Mexican cession and the Gadsden Purchase. Some 400,000 native people were confronted by the westward thrust of settler culture across the Great Plains, enforced by troops stationed west of the Mississippi.

In Florida, the Seminole people conducted a sustained resistance that was only ultimately suppressed in the 1840s. The forcible removal of the Cherokee to the unsettled "Indian Territory" of Oklahoma in 1838–39, after gold was found in their

original homelands, cost four thousand lives (the "Trail of Tears"). The Delaware, Wichita and many others suffered a similar fate. Settlers annexed native American lands with the support of the US government: a succession of bills enacted by Congress offering free land in return for minimal investment encouraged claims to be staked to territories on the Great Plains. Railroads further threatened the Plains peoples' main food source, the vast buffalo herds, already depleted by indiscriminate hunting. Atrocities peaked when the families of Arapaho and Cheyenne warriors who had assembled to sign a treaty at Sand Creek in Colorado in 1864 were slaughtered by a US cavalry contingent.

The Federal government tried to end the killing with an Indian peace commission. The Kiowa, Comanche and Arapaho reluctantly accepted reservation status at the Medicine Lodge Creek Conference (1867), while Sitting Bull's Dakota Sioux

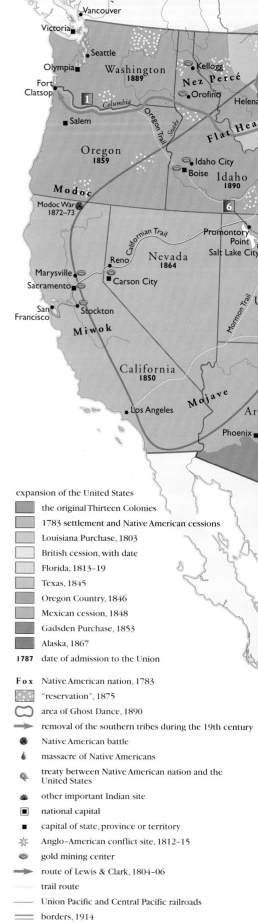

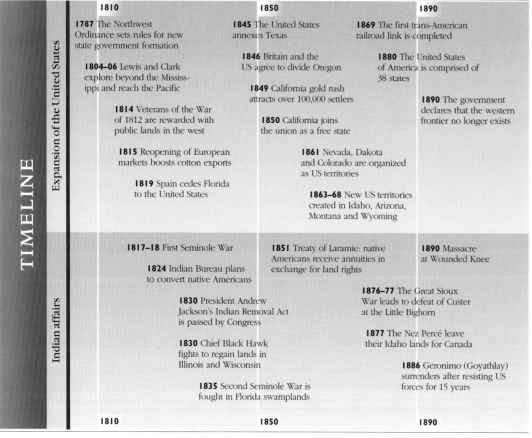

TIMELINE

Expansion of the United States

1810	1850	1890
1787 The Northwest Ordinance sets rules for new state government formation	**1845** The United States annexes Texas	**1869** The first trans-American railroad link is completed
1804–06 Lewis and Clark explore beyond the Mississippi and reach the Pacific	**1846** Britain and the US agree to divide Oregon	**1880** The United States of America is comprised of 38 states
1814 Veterans of the War of 1812 are rewarded with public lands in the west	**1849** California gold rush attracts over 100,000 settlers	**1890** The government declares that the western frontier no longer exists
1815 Reopening of European markets boosts cotton exports	**1850** California joins the union as a free state	
1819 Spain cedes Florida to the United States	**1861** Nevada, Dakota and Colorado are organized as US territories	
	1863–68 New US territories created in Idaho, Arizona, Montana and Wyoming	

Indian affairs

1810	1850	1890
1817–18 First Seminole War	**1851** Treaty of Laramie: native Americans receive annuities in exchange for land rights	**1890** Massacre at Wounded Knee
1824 Indian Bureau plans to convert native Americans		
1830 President Andrew Jackson's Indian Removal Act is passed by Congress		**1876–77** The Great Sioux War leads to defeat of Custer at the Little Bighorn
1830 Chief Black Hawk fights to regain lands in Illinois and Wisconsin		**1877** The Nez Percé leave their Idaho lands for Canada
1835 Second Seminole War is fought in Florida swamplands		**1886** Geronimo (Goyathlay) surrenders after resisting US forces for 15 years

expansion of the United States

- the original Thirteen Colonies
- 1783 settlement and Native American cessions
- Louisiana Purchase, 1803
- British cession, with date
- Florida, 1813–19
- Texas, 1845
- Oregon Country, 1846
- Mexican cession, 1848
- Gadsden Purchase, 1853
- Alaska, 1867

1787   date of admission to the Union

Fox   Native American nation, 1783

- "reservation", 1875
- area of Ghost Dance, 1890
- removal of the southern tribes during the 19th century
- Native American battle
- massacre of Native Americans
- treaty between Native American nation and the United States
- other important Indian site
- national capital
- capital of state, province or territory
- Anglo-American conflict site, 1812–15
- gold mining center
- route of Lewis & Clark, 1804–06
- trail route
- Union Pacific and Central Pacific railroads
- borders, 1914

Map labels

New Brunswick
Nova Scotia
Fredericton
Halifax
1842 to United States
Quebec (Lower Canada)
Québec
Ontario (Upper Canada)
CANADA to Britain, British dominion from 1867
Lake Winnipeg
Lake Winnipegosis
Saskatchewan
Manitoba
Lake Manitoba
Regina
Winnipeg
1818 to Canada
katchewan
Lake Superior
Vermont 1791
Maine 1820
Augusta
Montréal
Montpelier
New Hampshire 1788
Concord
Ottawa
Lake Huron
Toronto (York)
Lake Ontario
Albany
New York 1788
Boston
Massachusetts 1788
Providence
Rhode Island 1790
Hartford
Connecticut 1788
New York US capital 1785–90
Trenton
New Jersey
Philadelphia US capital 1790–1800
Red River Colony 1818 to United States
North Dakota 1889
Blackfoot
Paw Mountains
Ft Mandan
Bismarck
Minnesota 1858
Ojibwa
Michigan 1837
Lake Michigan
Wisconsin 1848
St Paul
Mississippi
Fox
Lansing
Madison
Chicago
Fallen Timbers 1794
Piankashaw
Ohio 1803
Columbus
Greenville 1795
Delaware
Pennsylvania 1787
Harrisburg
Baltimore
Annapolis
Dover 1787
Delaware 1787
Maryland 1788
Washington US capital from 1800
West Virginia 1863
Richmond
Missouri
Montana 1889
Little Bighorn 1876
Sioux
Standing Rock reservation
Deadwood
South Dakota 1889
Pierre
Black Hills
Wounded Knee 1890
oming 1890
Ft Laramie 1851, 1868
Platte
Nebraska 1867
California & Oregon Trails
Cheyenne
Omaha
Lincoln
Iowa 1846
Des Moines
Illinois 1818
Springfield
Indiana 1816
Indianapolis
Ohio
Shawnee
Tippecanoe 1811
Cumberland Road
Frankfort
Kentucky 1792
Charleston
Virginia 1788
Raleigh
North Carolina 1789
Cheyenne
Denver
Colorado 1876
Sand Creek 1864
Kansas 1861
Santa Fé Trail
Topeka
Kansas City
Jefferson City
Missouri 1821
St Louis
"Trail of Tears"
Nashville
Tennessee 1796
Cherokee
Columbia
South Carolina 1788
Arapaho
Medicine Lodge 1867
Oklahoma 1907
Oklahoma City
Little Rock
Memphis
Chickasaw
New Echota
Atlanta
Georgia 1788
Santa Fe
Kiowa
Canadian
Arkansas 1836
Mississippi 1817
Alabama 1819
Montgomery
vajo
New Mexico 1912
Red
Wichita
Jackson
Creek
Choctaw
Jacksonville
Tallahassee
Florida 1845
Comanche
Colorado
Brazos
Texas 1845
Austin
Louisiana 1812
Baton Rouge
New Orleans
Mobile
Rio Grande
Pecos
spanish Trail
Santa Fe
ache
leton
yon
MEXICO to Spain, 1821 independent
Gulf of Mexico
ATLANTIC OCEAN
Nassau
Bahamas to Britain
Havana
Cuba to Spain, 1898 independent

0　900 km
0　600 mi

ceased hostilities in return for permanent occupation of the Black Hills reservation. However, incursion by gold prospectors in 1874 provoked resistance by the Sioux aided by the Northern Cheyenne in 1876–77. They annihilated General Custer and 200 troopers at the Battle of the Little Bighorn, but their leaders Sitting Bull and Crazy Horse could not capitalize on this victory and were eventually forced to surrender.

The Blackfoot and Crow in Wyoming and Montana, the Modoc in Oregon, and the Nez Percé in Idaho met similar fates. Cochise and Geronimo of the Chiricahua Apaches in Arizona and New Mexico conducted guerrilla campaigns until forced to surrender (1872 and 1886 respectively).

Geronimo's surrender marked the end of the Indian Wars. For the first time in over a century the United States was at peace. However, despair at their situation led many native Americans to follow Wovoka, a Paiute religious leader. Wovoka conducted ghost dances which, he claimed, would make his

disciples immune to gunfire, and he promised that Sitting Bull would expel the whites. Sitting Bull was murdered while in custody and the US Seventh Cavalry massacred Sioux ghost dancers and their families at Wounded Knee Creek in December 1890.

Throughout this period the United States thrived. The northeast saw a stream of immigration from Europe, and new industries arose to feed, house and clothe the growing population. In the south, the high export prices of cotton brought the development of large plantations. The invention of the cotton gin in 1792 to separate cotton fiber from seeds stimulated production. Yet the plantation system relied on slavery, a growing point of contention between North and South. In the 1820s, many had hoped to liberate the plantation slaves, but three decades later the rising value of slaves made this less attractive. A compromise was reached when California was allowed to join the Union as a "free" state in 1850 in return for harsh laws against fugitive slaves, but the issue soon exploded into civil war.

1 The Columbia River was explored by Capt Robert Gray in 1792, who claimed it for the United States.

2 Meriwether Lewis and William Clark were commissioned by Thomas Jefferson to explore beyond the Mississippi in 1804.

3 The "Five Civilized Tribes" of the southeast United States – Choctaw, Cherokee, Chickasaw, Creek, and Seminole – were socalled for their adaptation to white culture. Even so, they were forcibly relocated in 1830.

4 The Indian Territory was set up as a homeland for native Americans in the 1830s, but the territory was shrunk in 1854 and 1890 and abolished in 1907.

5 Alaska was bought from czarist Russia in 1867 for US$7.2 million.

6 In 1869, the Union Pacific and the Central Pacific railroads met at Promontory Point in Utah.

See also 5.27 (American Civil War); 5.28 (US society to 1914)

The demand for cotton as an export crop made the economy of the states south of the Mason–Dixon line (the border between Pennsylvania and Maryland) dependent on the systematic exploitation of humanity. On plantations and farms and in cities and towns, four million black slaves were denied their rights to a family, education and citizenship. Slavery became a political issue during the westward expansion of the United States. In deference to southern interests, the Constitutional Convention of 1787 prohibited the importation of slaves, but protected slavery in the states from federal interference. In the Missouri compromise of 1820, which admitted Maine and the Louisiana Purchase lands (except Missouri) as free and proclaimed all states above latitude 36° 30' as free, a convention of balancing abolitionist and slave-owning interests was established.

Attitudes toward slavery were polarized; some demanded complete and immediate abolition, while others saw good economic and racial reasons for its retention. The issue was made even more divisive by a number of legislative decisions in the 1850s. The 1850 compromise admitted California as a free state, but took no action to curb slavery in the other territories ceded by Mexico after the war of 1846–48 (Utah and New Mexico). The Kansas–Nebraska Act (1854) gave settlers the right to decide whether or not to permit slavery in a new territory, a situation that led to open warfare between rival groups in "bleeding Kansas". Finally a Supreme Court ruling of 1857 – the "Dred Scott" case – declared that neither Congress nor the people of a territory could abolish slavery in the territories. This meant the Missouri compromise was unconstitutional and destroyed the artificial balance between free and slave states. This decision threatened the entire democratic foundation of the Union. Meanwhile, fugitive slaves escaped to the north via the "Underground Railroad" (a network of abolitionist households). In the 1860 presidential elections all the free states – except New Jersey – returned the Republican Abraham Lincoln, who refused to extend slavery to new territories.

On 20 December 1860 South Carolina seceded from the Union. Georgia, Alabama, Texas, Florida, Mississippi and Louisiana soon followed, creating a Confederacy and electing Jefferson Davis as their president. On 12 April 1861 Confederate forces began hostilities with a bombardment of Fort Sumter. Lincoln called for 75,000 northern volunteers, prompting Virginia, North Carolina, Tennessee and Arkansas to join the Confederacy. Yet not all the slave states seceded: Kentucky declared itself neutral; Delaware, Maryland and Missouri remained loyal, as did the northwestern counties of Virginia (which became the state of West Virginia in 1863).

The civil war that erupted was a devastating conflict: a quarter of all those who saw combat lost their lives. Confederate strategy was to defend itself and win international recognition as an independent state. The Union government thus had no option but to attack the south and restore the rebel states to the Union. The Union had a larger population, less vulnerable railroads and far greater industrial resources than the Confederacy. Lincoln was confident of achieving his two main objectives: to blockade the Confederate coastline and capture Richmond, the Confederate capital. However, superior Confederate generalship caused Union armies several early setbacks, notably their defeat at the two Battles of Bull Run, and their failure to take the key town of Fredericksburg. In January 1863, Lincoln espoused outright abolition in his emancipation proclamation, freeing all slaves in the Confederacy. Meanwhile, Confederate armies pushed north into Pennsylvania to take the war to the enemy. This aim was thwarted at the Battle of Gettysburg in July 1863, which marked a turning point in Union fortunes.

At the same time, Union armies were victorious in the west. Under the command of Ulysses Grant, they advanced down the Mississippi; after gaining

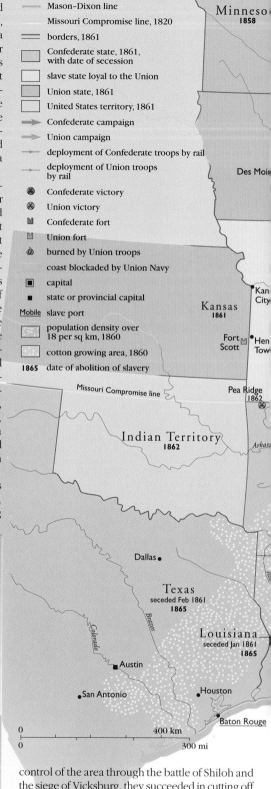

▨	Northwest Territory (slavery forbidden, 1787)
—	Mason–Dixon line
—	Missouri Compromise line, 1820
═	borders, 1861
▭	Confederate state, 1861, with date of secession
▭	slave state loyal to the Union
▭	Union state, 1861
▭	United States territory, 1861
➡	Confederate campaign
➡	Union campaign
→	deployment of Confederate troops by rail
→	deployment of Union troops by rail
⊗	Confederate victory
⊗	Union victory
⛫	Confederate fort
⛫	Union fort
◊	burned by Union troops
	coast blockaded by Union Navy
▪	capital
▪	state or provincial capital
Mobile	slave port
▨	population density over 18 per sq km, 1860
▨	cotton growing area, 1860
1865	date of abolition of slavery

Minneso 1858

Des Moi

Kansas 1861

Kan City

Fort Scott · Hen Tow

Missouri Compromise line

Pea Ridge 1862

Indian Territory 1862

Arka

Dallas ·

Texas seceded Feb 1861 1865

Colorado

Brazos

Louisiana seceded Jan 1861 1865

■ Austin

· San Antonio

· Houston

Baton Rouge

0 _____ 400 km
0 _____ 300 mi

control of the area through the battle of Shiloh and the siege of Vicksburg, they succeeded in cutting off Arkansas, Louisiana and Texas from the Confederacy. William Sherman's campaign in Georgia saw the destruction of Atlanta and the capture of Savannah. Grant fought a series of battles (Wilderness, Spotsylvania, Cold Harbor and Petersburg) against the Confederate commander Robert E. Lee, which left the south with barely 60,000 troops. Richmond fell on 3 April 1865 and Lee surrendered the Confederate army at Appomattox Court House on 9 April. Five days later, Lincoln was assassinated.

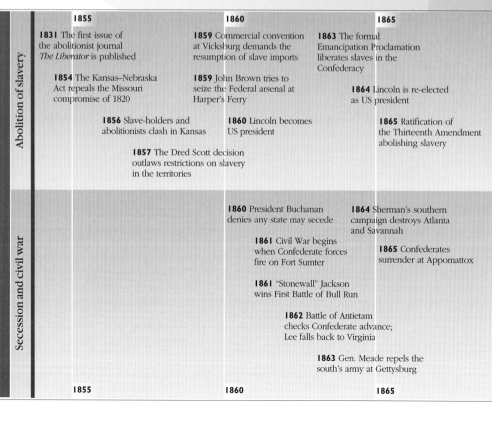

TIMELINE

Abolition of slavery

1831 The first issue of the abolitionist journal *The Liberator* is published

1854 The Kansas–Nebraska Act repeals the Missouri compromise of 1820

1856 Slave-holders and abolitionists clash in Kansas

1857 The Dred Scott decision outlaws restrictions on slavery in the territories

1859 Commercial convention at Vicksburg demands the resumption of slave imports

1859 John Brown tries to seize the Federal arsenal at Harper's Ferry

1860 Lincoln becomes US president

1863 The formal Emancipation Proclamation liberates slaves in the Confederacy

1864 Lincoln is re-elected as US president

1865 Ratification of the Thirteenth Amendment abolishing slavery

Secession and civil war

1860 President Buchanan denies any state may secede

1861 Civil War begins when Confederate forces fire on Fort Sumter

1861 "Stonewall" Jackson wins First Battle of Bull Run

1862 Battle of Antietam checks Confederate advance; Lee falls back to Virginia

1863 Gen. Meade repels the south's army at Gettysburg

1864 Sherman's southern campaign destroys Atlanta and Savannah

1865 Confederates surrender at Appomattox

1855   1860   1865

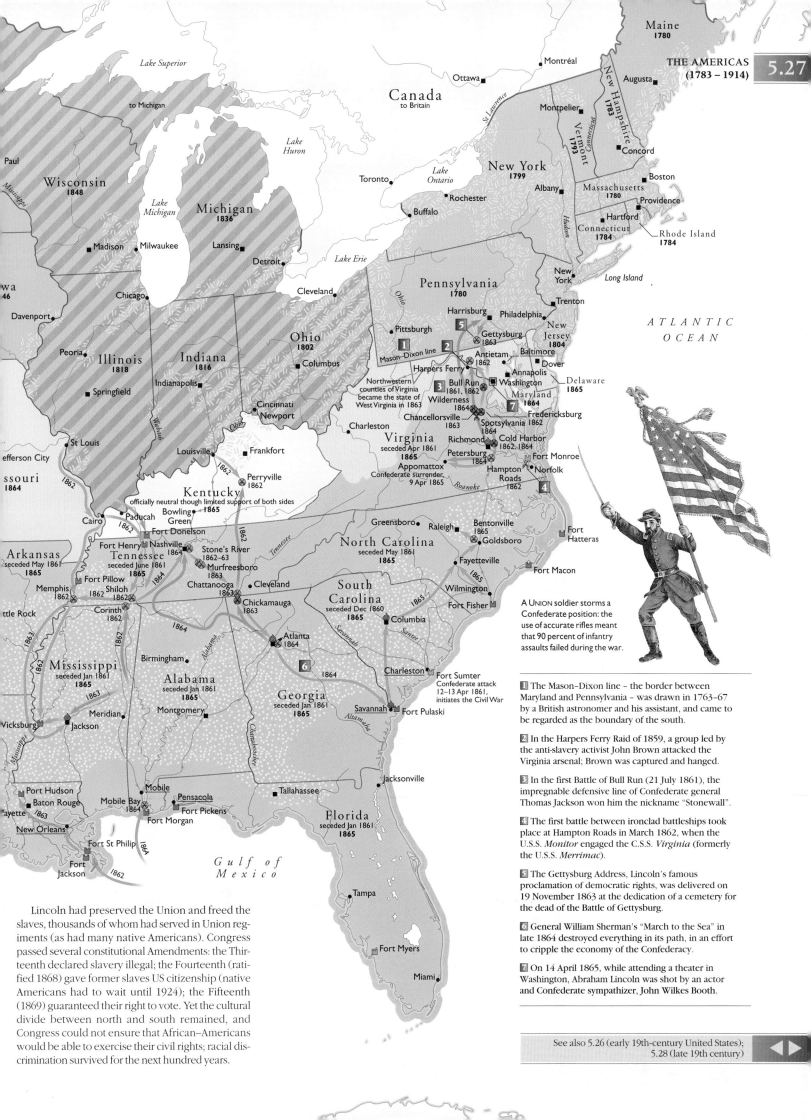

Lake Superior
to Michigan

Canada
to Britain

Maine
1780

Montréal

Ottawa

Augusta

New Hampshire
1783

Montpelier

Vermont
1793

Concord

Wisconsin
1848

Lake Huron

Lake Michigan

Michigan
1836

New York
1799

Toronto

Lake Ontario

Rochester

Albany

Massachusetts
1780

Boston

Providence

Hartford

Connecticut
1784

Rhode Island
1784

Madison

Milwaukee

Lansing

Detroit

Lake Erie

Buffalo

...wa
...46

Chicago

Cleveland

Pennsylvania
1780

Harrisburg

5

Philadelphia

Trenton

New Jersey
1804

ATLANTIC
OCEAN

Paul

St. Paul

Davenport

Illinois
1818

Indiana
1816

Ohio
1802

Pittsburgh

1

Gettysburg
1863

Mason–Dixon line

2

Antietam
1862

Baltimore

New York

Long Island

Peoria

Springfield

Indianapolis

Columbus

Harpers Ferry

Washington

Dover

Annapolis

Delaware
1865

Maryland

Cincinnati

Newport

Northwestern counties of Virginia became the state of West Virginia in 1863

3

Bull Run
1861, 1862

Wilderness
1864

7
1864

Fredericksburg 1862

St Louis

Louisville

Frankfort

Charleston

Chancellorsville
1863

Spotsylvania
1864

efferson City

Perryville
1862

Virginia
seceded Apr 1861
1865

Richmond

Cold Harbor
1862, 1864

Petersburg
1864

Fort Monroe

Norfolk

...ssouri
1864

1862

Kentucky
officially neutral though limited support of both sides
1865

Appomattox
Confederate surrender,
9 Apr 1865

Hampton Roads
1862

4

Roanoke

Cairo

Paducah

1862

Bowling Green

1865

Greensboro

Raleigh

Bentonville
1865

Fort Hatteras

Fort Donelson

Goldsboro

Arkansas
seceded May 1861
1865

Fort Henry
1864

Nashville

Stone's River
1862–63

North Carolina
seceded May 1861
1865

Fayetteville

Tennessee
seceded June 1861
1865

Murfreesboro
1863

1862

...ttle Rock

Fort Pillow
1862

Shiloh
1862

Chattanooga
1863

Cleveland

1865

Wilmington

Fort Fisher

Memphis
1862

Corinth
1862

1862

Chickamauga
1863

South Carolina
seceded Dec 1860
1865

1865

A UNION soldier storms a
Confederate position: the
use of accurate rifles meant
that 90 percent of infantry
assaults failed during the war.

1863

1864

Columbia

Charleston

1863

Atlanta
1864

6

1864

Savannah

Mississippi
seceded Jan 1861
1865

Birmingham

Alabama
seceded Jan 1861
1865

Montgomery

Georgia
seceded Jan 1861
1865

Charleston

Fort Sumter
Confederate attack
12–13 Apr 1861,
initiates the Civil War

Meridian

Jackson

Savannah

Fort Pulaski

1863

Vicksburg

1863

...ayette

Port Hudson

Baton Rouge

Mobile

Pensacola

Tallahassee

Jacksonville

New Orleans

Fort St Philip

Mobile Bay
1864

Fort Pickens

Fort Morgan

Florida
seceded Jan 1861
1865

Fort Jackson

1862

1864

*Gulf of
Mexico*

Tampa

Fort Myers

Miami

Lincoln had preserved the Union and freed the
slaves, thousands of whom had served in Union regiments (as had many native Americans). Congress
passed several constitutional Amendments: the Thirteenth declared slavery illegal; the Fourteenth (rati-
fied 1868) gave former slaves US citizenship (native
Americans had to wait until 1924); the Fifteenth
(1869) guaranteed their right to vote. Yet the cultural
divide between north and south remained, and
Congress could not ensure that African–Americans
would be able to exercise their civil rights; racial discrimination survived for the next hundred years.

1 The Mason–Dixon line – the border between
Maryland and Pennsylvania – was drawn in 1763–67
by a British astronomer and his assistant, and came to
be regarded as the boundary of the south.

2 In the Harpers Ferry Raid of 1859, a group led by
the anti-slavery activist John Brown attacked the
Virginia arsenal; Brown was captured and hanged.

3 In the first Battle of Bull Run (21 July 1861), the
impregnable defensive line of Confederate general
Thomas Jackson won him the nickname "Stonewall".

4 The first battle between ironclad battleships took
place at Hampton Roads in March 1862, when the
U.S.S. *Monitor* engaged the C.S.S. *Virginia* (formerly
the U.S.S. *Merrimac*).

5 The Gettysburg Address, Lincoln's famous
proclamation of democratic rights, was delivered on
19 November 1863 at the dedication of a cemetery for
the dead of the Battle of Gettysburg.

6 General William Sherman's "March to the Sea" in
late 1864 destroyed everything in its path, in an effort
to cripple the economy of the Confederacy.

7 On 14 April 1865, while attending a theater in
Washington, Abraham Lincoln was shot by an actor
and Confederate sympathizer, John Wilkes Booth.

See also 5.26 (early 19th-century United States);
5.28 (late 19th century)

At the end of the Civil War, the northern states experienced unprecedented prosperity as American and foreign speculators rushed to invest in a new wave of industrialization. Railroad construction drove the economy. The completion of the first transcontinental link in 1869 encouraged the development of other lines across America; three more were in operation by 1883. Urban centers and rural areas alike benefited; millions of cattle were transported to slaughterhouses in the new cities of Chicago and Kansas City. By opening up the west to profitable farming, railroads also hastened political change; by 1890 most of the western territories had been admitted as fully-fledged states of the Union. Yet the railroad boom was not without its negative aspects. Corrupt share-dealing provoked a panic and withdrawal of foreign capital in 1873.

The south had been devastated by the civil war. Its principal towns lay in ruins and its economic life destroyed. Opinion in the north was divided on how the rebel states should be treated. President Andrew Johnson (Lincoln's successor) favored reconciliation, while hardliners counseled repression. After a period of radical administration, conservatives reasserted white rule in the south, circumventing the constitutional rights guaranteed by Congress to freed blacks. Reconstruction proceeded slowly, and states were gradually readmitted to the Union.

Towns and cities grew with astonishing rapidity; by 1914, the United States had an urban population of 45 million, most of whom were immigrants. On five occasions the annual total of immigrants – from every corner of Europe – exceeded one million. Desperate for work and willing to take low-paid employment, the newcomers were quickly absorbed into the factories of New York, Chicago, Buffalo, Pittsburgh, Cleveland, Milwaukee, Cincinnati and St Louis. Appalling conditions prevailed in the crowded cities, polluted factories, primitive mining communities and harsh lumber camps. Immigrants often faced discrimination; as early as 1871, the Chinese who had entered through California to work in mining and on the railroads were the

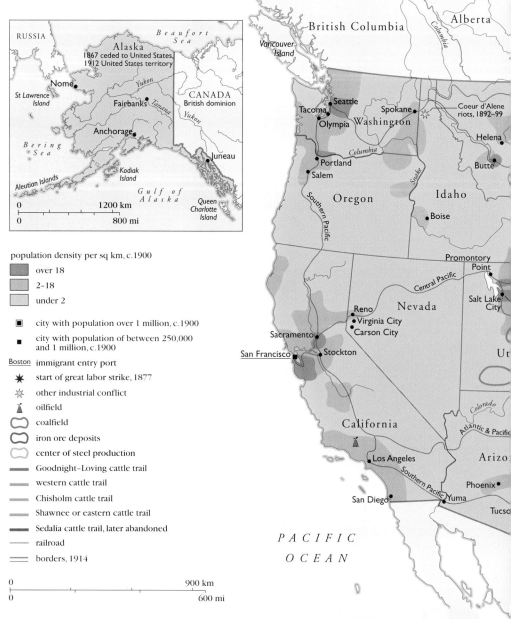

population density per sq km, c.1900

- over 18
- 2–18
- under 2

- ■ city with population over 1 million, c.1900
- ■ city with population of between 250,000 and 1 million, c.1900
- Boston immigrant entry port
- ✶ start of great labor strike, 1877
- ✳ other industrial conflict
- oilfield
- coalfield
- iron ore deposits
- center of steel production
- Goodnight–Loving cattle trail
- western cattle trail
- Chisholm cattle trail
- Shawnee or eastern cattle trail
- Sedalia cattle trail, later abandoned
- railroad
- borders, 1914

0   900 km
0   600 mi

1870

Social change

1865 Immigration increases after a decline during the Civil War

1866 Ku Klux Klan founded to oppose "Reconstruction" and freedoms for blacks

1870 A census shows US population at 40 million

1875 USA begins to restrict immigration by excluding "undesirables" (Chinese)

1877 600,000 black students attend schools in the south

1882 Immigration controls prevent entry for convicts, lunatics, idiots and those liable to be public charges

1890

1888 Dawes Act authorizes president to terminate native American tribal government

1890 Irish population of New York is twice that of Dublin

1892 The Ellis Island immigration reception center in New York is opened

1910

1902 The Chinese Exclusion Act is re-enacted indefinitely

1905 Over one million immigrants enter USA in a year

1910 Population is 92 million

1910 The Angel Island immigration center opens in San Francisco

Industrial change

1866–77 Congress attempts "Reconstruction" in the south

1870 John D. Rockefeller founds the Standard Oil Company of Ohio

1876 Alexander Graham Bell patents the telephone

1877 Thomas Edison invents the phonograph

1877 The great strike begins at Martinsburg, West Virginia

1880 US steel production exceeds 1.4 million tonnes

1882 Edison's Electric Illuminating Company supplies power to New York

1885 Bell and others create the American Telephone and Telegraph Company

1886 Haymarket Riot (Chicago) after police intervene in demonstration for an eight-hour day

1890 Anti-Trust Law passed to curb big-business power

1892 Riots at Homestead involve steel strikers and Pinkerton detectives

1894 3,400 special deputies are sworn in to break the Pullman strike

1901 United States Steel Corporation becomes the first billion-dollar company

1902 Strike in Pennsylvanian anthracite coal mines

1908 Henry Ford produces the first Model T automobile

1913–14 Violent strikes at Rockefeller-owned coal fields in Ludlow, Colorado

1870   **1890**   **1910**

Saskatchewan
Lake Winnipeg
Lake Winnipegosis
Manitoba
Lake Manitoba

Ontario (Upper Canada)

CANADA
British dominion

Quebec (Lower Canada)

New Brunswick
Nova Scotia

Maine
Augusta

Montpelier
Concord — New Hampshire
Vermont
Boston
Massachusetts

skatchewan

ntana
Great Northern
Northern Pacific

Lake Superior

St Lawrence

North Dakota
Bismarck

Minnesota

Wisconsin

Lake Huron

Michigan

Lake Ontario

Albany
Hartford
New York
5
Providence — Rhode Island
Connecticut

Buffalo

New York
Molly Maguire's
1862–76

Trenton

ssouri

Duluth

Lake Michigan

St Paul
Minneapolis
Mississippi

Madison

Lansing
Milwaukee

Detroit
Cleveland

Lake Erie

3
Pittsburgh
Homestead Strike
1892

Pennsylvania
Harrisburg

Philadelphia
New Jersey

Dover
Baltimore
Delaware

Washington

Annapolis
Maryland

South Dakota
Pierre

Iowa
Des Moines

Columbus

Ohio

West Virginia
Charleston

Richmond
Virginia

Wyoming

Nebraska
Omaha

Union Pacific

Pullman Strike
1894

Haymarket Riot, 1886
Chicago

Indiana
Indianapolis

Springfield

Cincinnati

Louisville
Frankfort

Raleigh

nion Pacific
Cheyenne

Platte

Lincoln

Illinois

Ohio

Kentucky

North Carolina

Denver

Leadville 1896

Cripple Creek 1894

Arkansas

Kansas Pacific
Topeka
Abilene
Sedalia

Kansas City

St Louis
Jefferson City

Missouri

Nashville

Tennessee

South Carolina
Columbia

Charleston

olorado
Pueblo

Ludlow 1913–14

Dodge City

Atchison, Topeka & Santa Fe

Kansas

1

Memphis

Santa Fe
Las Vegas
Albuquerque

Canadian

Oklahoma

4
Oklahoma City

Missouri, Kansas & Texas

Little Rock

Arkansas

Birmingham

Alabama

Atlanta

2

Savannah

Georgia

Jacksonville

New Mexico

Atchison, Topeka & Santa Fe

Red

Mississippi

Montgomery

El Paso

Pecos

Texas & Pacific
Fort Concho

Dallas

Colorado

Brazos

Texas

Austin
Houston
Galveston

Jackson

Vicksburg

Mobile

Louisiana
Baton Rouge
New Orleans

Tallahassee

Florida

Miami

Bahamas
to Britain

ATLANTIC OCEAN

Rio Grande
Southern Pacific

San Antonio

Laredo

MEXICO

Gulf of Mexico

Cuba

victims of race riots. Further Chinese immigration was blocked by the Chinese Exclusion Act of 1882.

The depression that affected Europe in the late 19th century had little effect on the vibrant US economy. This period saw the rise of magnates who made the United States into the world's great industrial power. John D. Rockefeller dominated the oil industry while Philip D. Armour controlled a meat-packing empire, the financier J. Pierpont Morgan underwrote railroads, and Andrew Carnegie was the leading figure in the steel industry. These men took advantage of low interest rates, cheap labor and a largely unregulated market. However, though employers used ruthless business methods and dealt summarily with discontent among their workforces, the age of American high capitalism had its benefits. The essential symbol of American enterprise and democracy was the Model T automobile, first made in 1908 by the Detroit mechanic Henry Ford. Also some multimillionaires, such as Carnegie, were philanthropists who gave away their fortunes.

Industrial growth brought labor problems. The

job losses resulting from the 1873 economic crisis made labor unions hostile to further immigration. Strikes were common, the most damaging in 1877. Railroad employees, enraged by a pay cut, withdrew their labor and were supported in their grievances by a large army of unemployed. Unrest spread to Pittsburgh, Chicago, St Louis, Kansas City, Galveston and San Francisco before militiamen were called out to suppress it. Although this dispute, the first general strike in American history, involved millions and even spread to Canada, its most significant feature was the Federal administration's use of troops. In 1892, workers at the Carnegie steel mill in Homestead were beaten by the state militia; two years later president Cleveland sent soldiers to put down a strike of railroad workers in Chicago.

The economy, though, stayed buoyant. By 1914, with a population over 97 million, the United States led the world in the manufacture of steel and lumber products, in meat-packing and precious metal extraction, and had the most telephones, telegraphs, electric lights and automobiles in the world.

1 Between 1867 and 1871, about 1.5 million head of cattle were herded on "long drives" along the Chisholm Trail to the railhead at Abilene, Kansas.

2 Atlanta had been razed by fire during the Georgia campaign of the civil war, but became the center of Federal government activity during reconstruction.

3 During the great strike of 1877, Pittsburgh was devastated by three days of rioting that destroyed much railroad property and almost leveled the city.

4 Oklahoma was opened to settlement in 1889; settlers raced across the prairie to stake their claims.

5 Ellis Island in New York Bay became the country's principal immigration station from 1892 onward.

6 Utah was admitted to the Union as a state in 1896, after its Mormon inhabitants had promised to relinquish the practice of polygamy.

See also 5.27 (American Civil War)

Cross-referencing
References to other dictionary entries are identified in small capitals (e.g. JOHN ADAMS); references to map spreads are denoted by the use of an arrow (e.g. ▷ 5.18).

Chinese spellings
Since 1979 the standard international system for the transliteration of Chinese names into Roman characters has been Pinyin, and this is the system used throughout this dictionary.

ABDUL HAMUD II
(1842–1918) The last Ottoman sultan. He succeeded his brother Murad V in 1876 and ruled autocratically until overthrown by ENVER PASHA, leader of the revolutionary YOUNG TURKS, in 1908. He abdicated in 1909, reviled as Abdul the Damned. His policies led to war with Russia (1877–78) and to massacres of Turkey's Armenian minority (1894–96). He modernized the Turkish army under the direction of a German military mission. ▷ 5.14

ABOLITIONISTS
Campaigners for an end to the slave trade and for the abolition of slavery. In Britain WILLIAM WILBERFORCE founded the movement that ended the West Indian slave trade in 1807. The 1833 Anti-Slavery Act abolished slavery in the British empire, with profound effects upon events in the West Indies and southern Africa. American abolitionists included W. L. Garrison, Frederick Douglass and JOHN BROWN. ABRAHAM LINCOLN abolished slavery with his Emancipation Proclamation (1863), which could not be implemented until after the AMERICAN CIVIL WAR. ▷ 5.17, 5.24, 5.27

ABOUKIR BAY, BATTLE OF
See NILE, BATTLE OF THE

ACT OF UNION (1801)
Law making Britain and Ireland one state. The 1798 UNITED IRISHMEN REBELLION and the threat of a French invasion convinced WILLIAM PITT that union was crucial for national security. It was enacted in August 1800 and came into force on 1 January 1801. It created the UNITED KINGDOM, abolished the Irish parliament and united the Church of Ireland and Church of England. Thirty-two Irish peers entered the UK House of Lords; 100 Irish MPs entered the UK House of Commons. ▷ 5.08

ADAMS, JOHN
(1735–1826) American lawyer and politician, and second president of the USA. A signatory of the 1776 Declaration of Independence, he became an American diplomatic representative in France and Holland and helped to negotiate the Treaty of Versailles (1783). Elected president after George Washington retired in 1796, he tried to win a second term of office in 1800 but lacked the support of his own Federalist Party and was defeated by THOMAS JEFFERSON. ▷ 5.26

ADAMS, JOHN QUINCY
(1767–1848) Son of JOHN ADAMS and president of the USA. He served as an American representative in the Netherlands and Russia, handled the crises over OREGON, Florida and Latin America, and helped draft the MONROE DOCTRINE. Elected president in 1824, he was defeated in 1828 by ANDREW JACKSON. He then devoted himself to minority rights and the ABOLITIONIST cause. ▷ 5.02

ADELAIDE
The first settlement and the capital of the colony of South Australia (from 1836). Edward Gibbon Wakefield's South Australian Association was authorized by the British Colonial Office to develop the township, swamped by 17,000 British immigrants unable to provide for themselves. Governor SIR GEORGE GREY (1841–45) resolved the crisis by forcing immigrants to leave Adelaide and farm outlying lands. ▷ 5.02, 5.18

ADOWA, BATTLE OF
(16 October 1896) Battle between the Ethiopian forces of EMPEROR MENELIK II and Italian invaders. It was the sole example of successful African resistance against a predominantly white army of a European power. It led to the 1896 Treaty of Addis Ababa, recognizing the independence of ETHIOPIA. ▷ 5.04, 5.16

AFGHAN WARS
Three wars fought by Britain to secure Afghanistan against Russian penetration. In the first war (1839–42) the British captured Kandahar and Kabul and exiled the ruler DOST MUHAMMED. His son, Akbar, recaptured Kabul, and most of the retreating British troops were massacred en route to Jalalabad. The second war (1878–80) saw the defeat of pro-Russian rulers and a British evacuation in 1881. Afghanistan's declaration of independence led to the third war (1919) before British recognition came in 1921. ▷ 5.02, 5.21

AFRIKANERS
See BOERS

AGADIR CRISIS
Crisis of 1911 when the German gunboat *Panther* visited this Moroccan port, ostensibly to protect the lives of German citizens and deter the French from annexing Morocco. The visit was interpreted by the French as an attempt to subvert agreements reached at the ALGECIRAS CONFERENCE and by Britain as a threat to Gibraltar and British trade routes. The crisis ended with Germany's acceptance of territory in the Congo in return for recognition of France's claim to Morocco. It drew Britain and France closer. ▷ 5.13

ALAMO, BATTLE OF THE
(23 February–6 March 1836) Battle in the TEXAN WAR OF INDEPENDENCE. American settlers in Texas, then ruled by Mexico, rebelled, and the Mexican president, ANTONIO DE SANTA ANNA, besieged 180 in the Alamo Mission, in San Antonio. None survived. During the siege, Texas declared its independence, secured at the BATTLE OF THE SAN JACINTO RIVER. ▷ 5.23

ALASKA
State of the USA in the northwestern corner of North America. Settled by Indians, Inuits and Aleuts, it was claimed for Russia by the Danish explorer Vitus Bering in 1741. Russian colonists founded Archangel (Sitka) in 1804. Fort Wrangel was constructed as a base against British trading ambitions. Russia sold Alaska to the USA in 1867 for $7.2 million. Gold was discovered in 1872. It achieved statehood in 1959. ▷ 5.05, 5.26, 5.28

ALBANIA
Balkan state, briefly independent in the 15th century and then under Ottoman rule until 1913. The League of Prizren (1878–81) demanded Albanian autonomy, but was crushed by Abdul Hamud I. After the BALKAN WARS, Austria sought an independent Albania to restrict SERBIAN expansion. The state was recognized by the Treaty of London (1913). ▷ 5.10, 5.13, 5.14

ALEXANDER I
(1777–1825) Czar of Russia (r.1801–25). Defeated by BONAPARTE at AUSTERLITZ (1805) and Friedland (1807), he made peace with France at TILSIT (1807). After the French withdrawal from Russia, he was among the victors at the BATTLE OF LEIPZIG (1813) and at the Treaty of Paris (1814). He founded the HOLY ALLIANCE and opposed all forms of national self-determination. ▷ 5.01, 5.02, 5.12

ALEXANDER II
(1818–81) Czar of Russia (r.1855–81). Fearing revolution, he emancipated the serfs in 1861; his Zemstvo Statute (1864) introduced district and provincial assemblies; his Duma Statute (1870) established DUMAS (self-governing councils) in larger towns. He reformed the imperial army and introduced conscription in 1874. He was assassinated by the terrorist Narodnaya Volya in 1881. ▷ 5.09, 5.12

ALEXANDER III
(1845–94) Czar of Russia (r.1881–94). He was autocratic and intolerant, persecuting nationalists, liberals and Jews. He rounded off the conquests of his predecessors in Central Asia, provoking a crisis with Britain when he advanced into Afghanistan in 1885. He signed the REINSURANCE TREATY (1887) with BISMARCK to replace the expiring DREIKAISERBUND; his close relations with France culminated in a military alliance in 1894. ▷ 5.12, 5.13

ALGECIRAS CONFERENCE
Conference in 1906 to settle the Moroccan crisis of 1905, when the German kaiser Wilhelm II arrived at TANGIER to oppose

French interests in Morocco. British support for France forced Wilhelm to accept the Act of Algeciras, permitting France and Spain to police Morocco under Swiss supervision. The affair emphasized the importance of the ENTENTE CORDIALE. ▷ 5.13

ALSACE-LORRAINE
French territory ceded to Germany in 1871 at the conclusion of the FRANCO-PRUSSIAN WAR and defined as an integral part of Germany in 1879. It was restored to France in 1919, lost to Germany in 1940 and regained in 1944. ▷ 5.09, 5.11

AMERICAN CIVIL WAR
(1861–65) Military conflict between the slave-owning American south (constituted as the breakaway CONFEDERATE STATES OF AMERICA) and the free industrialized north (fighting to preserve the Union). The north had an advantage in its industrial strength, but the generalship of the southerners THOMAS "STONEWALL" JACKSON and ROBERT E. LEE dominated from 1861 to 1863. Thereafter, the Union triumphed and under the command of ULYSSES S. GRANT and WILLIAM SHERMAN the northern armies overran the south, forcing the Confederates to surrender in 1865. More than 720,000 soldiers died. The northern victors created a social revolution in the south by emancipating its slaves. ▷ 5.27

AMIENS, TREATY OF
Treaty signed by Britain, France, Holland and Spain in 1802, marking a brief respite in the Napoleonic wars. George III, the British monarch, was required to abandon the title of king of France and restore Malta to the Knights of St John, the South African Cape to the Dutch and EGYPT to the Ottoman empire. Britain distrusted BONAPARTE's intentions in the Mediterranean and declared war on 16 May 1803. ▷ 5.07, 5.08

ANARCHISM
A political movement dedicated to the over-throw of the state and the substitution of government by free association of, and voluntary cooperation among, the people. Anarchists rarely agreed on strategy and tended to give prominence to direct action. Notable anarchists included the Frenchman Louis Blanqui (1805–81) and the Russian Mikhail Bakunin (1814–76). ▷ 5.10

ANGEL ISLAND
American immigration station opened in 1910, west of San Francisco. It was the west-coast equivalent of ELLIS ISLAND. Despite the Chinese Exclusion Act (1882), most of the immigrants processed were Chinese and of these 30 percent were excluded. Priority was given to Chinese who had a Chinese-American parent. ▷ 5.28

ANGLO-AMERICAN WAR
See WAR OF 1812

ANGLO-BOER WARS
Two wars fought in South Africa (1881 and 1899–1902). In the first, the BOERS demanded the independence of the TRANSVAAL, annexed by Britain in April 1877. They routed a British force at MAJUBA HILL and recovered their independence by the Convention of Pretoria (August 1881). The second war arose from plans by CECIL RHODES and his supporters to overthrow PAUL KRUGER, president of the Transvaal. Initial Boer successes were eventually reversed by hugely outnumbering British forces, and the final stage of the war saw KITCHENER defeat Boer commandos with blockhouses, barbed wire and concentration camps. Peace was signed at VEREENIGING (1902). ▷ 5.04, 5.17

ANGLO-JAPANESE NAVAL ALLIANCE
A diplomatic reaction in 1902 to Russian expansion in the Far East. In the event of war between an ally and one country, the other ally would remain neutral. If one ally were attacked by two enemies, the other would come to its aid. The Royal Navy was thus freed from major Far Eastern commitments and the Japanese navy had a free hand in operations against Russia. ▷ 5.13, 5.20

ANSEI TREATIES
Treaties between several western countries and Japan following MATTHEW PERRY's second visit to Japan in 1854. *Ansei* is the name of the era in which they were signed. There was pressure on Japan to establish full commercial relations, and in July 1858 the first US consul, Townshend Harris, concluded the US–Japan Treaty of Amity and Commerce. This and subsequent treaties were unequal, as the rights enjoyed by westerners in Japan were not reciprocated. ▷ 5.20

ANTIETAM, BATTLE OF
(17 September 1862) Battle of the AMERICAN CIVIL WAR, described as "the bloodiest day of the war". ROBERT E. LEE had crossed the Potomac to carry the war into the north. General McClellan faced Lee's 38,000 soldiers with 75,000 Union troops. There were 22,719 casualties. The Union regarded the outcome as a draw and ABRAHAM LINCOLN issued the Emancipation proclamation. ▷ 5.27

APACHE
Native American people of the southwestern United States, principally Arizona. Expert in guerrilla combat, the Apache fought on foot, using horses for personal transport. They resisted the US government and removal to reservations in three major wars (1861–71, 1873, 1885–86). Principal chieftains were COCHISE and GERONIMO. ▷ 5.26

APPOMATTOX
Village in Virginia where ROBERT E. LEE surrendered the CONFEDERATE army to the Union General ULYSSES S. GRANT, ending the AMERICAN CIVIL WAR on 9 April 1865, exactly four years to the day after the Confederates had decided to attack FORT SUMTER. ▷ 5.27

ARCOLA, BATTLE OF
(15–17 November 1796) Battle in BONAPARTE's north Italy campaign (1796–97). He defeated Austrian forces seeking to relieve Mantua in a three-day defensive battle regarded as his greatest achievement to date. The overall aim of the north Italy campaign was to crush Austria in a pincer attack that would meet with the French armies of the north in Vienna. ▷ 5.07

ARGENTINA
Republic in South America extending from Bolivia to Cape Horn. Indian resistance hindered Spanish colonization until the late 16th century. Nationalist rebellions began in 1810 and the country was independent by 1816. After the dictatorship of JUAN MANUEL ROSAS (1835–52), a liberal, federal constitution was adopted. Argentina was united under Bartolomé Mitre in 1862 and PATAGONIA was subjugated in 1879–80. ▷ 5.23

ASANTE WARS
Five wars (1824, 1826, 1863, 1874, 1900) between Britain and the Asante empire, a powerful west African state established by Osei Tutu in about 1675. British determination to end the Asante slave trade began the wars. The issue in later wars was Asante unwilling-ness to accept British protection. Asante warriors inflicted two defeats on British forces in 1863. A protectorate by 1901, Asante was annexed to the Gold Coast Colony in 1902. ▷ 5.01, 5.02, 5.03, 5.15, 5.16

ASSAM
Northeastern state of India founded by 13th-century Ahom invaders. Invaded by Burma in 1819 and occupied by Britain in 1824 during First Burma War (1823–26), it was ceded to Britain by Burma in the Treaty of Yandabu in 1826. Incorporated into the province of East Bengal and Assam in 1905, it was a separate province by 1919 but partitioned between India and Pakistan in 1947. ▷ 5.21, 5.22

ATCHISON, TOPEKA AND SANTA FE RAILROAD
US transcontinental railroad in the southwest founded in 1859. Beginning as a project to link Atchison and Kansas City with Santa Fe to exploit the winter wheat trade, it absorbed the Atlantic and Pacific Railroad to reach Los Angeles in 1887. Bankrupt by 1893, it was reorganized and profitable after 1895. ▷ 5.28

AUCKLAND
Major port on North Island, NEW ZEALAND. It was founded in 1845, as the capital, when SIR GEORGE GREY arrived as governor (1845–53) to deal with Maori unrest stirred by the behavior of the New Zealand Company. The capital was removed from Auckland to Wellington in 1865. ▷ 5.18

AUSGLEICH

The 1867 compromise between Austria and Hungary, lasting until 1918, that transformed the Austrian empire into the DUAL MONARCHY of AUSTRIA-HUNGARY. The privileged position of the kingdom of Hungary was resented by other nationalities and there were attempts to extend the Ausgleich to a separate Slav kingdom. ▷ 5.10, 5.11, 5.13

AUSTERLITZ, BATTLE OF

(2 December 1805) A tactical masterpiece for BONAPARTE and the decisive battle of the War of the Third Coalition, fought in Moravia, between Bonaparte and the Austro-Russian armies. He smashed the allied center, forcing the Austrians to surrender and the Russians to flee. The resulting peace at Pressburg (1805) gave Bonaparte control of most of Germany. ▷ 5.01, 5.08

AUSTRIA-HUNGARY

The dual state formed by the AUSGLEICH. Ruled by Emperor Francis-Joseph I and sharing a common foreign policy, it had a joint financial program and joint armed forces. Each state had its own prime minister and parliament, delegates from both meeting annually at Vienna or Budapest. ▷ 5.04, 5.05, 5,10, 5.13, 5.14

AUSTRO-PRUSSIAN WAR (THE SEVEN WEEKS WAR)

(June–August 1866) War fought by PRUSSIA and Italy against Austria and several smaller German states. Effective use of railroads and the electric telegraph by the Prussian general HELMUTH VON MOLTKE and rapid-fire breech-loading needle-guns enabled Prussia to win the decisive Battle of Königgrätz – and dominance of central Europe. ▷ 5.11

AYACUCHO, BATTLE OF

Final attempt by Spain to prevent the loss of its South American empire. Fought in PERU in 1824, after the Spanish armies had retreated into the hills east of Lima, it followed an earlier defeat at Junin. This too was a defeat. After heavy losses inflicted by General ANTONIO JOSÉ DE SUCRE, Spain evacuated Peru. Sucre then moved east to establish the Republic of BOLIVIA in 1825. ▷ 5.23

BADAJOZ, BATTLE OF

(19 April 1812) Battle of the PENINSULAR WAR. The DUKE OF WELLINGTON stormed Badajoz fortress which, together with Ciudad Rodrigo, controlled important passes on Spanish-Portuguese frontier. This led directly to victory at Salamanca and the capture of Madrid. ▷ 5.08

BAGHDAD RAILROAD

Railroad from Constantinople to Baghdad, agreed by German financiers and the Ottoman empire in 1899, linking with the Orient Express. It was seen as a potential threat by both British and Russian interests.

A small section of line was finished by 1914 and it was completed in 1918. ▷ 5.14

BALKANS

Term describing states located in the Balkan peninsula: modern Slovenia, Croatia, BOSNIA-HERZEGOVINA, Macedonia, Yugoslavia, BULGARIA, ROMANIA, Greece, ALBANIA and the European part of Turkey. In the 19th century, it was the scene of numerous nationalist revolts against the declining Ottoman empire and the source of major international tension, with hostility between AUSTRIA-HUNGARY and SERBIA finally precipitating the outbreak of World War I in 1914. ▷ 5.13, 5.14

BALKAN WARS

Two wars in the BALKANS. In the first (1912), BULGARIA, MONTENEGRO, SERBIA and Greece expanded their own territories at the expense of Ottoman Turkey. In Europe Turkey was left only with the Gallipoli peninsula. The great powers preserved the independence of ALBANIA (Treaty of London, 1913). The second (Bulgaria versus Greece and Serbia) resulted in defeat and territorial loss for Bulgaria (Treaty of Bucharest, 1913). ▷ 5.14

BALLARAT

City located in Victoria, Australia, northwest of Melbourne. It became the center of the 1851 gold rush six weeks after Victoria had become a separate colony. Thousands of prospectors worked the Ballarat alluvial deposits. These were soon exhausted but new deposits were found at Bendigo and Mount Alexander. Ballarat was later famous for the EUREKA UPRISING of 1854. ▷ 5.18

BAMBATA

Leader of the last ZULU revolt (1906–08) against white rule in the British colony of NATAL, South Africa. The Natal police had clashed with Zulus who refused to pay the poll tax, and summary executions of Zulus aroused widespread condemnation. Chief Bambata led a rebellion, cruelly crushed in the Nkandla forests. Bambata and 3,000 followers died. ▷ 5.16

BARBADOS

Island of the Lesser Antilles chain in the West Indies. Made a British crown colony in 1653, it retained a council and assembly and an enduring sense of independence. It opposed West Indian federation in 1876 but joined a new federation in 1958. It became independent on 30 November 1966. ▷ 5.24

BARTH, HEINRICH

(1821–65) Explorer commissioned by the British government to explore north and west Africa. He crossed the Sahara from Tripoli in 1850. His companions died en route but he reached Kano and penetrated as far as Yola on the River Benue before visiting Timbuktu in 1853 and returning along the River Niger in 1854. ▷ 5.15

BASTILLE

A French royal fortress in Paris. Used as a prison, it was stormed by Parisian workers from the Faubourg St Antoine on 14 July 1789. Their object was to capture weapons in the armory, not to release prisoners. Although the French Revolution had already begun, 14 July is celebrated as the national day of the French Republic and remains symbolic of the Revolution. ▷ 5.07

BASUTOLAND

Modern Lesotho, entirely surrounded by South Africa. Established by Moshoeshoe (c.1786–1870) in a mountain stronghold, it accepted many refugees during the MFECANE. It became a British protectorate in 1843, was annexed in 1868, made a separate colony in 1884 and given its independence in 1966. ▷ 5.02, 5.04, 5.15, 5.16, 5.17

BATAVIAN REPUBLIC

(1795–1806) The name given the Netherlands after its occupation by revolutionary France early in 1795. The republic was a satellite of France until 1806, when BONAPARTE made his brother, Louis Bonaparte, king of Holland. From 1810 to 1813 the Netherlands was part of the Napoleonic empire. ▷ 5.07, 5.08, 5.09

BAUTZEN, BATTLE OF

(20–21 May 1813) Battle between BONAPARTE and the armies of the Fourth Coalition in Saxony, Germany. He had captured Dresden, crossed the Elbe and planned to smash the Russo-Prussian armies as Marshal Michel Ney attacked simultaneously from the north. This plan failed, the enemy escaped and Bonaparte lost 25,000 men. ▷ 5.08

BECHUANALAND

Modern Botswana. Missionaries such as DAVID LIVINGSTONE crossed the area en route to MATABELELAND and MASHONALAND. CECIL RHODES urged its occupation to outflank the TRANSVAAL. It became a British protectorate in 1885 and base for the JAMESON RAID (1895–96). It achieved independence on 30 September 1966 with Seretse Khama as president and head of state. ▷ 5.16, 5.17

BELGIAN CONGO (CONGO FREE STATE)

Region of central Africa claimed by LEOPOLD II as a Belgian colony. He sponsored exploration there by H. M. STANLEY between 1879 and 1884. At the 1884–85 BERLIN CONFERENCE it was renamed the Congo Free State with Leopold as autonomous ruler. Atrocities against Africans led to its annexation by Belgium in 1908. Independent in 1960, it was renamed Zaire in 1971 and renamed the Democratic Republic of Congo in 1997. ▷ 5.04, 5.05, 5.16, 5.17

BELGIUM

Northwest European state bordered by Germany, France and the Netherlands, formerly the Austrian Netherlands. It was occupied by France in 1792 and incorporated into France in 1801. Unwillingly united with the Netherlands in 1815, it rebelled in 1830 and was recognized as an independent neutral in 1839 until invaded by Germany in 1914. ▷ 5.07, 5.09, 5.10

BELL, ALEXANDER GRAHAM
(1847–1922) Inventor of the telephone. Born in Edinburgh, Scotland, influenced by his father's work in speech therapy, he became a professor of vocal physiology in Boston, Massachussetts, specialized in teaching deaf-mutes. He patented the telephone in 1876, two hours before Elisha Gray patented his, and was renting out 54,000 instruments by 1880. He used wax cylinders to record sound in 1886 and made the first transcontinental call in 1915. ▷ 5.06, 5.28

BENTINCK, LORD WILLIAM CAVENDISH
(1774–1839) PENINSULAR WAR veteran and governor-general of India (1828–35). He reformed the Indian legal system and revenue collection, changed customs (suttee and thuggee) on humanitarian grounds and introduced English as medium of instruction in government-funded schools. He was convinced that western culture was superior to India's traditions and civilization. ▷ 5.21

BENZ, KARL
(1844–1929) German engineer who developed a two-stroke engine in 1879 but lacked financial backing. He built a three-wheel petrol-engined automobile in his new factory (Benz & Co, Mannheim) in 1885. The company built the prototype four-wheel automobile in 1889 and merged with Daimler Motoren-Gesellschaft in 1926. ▷ 5.10

BERLIN, CONGRESS OF
(1878) Congress called to revise the TREATY OF SAN STEFANO and establish a new frontier system in the BALKANS acceptable to the great powers. BULGARIAN territory was limited. ROMANIA, SERBIA and MONTENEGRO were recognized as independent. Austria occupied BOSNIA-HERZEGOVINA (still technically ruled by the Turks). Russia took BESSARABIA and Britain acquired CYPRUS. The congress was a success for BISMARCK that endured for 30 years. ▷ 5.06, 5.12, 5.13, 5.14

BERLIN CONFERENCE
(1884–85) Conference summoned by OTTO VON BISMARCK to reduce tension between the colonial powers during the scramble for central Africa. It recognized Belgium's right to the Congo and the freedom of all nations to use the Congo and Niger Rivers. It agreed that slavery should end and that colonial powers should enjoy their own spheres of influence to avoid future warfare. ▷ 5.04, 5.16

BERLIN DECREES
(21 November 1806) BONAPARTE's scheme to neutralize British seapower with land power.

Since TRAFALGAR (1805), he had no other way of combating the Royal Navy. He forbade commerce between Europe and Britain, but condoned smuggling, hoping to force up prices in Britain, create inflation, wreck industry and cause social unrest. ▷ 5.01, 5.08

BERNADOTTE, HOUSE OF
Ruling dynasty of Sweden since 1818, when the French marshal Jean-Baptiste-Jules Bernadotte succeeded the heirless Charles XII.

BESSARABIA
Region in southeast Europe running from the Black Sea to Poland, named after the 14th-century Basarabs of Wallachia. In 1812 it was ceded by Turkey to Russia, which in part surrendered it to Moldavia in 1856 but largely regained it at the CONGRESS OF BERLIN. It proclaimed its independence in 1917 but was united with ROMANIA in 1918. ▷ 5.08, 5.14

BISMARCK, PRINCE OTTO EDWARD LEOPOLD VON
(1815–98) Prussian statesman who unified Germany. A conservative royalist, he was elected to the Prussian Diet in 1847. He was contemptuous of the middle-class FRANKFURT NATIONAL ASSEMBLY (1851–59) and hostile to Austrian dominance. He became the chief minister in Prussia and saw victory in the SCHLESWIG-HOLSTEIN WAR (1864), AUSTRO-PRUSSIAN WAR (1866) and FRANCO-PRUSSIAN WAR (1870–71). Chancellor of the NORTH GERMAN CONFEDERATION (1867–71) and of the SECOND GERMAN EMPIRE (1871–90), he devised a system of alliances to isolate France: the DUAL ALLIANCE (with Austria, 1879); the TRIPLE ALLIANCE (with Austria and Italy, 1882); the REINSURANCE TREATY (with Russia, 1887). He secured a German colonial empire and achieved enduring social reforms: workers' sickness and accident insurance subsidized by employers, old age pensions and manhood suffrage. Quarrels with Kaiser William II led to his dismissal in 1890. ▷ 5.10, 5.11, 5.13

BISMARCK ARCHIPELAGO
Islands in western Pacific, part of Papua New Guinea since 1975. Claimed by Germany in 1884, they were occupied by Australia in 1914 and mandated to Australia as part of the New Guinea League of Nations Trust Territory in 1920. Invaded by Japan in 1942, they saw heavy fighting until liberated by the Allies in 1944. ▷ 5.22

BLANCO, GUZMAN
(1829–99) General in the Federal War and vice-president of VENEZUELA (1863–68). He established a Liberal autocracy in 1870, believing personal freedom less important than progress and social order. He introduced free compulsory primary education, began railroads and encouraged foreign investment. He held office three times (1873–77, 1879–84 and 1886–88) and is still esteemed in Venezuela. ▷ 5.23

BLOEMFONTEIN CONVENTION
(February 1854) Anglo-Boer agreement in which British renounced sovereignty over the ORANGE FREE STATE and guaranteed its independence. Britain signed the similar SAND RIVER CONVENTION with the TRANSVAAL. ▷ 5.17

BLÜCHER, GEBHARD LEBERECHT VON,
(1742–1819) Prussian field marshal and renowned opponent of BONAPARTE. He fought at Lützen and BAUTZEN, frustrating Bonaparte's plans at LEIPZIG. Defeated and wounded at Ligny (1815), he sent most of the Prussian army to the DUKE OF WELLINGTON's aid at WATERLOO in 1815 while he relieved pressure on the right. ▷ 5.08

BOERS
Descendants of Dutch, German and Swedish settlers landed by the Dutch East Indies Company at the Cape of Good Hope, South Africa, in 1652 and from French Huguenots (Protestant refugees) who arrived in 1688. They evolved Afrikaans, a version of Dutch spoken by master and slave, and took the name Afrikaners or Afrikanders (the people of Africa). They were also called Boers (from *boer* – Afrikaans for farmer). *Trekboers* (graziers and nomadic farmers) advanced deep into the interior. Britain occupied the Cape in 1806 and introduced 4,000 British settlers who diluted the established Boer culture. Britain's emancipation of the slaves in the 1830s prompted the VOORTREKKERS to undertake the GREAT TREK to the interior. Two Boer republics, the TRANSVAAL and the ORANGE FREE STATE, and two ANGLO-BOER wars resulted. ▷ 5.04, 5.15, 5.17

BOLÍVAR, SÍMON
(1783–1830) Latin American revolutionary, general and writer who invaded VENEZUELA in 1813 and captured Caracas. Defeated by the Spanish, he raised a new army of liberation and crossed the Andes to defeat the Spaniards at Boyocá (1819). He created the state of GRAN COLOMBIA (Venezuela, ECUADOR, and COLOMBIA) in 1820 and liberated upper Peru, renamed BOLIVIA in his honor in 1825. ▷ 5.23

BOLIVIA
West-central South American republic, part of the Inca empire before the Spanish conquest under Hernando Pizzaro in the 1530s. It was integrated into the viceroyalty of Buenos Aires in 1776. Independent in 1825, it lost access to the sea in the WAR OF THE PACIFIC (1879–83). ▷ 5.02, 5.03, 5.04, 5.23,

BOMBAY
Former state in western India. The island of Bombay was acquired by Britain in 1662, and it become a key trading area from 1677, a fortified naval base and the headquarters of the East India Company from 1687. Apart from two battalions, Bombay sepoys (Indian troops serving in the East India Company's army) remained loyal during the INDIAN

MUTINY. Bombay became part of an independent India on 15 August 1947. ▷ 5.21

BONAPARTE, JOSEPH

(1768–1844) Eldest brother of NAPOLEON BONAPARTE. A lawyer, he signed the TREATY OF AMIENS (1802). Bonaparte made him ruler of the TWO SICILIES in 1805, king of Naples in 1806 and king of Spain in 1808. Militarily incompetent, he escaped to the USA in 1815 and became a US citizen. ▷ 5.08, 5.23

BONAPARTE, NAPOLEON (NAPOLEON I)

(1769–1821) Emperor of France (r.1804–14, 1815). Born in Corsica, he joined the French army in 1785. An artillery expert, he dispersed a rebellion against the revolutionary government (5 October 1795). He was appointed commander of the Army of Italy and married Josephine de Beauharnais in 1796. He led the unsuccessful EGYPTIAN expedition (1798–99) and returned to overthrow the DIRECTORY in 1799 and become First Consul in 1800. He invaded Italy and won at MARENGO (leading to the TREATY OF AMIENS, 1802), becoming emperor of the French in 1804. He prepared an abortive invasion of Britain (1805), led the Grand Army to Vienna and victory at AUSTERLITZ, ending the Holy Roman empire (1806). After JENA his power was at its height. Meanwhile, he introduced numerous domestic reforms, particularly a new civil code (the Code Napoléon) that made a permanent impact on French and European society. The failure of his CONTINENTAL SYSTEM and the PENINSULAR WAR weakened his resources, though he defeated the Austrians at WAGRAM (1809). To enforce the Continental System he invaded Russia in 1812, but retreated from Moscow and was defeated at LEIPZIG (1813). He abdicated in 1814, and was exiled to Elba but escaped to fight and lose at WATERLOO (1815), after which he was exiled to St Helena. ▷ 5.01, 5.07, 5.08, 5.09

BORODINO, BATTLE OF

(5–6 September 1812) Inconclusive battle in BONAPARTE's invasion of Russia that seriously weakened the French army before it entered Moscow. General Kutuzov made a stand at the Borodino strongpoint before gradually withdrawing to Moscow. The French losses were 30,000; the Russian 60,000. ▷ 5.08

BOSNIA-HERZEGOVINA

A constituent republic of Yugoslavia from 1946, which declared its independence in 1992. The Ottoman empire took Bosnia in 1463 and Herzegovina in 1482. The two tried to unite with SERBIA in 1875 but in 1878 became a province of AUSTRIA-HUNGARY, which formally annexed the country in 1908. Sarajevo, its capital, was the scene of the Austrian archduke Francis Ferdinand's assassination in 1914. Since independence the country has seen bitter inter-ethnic conflict between its mixed Muslim, SERBIAN and Croat population. ▷ 5.13, 5.14

BOTANY BAY

Bay south of Sydney, NEW SOUTH WALES, Australia, where Captain James Cook landed in 1770. The British prime minister WILLIAM PITT envisaged New South Wales as a penal settlement and authorized Captain Arthur Philip (1738–1814) to found one at Botany Bay. The first fleet arrived on 18 January 1788, but the site was abandoned and Philip transferred the convicts to Sydney. ▷ 5.18

BOTHA, LOUIS

(1862–1919) BOER general in the SECOND ANGLO-BOER WAR (1899–1902). He besieged LADYSMITH and blocked British relief attempts at COLENSO, SPION KOP and Vaal Krantz but was defeated at Tugela River and Bergenda. He led the guerrilla forces in the TRANSVAAL and was the first prime minister of the UNION OF SOUTH AFRICA. ▷ 5.17

BOXER REBELLION

(1898–1900) Chinese movement dedicated to the destruction of all foreign influence. Led by the League of Harmonious Fists, it began in Shandong. Boxers tore up the railroad into Beijing, entered the city and besieged the diplomatic legations. In 1901, after an intervention force relieved the legations, an international protocol was imposed on China, together with an indemnity and a western military presence. ▷ 5.04, 5.19, 5.20

BOYACÁ, BATTLE OF

(17 August 1819) Battle of the Colombian War of Independence. Revolutionaries led by SÍMON BOLÍVAR cut off a Spanish force and won a decisive victory. Bolívar optimistically proclaimed the UNION OF GRAN COLOMBIA, then still partly occupied by Spain. ▷ 5.23

BRAGANZA DYNASTY

Portuguese royal family (r.1640 to 1910). A British link was established with the 1662 marriage of Charles II and Catherine of Braganza, daughter of John IV of Portugal. France occupied Lisbon in 1807 and the family escaped to BRAZIL, escorted by the Royal Navy. Joao VI returned in 1821. His son became PEDRO I, emperor of Brazil. ▷ 5.23

BRANDENBURG-PRUSSIA

German state in north-central Europe, formed when the elector of Brandenburg inherited the duke of Prussia's territories in 1618. Transformed into a major military power by Frederick William (1640–88), it became the kingdom of PRUSSIA under Frederick I in 1701. Frederick II the Great (1740–86) annexed West Prussia, SILESIA and East Frisia. Prussia gained the Rhineland and Saxony at the CONGRESS OF VIENNA in 1815. The German empire was proclaimed in 1871 with the Prussian king as Emperor William I. ▷ 5.07

BRAZIL

Federal republic in South America. Portuguese coastal settlements in the 1530s expanded into the interior during the 18th century. Its capital, Rio de Janeiro, became the refuge of the BRAGANZA DYNASTY in 1808. It joined the Allies in 1917 during World War I and in 1942 during World War II. Brasília became the capital in 1960. ▷ 5.23, 5.24

BRITISH COLUMBIA

Canadian province on the Pacific coast. Indigenous peoples, mainly Nootka, Haida and Kwakiutl, were encountered by English mariners: Sir Francis Drake (1578–79) and James Cook (1778). American and British explorers traversed the region from 1793 to 1811 and the OREGON TERRITORY was claimed by the USA. Partitioned in 1846, the Oregon country north of the 49th parallel became New Caledonia in 1849, then the crown colony of British Columbia in 1858 and a Canadian province in 1871. ▷ 5.03, 5.25

BRITISH EAST AFRICA

General term for the British colonies of Kenya, Uganda, Tanganyika and ZANZIBAR; also a specific term for Kenya. The British East Africa Company supervised settlements in Uganda until 1895, when the region was reorganized as the British East Africa Protectorate. The coastal section, named the Kenya Protectorate, was settled after 1902. It became a crown colony in 1905, independent in 1963. ▷ 5.04, 5.05, 5.16

BRITISH HONDURAS

Modern Belize: Central America east of Guatemala. Heavily populated by Mayan Indians before English settlers arrived in 1638, it became a colony in 1862, governed from Jamaica, until a separate colony was established in 1871. It was granted internal self-government in 1964 with independence in 1981. It has frontier disputes with its neighbor Guatemala. ▷ 5.23

BRITISH NORTH BORNEO

British colony in the Malay Archipelago, originally part of the sultanate of BRUNEI, since 1963 a member of the independent Malaysian Federation. Governed by the British North Borneo Company from 1881, it was invaded by Japan in 1942. The region was a crown colony from 1946 until 1963. ▷ 5.22

BROOKE, JAMES

(1803–68) Rajah of Sarawak. A former officer in the East India Company army, he arrived in 1839 and settled a conflict between the Dyak peoples and the unpopular viceroy of the sultan of Brunei. The sultan awarded him the title of rajah. He abolished headhunting and piracy and extended the area under his direct rule. It became a British protectorate in 1888. His descendants ruled Sarawak until the Japanese invasion in 1942. ▷ 5.22

BROWN, JOHN

(1800–59) Militant American ABOLITIONIST who proposed a mountain fortress in Virginia for escaped slaves. To promote a slave insurrection, he raided a US armory at HARPER'S FERRY, where he was besieged in an engine-house by ROBERT E. LEE and wounded. Tried for treason and murder, he was hanged at Charlestown, Virginia. ▷ 5.27

BRUNEI
Independent sultanate in northeast Borneo. It was an important South China Sea state before the 15th century. The sultan ceded Labuan to Britain in 1847 and it became a British protectorate in 1888. Oil strikes were made in 1929. Invaded by Japan in 1941, it was liberated by Australian troops in 1945. It refused to join the Malaysian Federation in 1963 and became independent in 1984. ▷ 5.22

BUCHANAN, JAMES
(1791–1868) The 15th president of the USA. He negotiated the first American commercial treaty with Russia and settled the OREGON boundary dispute. Elected Democratic president in 1856, he opposed the ABOLITIONISTS, arguing that Kansas should be a slave state. He denied that states had a right to secede from the Union but he failed to secure a political compromise. He retired in 1861 and published a justification of his policies after the AMERICAN CIVIL WAR. ▷ 5.26

BUGANDA
Former African kingdom, now in southeast Uganda. It had a long tradition of centralized government, with clans owing allegiance to the kabaka (king). Threatened by the rise of Bunyoro, it was saved by the arrival of the British. A protectorate in 1900, it became a constitutional kingdom in 1955 and then part of independent Uganda in 1962. ▷ 5.15

BULGARIA
Republic in southeastern Europe south of Romania. It was conquered by Turkey in the 14th century, and the Bulgarian Revolt (1875–76) led to the Russo-Turkish War, ended by the TREATY OF SAN STEFANO (1878). It created the "large Bulgaria" later reduced in size by the CONGRESS OF BERLIN. Effectively independent in 1885, it sided with Germany in World War I (1915–18). Invaded by the Soviet Union in 1944, it was a communist people's republic from 1946 to 1991. ▷ 5.10, 5.13, 5.14

BULL RUN, BATTLES OF
Two major battles in the AMERICAN CIVIL WAR (21 July 1861 and 30 August 1862). Both were fought along the Bull Run River to the west of Washington DC. Both were CONFEDERATE victories, the second a defeat for the newly created Federal Army of the Potomac. ▷ 5.27

BÜLOW, BERNHARD, FÜRST VON
(1849–1929) German statesman appointed foreign minister in 1897 and charged with implementing the kaiser's wish to pursue an ambitious policy in both colonial and middle European affairs. Regarded as an aggressive

politician, particularly over the 1905 Moroccan crisis, he was chancellor from 1900 to 1909, then lost the kaiser's support. ▷ 5.16

BURGOS, BATTLE OF
(November 1812) Battle in the PENINSULAR WAR. After his victory at Salamanca, the DUKE OF WELLINGTON took Madrid only to face superior French forces at Burgos. Defeated, he withdrew to Ciudad Rodrigo to regroup and prepare for the successful offensives of 1813. ▷ 5.08

BURKE, ROBERT O'HARA
(1820–61) Explorer of Australia. He migrated to Australia in 1853 and became an inspector of police. He then led a well-equipped expedition, with WILLIAM WILLS (1834–61), to accomplish the first south–north crossing of Australia (1860–61). Only one man, John King, survived the return journey and an inquiry blamed Burke for the tragedy. ▷ 5.18

BURUNDI
Central African republic, south of Rwanda. Formerly Urundi, the region was settled in the 15th and 16th centuries by Nilotic Tutsi (a military society) and their serfs, the Bantu Hutu. Part of German East Africa, it was passed to Belgium as a League of Nations mandate after World War I and became a United Nations Trust territory in 1946. Independent in 1962, it saw ethnic conflict and genocide in the 1990s. ▷ 5.01, 5.15

CACIQUE
A chief or prince among the Arawak peoples encountered by the first European explorers in the Caribbean and Bahamas. Each Indian village had its cacique, who ruled by the authority of a greater cacique in Cuba.

CAMBODIA
Kingdom in southeast Asia, successor of the medieval Khmer empire. A French protectorate from 1863, it was occupied by Japan (1940–45) and reoccupied by France in 1946 until independence in 1954. Cambodia was destabilized during the Vietnam War as result of intervention by US forces. In 1975 the Khmer Rouge under Pol Pot came to power, changing the country's name to Democratic Kampuchea. Around one-third of the population died in the reign of terror that followed. The Khmer Rouge regime was overthrown by Vietnam in 1979 but stable government and prosperity still eluded Cambodia in the late 1990s. ▷ 5.22

CAMEROON
Republic on the Gulf of Guinea, west Africa, and home of African kingdoms to which FULANI traders brought Islam. It had a long history of slave trading. A German colony (Kamerun) from 1884, it was invaded by west African troops under British command in 1914. Cameroon became a League of Nations Trust mandate to France in 1922 and a UN

Trust Territory in 1946, achieving independence in 1960. ▷ 5.16

CAMPO-FORMIO, TREATY OF
(18 October 1797) Treaty arranged by BONAPARTE between France and Austria at the end of the War of the First Coalition. France gained BELGIUM, the Ionian Islands and the CISALPINE REPUBLIC. Austria gained VENETIA, Istria and Dalmatia. The treaty was approved by the DIRECTORY, which then appointed Bonaparte to lead an invasion of Britain. ▷ 5.07

CANADA, DOMINION OF
Federation occupying most of the northern two-thirds of North America. The indigenous peoples are Inuit and Indian. French colonists applied the name Canada to the St Lawrence River valley, part of the colony of New France from 1608, which included Acadia – modern Nova Scotia and part of NEW BRUNSWICK – dating from 1604. In 1713 France yielded all claim to Newfoundland, Hudson Bay and most of Acadia to England. In 1760 Britain completed a conquest of the St Lawrence River valley, and in 1791 divided the valley and the Great Lakes region into UPPER AND LOWER CANADA. These emerged under the British North America Act (1867) as the provinces of ONTARIO and Québec, joined with NEW BRUNSWICK and Nova Scotia in the dominion of four provinces from which the country eventually expanded to its present ten provinces and two far-northern territories, including all British possessions in North America not absorbed by the USA. It was the first part of the British empire to adopt dominion status – independent (though Britain continued to take some responsibility for foreign relations until 1931) but retaining the British monarch. Without success Canada has attempted in recent decades to reformulate its constitution, in terms acceptable to all provinces, to meet aspirations of French-speaking Québec for a special status. ▷ 5.25, 5.26

CANADA, UPPER AND LOWER
Two colonial provinces created by Britain in 1791 in the St Lawrence River valley and the Great Lakes region of modern Canada. Lower Canada (main towns Québec and Montréal) had a mainly French population. Upper Canada (main town York, later Toronto) had been settled over the previous 20 years by American refugees still loyal to the British crown and by British immigrants. After the DURHAM report, advocating cultural absorption of the French, they became Canada West and Canada East under a single parliament (1841), self-governing from 1848. However, the French had as many parliamentary seats as the "English", and would not agree to the coming confederation of all British North American colonies unless allowed a province of their own. In 1867 Canada East thus entered the DOMINION OF CANADA as Québec, Canada West as ONTARIO. ▷ 5.25

CANNING, GEORGE
(1770–1827) British foreign minister from 1807 and foreign secretary from 1822. He reduced commercial tariffs and was the first to recognize newly independent states in South America. He supported the GREEK WAR OF INDEPENDENCE and Catholic emancipation and advocated the repeal of the CORN LAWS. He was briefly prime minister in 1827. ▷ 5.09

CAPE BRETON ISLAND
Island in Nova Scotia, eastern CANADA. Settled by France in the 17th century it was ceded to Britain at end of Seven Years War in 1763. Governed first as separate province, it became part of Nova Scotia in 1820. ▷ 5.25

CAPE ST VINCENT, BATTLE OF
(14 February 1797) Sea battle of the FRENCH REVOLUTIONARY WARS off the Portuguese coast between British and Spanish fleets. Admiral Sir John Jervis engaged a superior Spanish fleet with his 15 ships of the line and five frigates. It was a major defeat for Spain, and frustrated Franco-Spanish plans for an invasion of England. ▷ 5.07

CARABOBO, BATTLE OF
(24 June 1821) Battle in northern VENEZUELA between SÍMON BOLÍVAR's army of 8,000 (including the veteran British Legion) and General Miguel La Terre's 5,000 troops guarding the route to Caracas. Bolívar's victory and the headlong Spanish retreat enabled him to enter Caracas and declare Venezuela's independence. ▷ 5.23

CARBONARI
Literally "the charcoal burners", a secret society begun during the Napoleonic wars and formally established as a revolutionary body after the return of the unpopular Bourbons to Naples in 1815. They instigated the 1820 Naples revolt, the 1821 Piedmont revolt and widespread uprisings in 1831. They sought national unity but lacked effective leaders. ▷ 5.09

CARNEGIE, ANDREW
(1835–1919) Scottish immigrant to the USA (1848) who built an industrial empire (1873–1901) to become the most important steel producer in the world. When he sold his business to the US Steel Corporation he retired a dollar billionaire. A prominent philanthropist, he endowed academic institutions in the USA and Britain. ▷ 5.28

CARTWRIGHT, EDMUND
(1743–1823) English inventor of the power loom (1785), inspired by a visit to Arkwright's spinning factory. His first factory was established at Doncaster, England, in 1787. Power looms were widely adopted by factories, transforming the weaving process during the Napoleonic wars. He applied to Parliament for a reward in 1809 and received a grant of £10,000. ▷ 5.10

CASTLE HILL UPRISING
Rebellion in 1804 against punishments levied by the magistrate Samuel Marsden in an agricultural settlement northwest of Sydney where Irish nationalists had been transported to Australia for their part in risings against Britain. About 300 men assembled to protest against the colony's government. Soldiers killed several and six were hanged. They entered Australian popular history as defenders of liberty. ▷ 5.18

CAVOUR, CAMILLO DI
(1810–61) Italian statesman who founded the newspaper *Il Risorgimento* (Resurgence) in 1847. As prime minister of Piedmont (1852–61) he carried out reforms and, seeking allies in his quest to unify Italy, joined France and Britain in the CRIMEAN WAR. He secured the Plombières Agreement with NAPOLEON III (1858) for a Franco-Piedmontese War against Austria (1859). He united Piedmont with Parma, Tuscany, Modena and the Romagna (1860). His linking with GIUSEPPE GARIBALDI on the VOLTURNO RIVER led to an Italian parliament and the accession of Victor Emmanuel as king of Italy 1861. ▷ 5.09

CETSHWAYO
(1827–84) ZULU monarch, an outstanding general against tribal factions, notably at the Battle of Ndondakusuka where he massacred the iziGqoza (2 December 1856). King of ZULULAND by 1872, he refused to accept British protection. He escaped from ULUNDI (1879) before the decisive battle. Captured and imprisoned by the British, he was released in 1883 in the hope he would restore order among the disturbed Zulu clans. ▷ 5.17

CHACABUCO, BATTLE OF
(12 February 1817) Battle of the CHILEAN struggle for independence, fought north of Santiago. BERNADO O'HIGGINS and JOSÉ DE SAN MARTÍN defeated the Spanish and occupied Santiago, where Chilean independence was proclaimed in 1818. ▷ 5.23

CHANCELLORSVILLE, BATTLE OF
(1–3 May 1863) Battle of the Chancellorsville campaign in the Wilderness region of Virginia (April–May 1863), marked by a series of brilliant countermarches on both sides. It was ROBERT E. LEE's greatest defensive victory and enabled him to advance to GETTYSBURG. The Union commander General Joseph Hooker squandered his tactical advantages by pausing to construct a defensive position at Chancellor farm. GENERAL THOMAS "STONEWALL" JACKSON died of his wounds. ▷ 5.27

CHARLES X
(1757–1836) King of France (r.1824–30). He fled to Edinburgh during the French Revolution and returned in 1814 to succeed his brother Louis XVII. Public opinion was enraged when he compensated émigrés and dismissed Bonapartist officers from the army.

He blocked political reform and, aided by his prime minister, Prince Jules de Polignac (1780–1847), attempted to govern by decree. This sparked the JULY REVOLUTION of 1830, and once again he fled to Edinburgh. ▷ 5.09

CHARTISTS
English radical movement demanding political reforms expressed in a six-point 1838 charter: manhood suffrage, a secret ballot, annual parliaments, equal electoral districts, and salaried Members of Parliament who would not be required to meet property qualifications. Its three petitions to Parliament (1839, 1842 and 1848) were rejected. ▷ 5.09

CHATTANOOGA, BATTLE OF
(24–25 November 1863) Climax of the Chattanooga campaign in the AMERICAN CIVIL WAR (June–December 1863). WILLIAM SHERMAN defeated CONFEDERATE forces in a two-day battle as a result of which the South lost Tennessee and the way was opened for the Union march into Georgia. ▷ 5.27

CHICAGO
American city on Lake Michigan. Originally a military post (Fort Dearborn) built on a strategic lake site in 1803. A major inland port after the Illinois and Michigan Canal was built in 1848, it was long a center of social and industrial violence: the Haymarket riot (1886), the Pullman strike (1894), race riots in 1919, a gangster era during Prohibition. ▷ 5.28

CHICKAMAUGA, BATTLE OF
(18 September 1863) Battle of the AMERICAN CIVIL WAR at Chickamauga Creek in northwestern Georgia during the CHATTANOOGA campaign. The army of Tennessee under General Braxton Bragg (1817–76), pursued by Unionists under General William Starke Rosencrans (1819–98), unexpectedly turned and defeated the North. The Unionists were forced back to Chattanooga and Rosencrans was relieved of his command. ▷ 5.27

CHILE
South American republic. Spanish settlements began in 1541. Nationalist revolts began in 1810 and independence came in 1818 after the decisive BATTLE OF CHACABUCO. Ruled by BERNADO O'HIGGINS until 1823, it acquired coastal nitrate fields from BOLIVIA and PERU in the WAR OF THE PACIFIC. It achieved its present borders in 1902 with the annexation of southwestern PATAGONIA. ▷ 5.23

CHISHOLM TRAIL
A Texas cattle trail from San Antonio to Ellsworth and Abilene on the Kansas Pacific Railroad, opened by Jesse Chisholm, a part-Cherokee cattleman. In 1867, 35,000 cattle came up the trail for shipment east. ▷ 5.28

CHOSHU
Former province in Nagato, Honshu, Japan, and the feudal territory of a major Japanese

clan. Choshu led attacks against foreign ships (1862–63), united with Satsuma in 1866 to restore the emperor to power and led the 1868 palace coup leading to the MEIJI RESTORATION. Choshu provided numerous military and political rulers thereafter. ▷ 5.20

CISALPINE REPUBLIC

Province in northern Italy, formed by BONAPARTE's union of the Cispadane Republic and the Transpadane Republic in 1797. Recognized by Austria at CAMPO-FORMIO, it was renamed the Italian Republic (1802–04) and incorporated into the kingdom of Italy (1804–15). ▷ 5.07

CIXI

(1835–1908) Empress of China (r.1862–1908), consort of Emperor Xianfeng (1851–62). In retirement at the Summer Palace from 1889 onward, she nevertheless dominated the young emperor Tongzhi. She suggested modernizing reforms in 1898 but sympathized with the BOXER REBELLION. She initiated piece-meal reform (1901–05) but never desired a truly constitutional monarchy. ▷ 5.19

CLARK, WILLIAM

(1770–1838) Soldier and explorer who joined MERIWETHER LEWIS to explore the far north-west of the territories claimed by the USA (1804–06). A cartographer and expert in Indian affairs, he became principal Indian agent, a brigadier-general and joint founder of the Missouri Fur Company. Governor of Missouri Territory from 1813, he organized the defense of the Mississippi, employing gun-boats and blockhouses, during the WAR OF 1812. ▷ 5.26

CLEVELAND, STEVEN GROVER

(1837–1908) The 22nd and 24th president of the USA (1885–89 and 1893–97). A Democrat, he advocated the restoration of federal lands illegally acquired by railroads and cattle barons and made tariff reform a major political issue. He stated that, by virtue of the MONROE DOCTRINE, the USA had the right to settle Britain's territorial dispute with VENEZUELA in 1895. ▷ 5.28

COCHIN CHINA

Former French colony, comprising mainly the alluvial plains of the Mekong Delta. Part of the empire of Annam, it was occupied by France in 1859 and united with the protectorates of CAMBODIA, Tonking and Annam to form the French INDO-CHINESE UNION. This was expanded in 1893 to include Laos. It became a republic within the French Union in 1946 and part of South Vietnam in 1954. ▷ 5.03, 5.04

COCHISE

(d.1874) Chiricahua APACHE chief. After escap-ing from wrongful imprisonment in 1861, he led Apache warfare against the US govern-ment for ten years, though sometimes facing

howizers (Battle of Apache Pass, 1862, against General James Carleton), and died on a reservation in 1874. ▷ 5.26

COLENSO, BATTLE OF

(15 December 1899) Attempt in the SECOND ANGLO-BOER WAR to relieve LADYSMITH – one of three battles lost by the British during "Black Week", leading to a reorganization of their command. General Sir Redvers Buller crossed the Tugela River and tried to turn the flank of the Boer general LOUIS BOTHA, but met superior small-arms fire. ▷ 5.17

COLOMBIA

South American republic. The region was conquered by Spain (1536–38), becoming the Spanish colony of New Granada. In 1819 it became part of GRAN COLOMBIA. By 1830 Gran Colombia had disintegrated, with ECUADOR and VENEZUELA independent. In a civil war (1899–1903) Panama broke away from Colombia with American help. Colombia has continued to suffer political instability in the 20th century. ▷ 5.23

CONCERT OF EUROPE

General consensus among post-Napoleonic monarchies that leading European powers should act in concert to maintain the status quo. The great powers assumed the right to intervene in the internal affairs of states threatened by revolution. Maintained by the CONGRESS SYSTEM, it was a major influence on European politics in the 19th century. ▷ 5.09

CONFEDERATE STATES OF AMERICA

The eleven states that fought during the AMERICAN CIVIL WAR to secede from the USA: South Carolina, Georgia, Alabama, Florida, Mississippi, Louisiana, Texas, Virginia, Arkansas, Tennessee, North Carolina. ▷ 5.27

CONFEDERATION OF THE RHINE

Confederation created by BONAPARTE in the Treaty of Paris (17 July 1806) to mark his victory at AUSTERLITZ and his control of the western regions of Germany. Baden, Hesse-Darmstadt, Würtemburg, Bavaria and a dozen smaller states were united to become part of the French empire and provide him with an army of 63,000. It ended after his defeat at LEIPZIG (1813). ▷ 5.01, 5.08

CONGRESS

The American national legislature that first met on 4 March 1789. It consists of the House of Representatives (composed of 435 members elected for four years and allocated to the states according to their population) and the Senate (100 members elected for 6 years). An Act of Congress must pass both houses. Congress meets in the Capitol building, Washington DC.

CONGRESS OF VIENNA

(1814–15) Congress convened to settle post-war Europe after the Napoleonic wars. It was

interrupted by BONAPARTE's escape from Elba and his return to France. Its Final Act (9 June 1815), known as the Treaty of Vienna, created CONGRESS POLAND, Lombardy-Venetia, the kingdom of the Netherlands (Holland, BELGIUM, Luxembourg) and the GERMAN CONFEDERATION. It unified NORWAY and Sweden and and recognized the Swiss Confederation as perpetually neutral. ▷ 5.09

CONGRESS POLAND

An autonomous kingdom under the rule of the Russian czar, defined by the Treaty of Vienna (1815). An unsuccessful revolt in 1830–31 led to the loss of its autonomy. A revolt in 1863–64, caused by Russian conscription policies, was crushed and Poland was reduced to a province. This was followed by an attempt to Russify the country by redistributing land from the aristocracy to the peasantry. ▷ 5.09

CONGRESS SYSTEM

A term describing the conduct of diplomatic affairs in Europe in the decade (from 1815 to 1825) that followed the CONGRESS OF VIENNA. The Quadruple Alliance prevented a resurgence of French power and regular congresses discussed European problems. The system broke down after the CONGRESS OF VERONA but the idea persisted in the CONCERT OF EUROPE.

CONSERVATIVE PARTY

In the UNITED KINGDOM, traditionally the party favoring pragmatism and non-doctrinaire policies. It is usually identified with free enterprise and the free market and often known from its historical roots as the Tory Party. Under BENJAMIN DISRAELI's leadership, it developed strong links with industry and finance. Its first long period of office was from 1886 to 1906. Apart from three years in opposition, it was in power from 1915 to 1945, again from 1951 to 1964 and from 1979 to 1997 under Margaret Thatcher and John Major, until defeated in the Labour landslide victory 1 May 1997.

CONTINENTAL SYSTEM

BONAPARTE's attempt to destroy the British economy, initiated by the BERLIN DECREES (21 November 1806). Designed to close the Continent to British trade, it extended from the Russian coast in 1807 to the Iberian peninsula by 1808. European ships were forbidden to trade with Britain (Milan Decrees, 1807). The system hurt the French economy more than the British and Bonaparte's attempt to enforce it led to his disastrous invasion of Russia in 1812. ▷ 5.08

COPENHAGEN, BATTLES OF

Three battles involving the Danish capital. Charles X of Sweden besieged the city in July 1658 during the First Northern War (1655–60). It was relieved by two Anglo-Dutch inter-ventions. The British admiral LORD HORATIO

NELSON attacked the city on 2 April 1801, during the War of the Second Coalition. The Confederacy of the North (Denmark, Russia, Sweden) had resolved in 1801 to bar Britain from the Baltic trade. Nelson entered Copenhagen harbor with 12 ships, smashed the Danish fleet and was about to sail to the Russian coast when an armistice terminated hostilities. In September 1807 a British combined operation attacked Copenhagen with rockets to capture the Danish fleet and deny its use to the French. ▷ 5.08

CORN LAWS
Duties first introduced in 1804 to protect British grain prices against foreign imports. The 1815 Corn Law was more drastic in that it permitted free import of foreign wheat only after wheat had reached 80 shillings a quarter. This made bread expensive and caused immense social distress, partially relieved by a sliding scale of duties (1828). Poor harvests and the Irish potato famine led to the repeal of the Corn Laws in 1846. ▷ 5.10

CRAZY HORSE
(c1849–1877) Oglala Sioux war chief. Victorious in several firefights against the US cavalry, he defied their invasion of the sacred Black Hills (1875–77). Allied with the Cheyenne, his 25,000 warriors annihilated LIEUTENANT COLONEL GEORGE ARMSTRONG CUSTER's 200 men at the BATTLE OF THE LITTLE BIGHORN. He surrendered in 1877 and was murdered. ▷ 5.26

CRIMEAN WAR
(1854–56) War in which Britain and France sought to limit Russian power. After a Russian squadron destroyed the Turkish fleet at Sinope (30 November 1853), France and Britain landed forces on the Crimean peninsula (14 September 1854), intending to capture the Russian naval base at Sevastopol. Three major battles (the Alma, Balaclava, Inkerman) were fought from September to November in 1854, but Sevastopol did not surrender until September 1855. The Vienna Agreement (February 1856) secured a temporary peace, followed by the Treaty of Paris (March 1856) that neutralized the Black Sea. ▷ 5.12, 5.13, 5.14

CUSTER, GEORGE ARMSTRONG
(1839–76) American soldier who fought at FIRST BULL RUN, ANTIETAM, Fredericksburg, CHANCELLORSVILLE and GETTYSBURG during the AMERICAN CIVIL WAR. Commanding the 7th Cavalry in 1866 he recklessly attacked the Sioux at the LITTLE BIGHORN and was killed in the fighting. ▷ 5.26

CUSTOZZA, BATTLES OF
Two battles in northern Italy. The first (24 July 1848) was fought during the Italian wars of independence when Milanese rebels, aided by Piedmont and Lombardy volunteers, were defeated by Austria. The second battle

(24 June 1866) was fought during the AUSTRO-PRUSSIAN WAR. It was a major Austrian victory over an Italian army led by General Alfonso de la Marmora. ▷ 5.11

CYPRUS
Island in the eastern Mediterranean, divided into two republics, one Greek (Kypriaki Dimokratia) the other Turkish (Kibris Cumhuriyeti). Colonized by Greeks before 1000 BC, Cyprus belonged to a succession of empires. Under Turkish rule from 1571 to 1914, though a British base after 1878, it was annexed by Britain in 1914 and became a crown colony by 1925. Independence came in 1960. Violations of the constitution by the Greek majority led to a Turkish invasion and partition of the island in 1974. ▷ 5.13, 5.14

DAIMLER, GOTTLIEB
(1834–1900) German engineer who worked with NIKOLAUS OTTO and Eugen Langen on engine design. He invented a high-speed internal combustion engine fitted to a motor-boat in 1883, then adapted it to power a cycle in 1884. He applied it to a four-wheeled vehicle in 1886 to create one of the first automobiles and founded the Daimler Motoren-Gesellschaft at Kannstatt in 1890. ▷ 5.06, 5.10

DAVIS, JEFFERSON
(1808–89) American politician and soldier. He served in the MEXICAN-AMERICAN WAR and became secretary of war (1853–57). He was appointed president of the CONFEDERATE STATES in 1861 and was captured by Federal troops in May 1865. Indicted for treason, he was granted an amnesty in 1868. Though devoted to the Confederate cause, Davis was quarrelsome and intolerant of opposition. As a result his government was staffed by sycophants and he was unable to win support for unpopular but necessary war measures, such as conscription. ▷ 5.27

DE BEERS
Diamond mining company formed by CECIL RHODES in 1880, named after a BOER farmer on whose land diamonds were found. By amalgamating several companies operating in the KIMBERLEY area of Cape Province, South Africa, Rhodes created De Beers Consolidated Mines in 1887 and monopolized southern Africa's diamond trade. ▷ 5.17

DECEMBRIST REVOLT
(December 1825) Revolt by discontented Russian army units against the young CZAR NICHOLAS I. It was led by Russian officers who had served in France and saw that improvement in the condition of the Russian people was long overdue. Nicholas hanged the leaders, demoted others to the status of peasant and sent the rest to Siberia. ▷ 5.12

DECLARATION OF THE RIGHTS OF MAN
(27 August 1789) Declaration issued by the NATIONAL ASSEMBLY of France, effectively

ending the feudal system. Influenced by the American example of 1776, it proclaimed that "all men, being born equal, should have equal rights." In practice, the new legislative chamber would be elected not by universal suffrage, but by "active citizens" (taxpayers), thus reducing the French electorate to around 4 million. ▷ 5.07

DESSALINES, JEAN-JACQUES
(c1758–1806) African-born emperor of HAITI. Bought as a slave, he had adopted his master's name. He succeeded TOUSSAINT L'OUVERTURE who had led the 1791 slave rebellion. After exterminating most of his opponents, he proclaimed himself Jacques I, emperor of Haiti, in 1804. He was assassinated in 1806. ▷ 5.24

DEWEY, GEORGE
(1837–1917) American admiral who fought in the AMERICAN CIVIL WAR and commanded the US Asiatic Squadron during the SPANISH-AMERICAN WAR. After destroying the Spanish fleet in MANILA BAY in 1898 without suffering any casualties, he supported US landing forces. ▷ 5.22

DIAZ, JOSÉ DE LA CRUZ PORFIRIO
(1830–1915) Mexican president. He fought in the MEXICAN-AMERICAN WAR and opposed MAXIMILIAN I. He seized power in 1876, was elected president in 1877 and carried out reforms. Apart from 1880–84, he was in office until 1911, when overthrown by FRANCISCO MADERO. ▷ 5.23

DIRECTORY
Government in the First Republic of France (August 1795–November 1799) composed of five directors (the executive), a Council of Ancients and a Council of the Five Hundred (the legislature). Unpopular because of its corruption and inability to handle local tensions (the VENDÉE uprisings) it was overthrown by BONAPARTE. ▷ 5.07

DISRAELI, BENJAMIN
(1804–81) British CONSERVATIVE politician and novelist. He entered Parliament in 1837 and led the Conservatives after a split over the repeal of the CORN LAWS in 1846. Chancellor of the exchequer three times (1852, 1858–59, 1866–68), he was prime minister in 1868 and from 1874 to 1880. Concerned with social reform and imperialism, he secured a controlling interest in the SUEZ CANAL, made QUEEN VICTORIA empress of India and acquired the right to occupy CYPRUS. ▷ 5.21

DOST MUHAMMED
(1783–1863) Ruler of Afghanistan (r.1826–38 and 1843–63). He captured Kabul in 1826, occupied most of the country and established friendly relations with Russia. This aroused British anxieties and led to the FIRST AFGHAN WAR and his capture. Restored, he was regarded as a British ally after 1855. ▷ 5.21

DREADNOUGHTS
Battleships modelled on HMS *Dreadnought*, launched by Britain in 1906, whose large guns, thick armor and fast speed made every other battleship in the world obsolete, precipitating a naval arms race between Britain and Germany. ▷ 5.13

DREIKAISERBUND
A "League of the Three Emperors" created by OTTO VON BISMARCK to maintain the status quo in Europe while isolating France. The first understanding was made between Kaiser Wilhelm II, CZAR ALEXANDER II and Emperor Francis Joseph in 1873. Bismarck upgraded this to an alliance in 1881. It promised that if one signatory were at war with a fourth power (other than Turkey) the others would remain neutral. It was renewed in 1884 but abandoned in 1887 when Bismarck signed the REINSURANCE TREATY with Russia. ▷ 5.13

DREYFUS, CAPTAIN ALFRED
(1859–1935). A Jewish officer in the French army jailed for treason. Retried in 1906, he was declared innocent, promoted and awarded the Legion of Honor. Known as *l'affaire*, the Dreyfus case deeply divided France into Dreyfusards (a socialist and intellectual faction) and the anti-Dreyfusards (Catholics and the military).

DUAL ALLIANCE
(1879) BISMARCK's secret agreement with Austria promising support if either signatory were attacked by Russia. Joined by Italy in 1882 (making it the TRIPLE ALLIANCE), it was in effect until 1918. A Franco-Russian Dual Alliance was signed in 1894 to counteract the Triple Alliance. ▷ 5.13

DUAL MONARCHY
The arrangement reached in 1867 whereby the Habsburg sovereign ruled both as the emperor of Austria and as the constitutional king of Hungary. Each country had its own parliament but there were joint ministries for foreign affairs, the budget and the armed services. The Hungarians enjoyed an equality with the Austrians that was envied by other ethnic groups in AUSTRIA-HUNGARY. ▷ 5.11

DUMA
A self-governing council such as offered to larger towns by CZAR ALEXANDER II in his Duma Statute (1870). After the 1905 Russian revolution the term was used to describe four parliaments (1906–07, 1907, 1907–12, 1912–16), none of which achieved the scale of reform desired by the Russian people. ▷ 5.12

DURHAM, LORD
(1792–1840) Briefly governor-general of CANADA in 1838, charged to investigate the MACKENZIE and PAPINEAU rebellions. Censured for his leniency toward the rebels, he resigned and returned to Britain where he published the Durham Report, which recommended responsible government and the assimilation of French Canadians to English culture. ▷ 5.25

DUTCH EAST INDIES
Modern Indonesia, exploited by the Dutch East India Company in the 17th century. It was occupied by Britain in 1798 and restored to the Netherlands in 1816, falling under Japanese control from 1942 to 1945. After World War II, nationalists resisted Dutch attempts to retain control. Independent in 1949, it annexed Portuguese Timor (1975–76), provoking fierce local resistance. ▷ 5.22

ECUADOR
South American republic. Under Inca control when the Spaniards began their conquest in 1525, it became part of the viceroyalty of PERU and a lucrative source of gold. It won its independence from Spain and joined GRAN COLOMBIA until 1830 when it became a separate republic. ▷ 5.23

EDISON, THOMAS
(1847–1931) The most successful American inventor, with 1,300 patents to his credit. He improved the telegraph service and was able to fund his own research laboratory. He invented the phonograph, motion pictures, the carbon microphone and the incandescent lamp. He discovered the "Edison effect" (1883) that led to the radio valve. ▷ 5.28

EDWARD VII
(1841–1910) King of Britain (r.1901–10), who married Princess Alexandra of Denmark in 1863 and succeeded his mother, VICTORIA. He was self-indulgent, and his behavior sometimes scandalized London society. Strongly francophile, in 1903 he made a visit to Paris that helped set the tone for discussions leading to the ENTENTE CORDIALE.

EGYPT
Arab republic in north Africa. Center of one of the earliest civilizations (from c.3000 BC), it was technically part of the Ottoman empire from 1517 to 1914. Following BONAPARTE's unsuccessful invasion in 1798, the Ottomans appointed MEHMET ALI as governor, under whom Egypt became an autonomous province within the empire (1805). The building of the SUEZ CANAL (1859–69) greatly increased Egypt's strategic importance, and it became a British protectorate in 1882. Egypt became an independent monarchy in 1922 but British garrisons remained until after World War I. The Egyptian king was overthrown in 1952–53 and President Nasser's nationalization of the Suez canal provoked an unsuccessful Anglo-French invasion in 1956. Egypt has fought four wars against Israel (1948, 1956, 1967 and 1973). ▷ 5.14

ELLIS ISLAND
Island in Upper New York Bay, from 1892 the site of the Ellis Island Immigration Station. When it closed in 1954 it had processed 12 million immigrants. One million arrived in 1907 alone and today 40 percent of Americans are descended from those who entered the USA through Ellis Island. ▷ 5.28

EMS TELEGRAM
(13 July 1870) Telegram sent from the German spa of Ems by the Prussian kaiser WILHELM I to his minister BISMARCK. It refused the French ambassador's request for a guarantee that a HOHENZOLLERN would never seek the Spanish throne. Bismark altered the text of the telegram so as to infuriate French and German public opinion when it appeared in the press. This led directly to a French declaration of war, the start of the FRANCO-PRUSSIAN WAR. ▷ 5.11

ENGELS, FRIEDRICH
(1820–95) Co-author with KARL MARX of the *Communist Manifesto* (1848). Born in Germany, he visited Manchester, England, as an agent of his father's prosperous textile firm and became interested in CHARTISM. He funded Marx's research and assisted with the compilation of *Das Kapital* and, after Marx's death, completed the work in 1883. ▷ 5.10

ENTENTE CORDIALE
(1904) the "friendly understanding" between Britain and France that settled disputes over SIAM, MADAGASCAR, the New Hebrides, the Newfoundland fisheries and west Africa. It defined EGYPT as a British sphere of influence and Morocco as a French sphere of influence. ▷ 5.13, 5.16

ENVER PASHA
(1881–1922) A Turkish soldier who led the 1908 YOUNG TURK Revolt. He was prominent during the BALKAN WARS and organized the military alliance that took Turkey into World War I on Germany's side. Dismissed as minister of war in 1918, he was killed in the 1922 Turkestan rebellion. ▷ 5.14

ERITREA
Independent state on the shores of the Red Sea north of Ethiopia. Part of the ancient Ethiopian empire, it was occupied by Italy and became an Italian colony in 1890. Occupied by British and imperial troops in 1941, it became a province of Ethiopia in 1962 and independent in 1993. ▷ 5.15

ESTATES-GENERAL
An assembly of provincial representatives called by the French king to approve taxes. It had three houses: the First Estate (clergy); the Second Estate (nobility); and the Third Estate (commoners). The meeting of the Estates-General in 1789, the first since 1614, culminated in the French Revolution. ▷ 5.07

ETHIOPIA
East African state founded in the 12th century. Christian, it allied with the Portuguese against its Muslim neighbors in the 16th century. It

was the only African state to resist European colonialism in the 19th century, defeating an Italian invasion at ADOWA (1896). It was eventually annexed by Italy in 1936 and liberated by the British in 1941. Emperor Haile Selassie was deposed in 1974 and the monarchy abolished in 1975. ▷ 5.15

EUREKA UPRISING

(1854) Rebellion in the BALLARAT goldfield of Victoria, Australia, by miners resentful of heavy license fees and demanding democratic rights. The uprising, in which 45 miners died when troopers attacked their makeshift stockade, took its name from the local hotel. Within a year, Victoria had its own parliament. ▷ 5.18

EYRE, EDWARD JOHN

(1815–1901) Australian explorer who made three attempts to cross the Nullabor Plain to ADELAIDE. The first two, by a a northern route, were unsuccessful Then in 1841 he set out from Perth and, by hugging the southern coastline, was the first European to cross the plain. He was later governor of NEW ZEALAND and Jamaica. ▷ 5.18, 5.24

FALKLAND ISLANDS (ISLAS MALVINAS)

British colony in the South Atlantic. Briefly colonized in 1764 by French sailors from St Malo (*Malouins* who called the islands Les Malouines, from which the Spanish name Islas Malvinas derives). The islands were claimed by Britain (1765), by Spain (1767) and, after its independence from Spain, by ARGENTINA (1820). An Argentinian colony was established in 1826 but in 1833 the settlers were forced to leave by the British who in turn established a colony. In 1982 Argentina invaded the islands in pursuance of its territorial claim but its forces were quickly expelled by a British task force. ▷ 5.23

FASHODA CRISIS

(1898) Incident in small town on the upper Nile River. British troops under KITCHENER encountered a French force there and after diplomatic exchanges France was forced to withdraw and abandon all claims to the Nile valley in 1899. ▷ 5.13, 5.16

FENIAN BROTHERHOOD

(From *Fianna* – Irish folk heroes) The name used in 1858 by James Stephens (1824–1901) for his revolutionary Irish nationalist move-ment in America. His aim was secure a republican government in Ireland through direct action. American Fenians attacked across the Canadian border (1866–70); Irish Fenians attacked Clerkenwell Jail in London in 1867, killing 20 people. ▷ 5.09, 5.25

FIRE IN THE FERN

(1860–72) the unified Maori resistance move-ment in NEW ZEALAND that began with the KING MOVEMENT in 1858. It flared into armed conflict after a land dispute at Waitara, with

12 years of inconclusive warfare in the moun-tains, during which the colonial government confiscated vast tracts of Maori land. ▷ 5.18

FIRST OF JUNE, BATTLE OF THE

(29 May–1 June 1794) Sea battle between Britain and France. When 130 French grain-ships sailed from New York in April a French fleet sailed into the Atlantic as escort. Admiral Sir Richard Howe intercepted this fleet and captured or dispersed the French warships. As the battle raged, the grainships docked safely at Brest. ▷ 5.07

FIVE CIVILIZED TRIBES

The Cherokee, Chickasaw, Choctaw, Creek and Seminole nations of southeastern North America. They were termed "civilized" because of their willingness to adopt western culture. Nevertheless, they were relocated to the INDIAN TERRITORY and en route the Cherokee experienced their TRAIL OF TEARS (1838–39). ▷ 5.26

FLINDERS, MATTHEW

(1774–1814) The first circumnavigator of Australia (1801–03) and the first to carry out a detailed survey of the shape of the continent. In 1798 Flinders and George Bass had sailed through the Bass Strait to prove that Tasmania was a separate island. ▷ 5.18

FORD, HENRY

(1863–1947) Pioneering automotive manu-facturer. Born in Michigan, USA, a first class mechanic, he created an automobile company in Detroit in 1899, named the Ford Motor Company in 1903. His third design, the Model T, appeared in 1908 and was in production until 1925, when a new Model T rolled off the assembly line every 15 seconds. He was regarded as the most original manufacturer of his day, and his factories played an important role in World War I. ▷ 5.28

FORT SUMTER

Military base in Charleston Harbor, South Carolina, USA. It was the scene of the first action in the AMERICAN CIVIL WAR, when rebel artillery began shelling the fort at 4.30 am, 12 April 1861. The Federal garrison surrendered and departed. PRESIDENT ABRAHAM LINCOLN called for volunteers to fight the south. ▷ 5.27

FRANCIA, JOSÉ

(1766–1840) A university-educated Creole, architect of the PARAGYUAN revolution who as El Supremo (r.1814–40) wielded absolute power by eliminating all his enemies. He accomplished a social revolution in Paraguay, isolating its people from the rest of South America. ▷ 5.23

FRANCO-PRUSSIAN WAR

(1870–71) War occasioned by a Franco-Prussian quarrel over the HOHENZOLLERN candidature for the Spanish throne and by the EMS TELEGRAM, deliberately provoked by

BISMARCK to secure the predominance of PRUSSIA in Europe. The French, unprepared for Prussia's methods of waging war, suffered heavy defeats and the humiliating Treaty of Frankfurt (10 May 1871). France surrendered ALSACE-LORRAINE and agreed to pay an indemnity of 5 billion francs. ▷ 5.11

FRANKFURT NATIONAL ASSEMBLY

(18 May 1848–18 June 1849) Assembly of elected representatives during the German Revolution, meeting to draft a federal constitution for a united Germany. The constitution was agreed by March 1849 and Frederick William of PRUSSIA was elected emperor. However, in April 1849 he refused the crown and this attempt at German unity failed.

FRANZ-JOSEPH I

(1830–1916) Emperor of Austria (r.1848–1916) and king of Hungary (r.1867–1916). He opposed nationalist groups within the empire, survived military defeat in the AUSTRO-PRUSSIAN WAR (1866) and accepted the 1867 AUSGLEICH. He ruled longer than any other European monarch. ▷ 5.09, 5.11, 5.13

FRASER RIVER GOLD RUSH

GOLD RUSH on the Fraser River, beginning in 1856 and peaking in 1858, when thousands of immigrants settled in the region. Their presence created an administrative problem for the Hudson's Bay Company, solved by creating the Crown Colony of BRITISH COLUMBIA in 1858. ▷ 5.25

FREDERICK WILLIAM IV

King of PRUSSIA (r.1840–61), the son of Frederick William III (r.1797–1840). His reign included his momentary conversion to the idealism of the 1848 German Revolution, whose leadership he assumed until formally offered the crown in 1849. Illness forced him to abdicate in 1861. ▷ 5.09

FREMANTLE

Port in southwestern Australia south of Perth, founded in 1829 when the first colony on the SWAN RIVER was established. In 1850 Britain allowed the resumption of convict labour and every year ships bearing 500 convicts docked in Fremantle harbor. The last, the *Hougoumont*, berthed in 1868. ▷ 5.18

FRENCH EQUATORIAL AFRICA

Four French colonies in equatorial Africa, where France first established its presence in 1841. In 1910 three colonies, Ubangi-Shari, Gabon and Middle Congo, were created. Chad was added in 1920. They won their independence in 1960: as the Central African Republic, Gabon, Congo, and Chad respectively. ▷ 5.16

FRENCH INDO-CHINA

Four French colonies: COCHIN CHINA, Annam, CAMBODIA and Tonking, administratively united in 1887. Laos was added in 1893. After the defeat of France in World War II, it was occupied by Japan (1940–45). Indo-China was restored to the French in 1946, but they withdrew after their defeat by a communist Viet Minh army at Dien Bien Phu in 1954. ▷ 5.22

FRENCH REVOLUTIONARY WARS
Wars that followed when Austria and PRUSSIA, alarmed by the French Revolution and fearful for the fate of LOUIS XVI, issued the Pillnitz Declaration (August 1792), declaring that they would restore the French monarchy. The French Legislative Assembly organized defensive armies and two international coalitions, including Britain, were assembled to fight them: the First Coalition (1792–98) and the Second (1798–1800). ▷ 5.07

FRENCH SUDAN
Modern Mali. Center of the empire of Mali under Mansa Musa (r.1312–37). Involved in Samouri Touré's resistance against the French (1882–98), it became a colony in 1904. It won independence in 1960. ▷ 5.16

FRENCH WEST AFRICA
Federation of French colonies (Mauretania, SUDAN, Senegal, Guinea, Ivory Coast, Upper Volta, Niger and Dahomey) developed by 1895 and reorganized in 1904. Its administrative capital was Dakar. By 1959 it had dissolved into several independent states: Mauretania, Mali, Senegal, Guinea, Ivory Coast, Burkina Faso, Niger, Dahomey. ▷ 5.26

FULANI
People of the west African Sahel. Muslim since the 11th century, they reached the peak of their power after the jihad of Usman dan Fodio, who created the SOKOTO CALIPHATE in the early 19th century. ▷ 5.15, 5.16

GADSDEN PURCHASE
Purchase from Mexico negotiated by James Gadsden (1788–1858) in which the USA received 77,700 square kilometers (30,000 square miles) of territory in 1853 for just $10 million. This made it possible to build the Southern Pacific transcontinental railroad through modern Arizona and New Mexico by way of El Paso and Tucson. ▷ 5.26, 5.28

GAMBIA
Republic in west Africa, surrounded by Senegal apart from its outlet to the Atlantic. Once part of the Mali empire, it was visited by Portuguese in the 15th century, and a British fort was built on James Island in 1618. Gambia became a British colony in 1843, a full protectorate in 1894 and independent in 1965. It became a republic in 1970. ▷ 5.16

GARIBALDI, GIUSEPPE
(1807–82) Italian soldier and patriot born in Piedmont. He defended the Roman Republic in 1849, fought the Austrians in 1859 and in 1860 led his Thousand Redshirts to invade SICILY and Naples in their quest for a united Italy. He then offered the conquered territories to VICTOR EMMANUEL II of Piedmont who became king of Italy. ▷ 5.09

GAZA EMPIRE
Southern African empire located in modern Zimbabwe and Mozambique. It was founded by Ndwandwe migrants led by Soshangane (d.1858), an ambitious African imperialist who named it Gaza in honor of his grandfather. He vanquished the Shona and Tonga and tried to assimilate them into a single nation. ▷ 5.02

GENEVA CONVENTION
International agreements on the conduct of war formulated in 1864 and modified at conventions held in 1906, 1929, 1949 and 1977. Initially concerned with wounded soldiers and the immunity of the RED CROSS, the agreements also cover prisoners of war and the protection of civilians.

GEORGE IV
(1762–1830) King of Great Britain (r.1820–30), and prince regent (1811–20) during his father's illness. Unpopular because of his attempt to divorce Queen Caroline in 1820 and hostile to the reforms advocated by his ministers, he is remembered for his tasteful support of the Brighton pavilion and improvements to the West End of London.

GEORGE V
(1865–1936) King of Great Britain (r.1910–36), who married Princess Mary in 1893. He was careful to act as a constitutional monarch and when he intervened in political affairs such as the Parliament Act (1911) and the Irish crisis of 1914, he did so entirely on the advice of his ministers. ▷ 5.13, 5.21

GEORGETOWN
Capital of the South American state, Guyana. Founded by the British in 1781 and occupied by the Dutch (1784–1812), it became an entry port for former slaves, Chinese and Madeirans seeking work on plantations. It saw major trade union unrest in 1906. ▷ 5.24

GERMAN CONFEDERATION
Confederation created at the CONGRESS OF VIENNA (June 1815) in an attempt to fill the vacuum caused by BONAPARTE's destruction of the Holy Roman empire in 1806. Its aim was to maintain the security and independence of its 39 component states through its diet (the Bundestag) at Frankfurt. Initially under Austrian control but threatened by the rise of PRUSSIA, it was abolished in 1866. ▷ 5.09, 5.11

GERMAN EMPIRE (SECOND REICH)
Second of three German *Reiche* (empires). The First Reich was the Holy Roman empire (962–1806). BISMARCK created the Second Reich (1871–1918), during a period of unification that reached its climax in the FRANCO-PRUSSIAN WAR. This empire ended with German defeat in World War I. The Third Reich (1933–45), was created by Adolf Hitler. ▷ 5.11, 5.13

GERMAN SOUTH WEST AFRICA
Modern Namibia when colonized by Germany (1885–1914). Traditional home of the San, Khoikhoi, NAMA and Herero, they rebelled against German rule (1904–1909). The area was occupied by South African forces during World War I and mandated to South Africa by the League of Nations. ▷ 5.15, 5.16, 5.17

GERONIMO (GOYATHLAY)
(1829–1909) Chiricahua APACHE leader, an outstanding guerrilla fighter, whose name Goyathlay means "one who yawns". He raided into Mexico, Arizona and New Mexico. Escaping from his reservation, he fought in the 1885–86 Apache War. He surrendered in 1886 and dictated his memoirs in 1906. ▷ 5.26

GETTYSBURG
Town in Pennsylvania, the scene of an important battle in the AMERICAN CIVIL WAR and of

HANOVERIAN DYNASTY 1820–1901

GEORGE IV 1820–30		1854	Crimean war begins,
			Battles of the Alma, Balaclava, Inkerman
1829	Catholic emancipation	1857	Indian Mutiny begins
		1867	Second Reform Act
WILLIAM IV 1830–37			Fenian rising
		1874	Fourth Asante War
1832	First Reform Act	1875	Suez Canal shares purchased
1833	Slavery abolished in British empire	1878	Second Afghan War begins
		1881	First Anglo-Boer War
VICTORIA 1837–1901			The Mahdi's Rebellion begins
		1884	Third Reform Act
1839	First Afghan war begins,	1895	Jameson Raid
	First Chartist petition	1898	Battle of Omdurman
	First Opium War begins		Fashoda crisis
1845	Irish famine begins	1899	Second Anglo-Boer War begins
1846	Corn Laws repealed	1900	Relief of Ladysmith and Mafeking

a famous address by ABRAHAM LINCOLN. The battle (1–3 July 1863) was between the Army of the Potomac and the CONFEDERATE Army of Virginia. It revolved around the town and the ridge beyond and was notable for "Pickett's charge" by the Confederates, a desperate attack which was shattered by Union rifle fire. Both sides suffered heavy casualties and the south never again fielded a comparable force. Dedicating the battlefield as a national cemetery, President Lincoln delivered the Gettysburg Address on 19 November 1863, emphasizing the democratic principles and moral values enshrined in the American constitution. ▷ 5.27

GHOST DANCE
Ritual of the Sioux Ghost Dance Movement (1889–90). Wovoka, calling himself the new messiah, offered to bring the Sioux, traumatized by white aggression, a vision of a joyful future by joining his movement. The dances, lasting several days and involving religious fervor, caused trances and even deaths. ▷ 5.26

GILES, ERNEST
(1829–1909) Australian explorer. Using a camel train, he crossed the Nullabor Plain in 1875 from Beltana, north of Port Augusta in South Australia, to Perth. He then went on to cross the Gibson and Great Victoria Deserts. ▷ 5.18

GLADSTONE, WILLIAM EWART
(1809–98) British chancellor of the exchequer (1852–55 and 1846–52) and Liberal prime minister (1868–74, 1880–85, 1886, 1892–94). His major reforms included Forster's Education Act (1870), the Secret Ballot Act (1872) and the third parliamentary reform act (1884). He dedicated himself to home rule for Ireland and was defeated twice on this issue (1886 and 1893). His debates, especially when opposed by BENJAMIN DISRAELI, aroused great public interest.

GOKHALE, GOPAL
(1866–1915) Indian nationalist and social reformer. He was president of the Indian National Congress and sought independence within the British empire. He acted as a political advisor to Mahatma Gandhi. ▷ 5.21

GOLD RUSHES
Short periods of gold prospecting fever that opened up world gold reserves and new regions for settlement and farming. They were facilitated by improvements in shipping and railroads. Spectacular gold rushes included California (1848–49); Bathurst, New South Wales (1851); Witwatersrand, South Africa (1886); the KLONDIKE and YUKON Rivers, Canada (1896). ▷ 5.17, 5.18, 5.20, 5.25, 5.26

GORDON, CHARLES
(1833–85) British soldier. He fought in the CRIMEAN WAR and in the TAIPING REBELLION before he was ordered to the SUDAN in 1884

to rescue British garrisons isolated by the MAHDI in 1882. He was besieged and killed in KHARTOUM, his death leading to criticism of the prime minister WILLIAM GLADSTONE, who had failed to send a relief force. ▷ 5.16

GRAN COLOMBIA
Quito, VENEZUELA and New Granada united as one republic by SÍMON BOLÍVAR in 1819. The union ended in 1830 and the name COLOMBIA was adopted by New Granada. ▷ 5.23, 5.24

GRANT, ULYSSES S.
(1822–85) American soldier and Republican president of the USA (1868–77). A Union major-general in the AMERICAN CIVIL WAR, victorious at VICKSBURG and CHATTANOOGA (1863), he commanded the Union armies (1864–65). He received the CONFEDERATE surrender at APPOMATTOX (1865). His presidency was beset by scandals and though he was honest his cabinet colleagues were sometimes corrupt. ▷ 5.27

GREAT TREK
The migration to the interior of South Africa of 10,000 BOERS from Cape Colony (1836–37) to escape the authority of the British government. They founded two republics, the ORANGE FREE STATE and the TRANSVAAL. A third party settled in NATAL. ▷ 5.17

GREEK WAR OF INDEPENDENCE
Greek patriot struggle (1821–32) against Turkish rule. An initial Greek advantage was lost after EGYPT's intervention in 1825, but Britain, France and Russia sent warships to defeat the Turkish-Egyptian fleet at NAVARINO (1827). Greek independence was confirmed by the Treaty of London (1832). ▷ 5.09, 5.14

GREENVILLE, TREATY OF
(3 August 1795) Treaty signed after the American general Anthony Wayne had defeated western Indians at the Battle of Fallen Timbers (1794). The council held at Wayne's headquarters in Greenville, Ohio, transferred Indian rights in the Northwest Territory to the USA. ▷ 5.26

GREY, SIR GEORGE
(1822–85) British colonial governor and prime minister of NEW ZEALAND. A troubleshooter for the British government's colonial office, he was successively governor of South Australia, New Zealand and Cape Colony. He dealt with the Maori problems during the FIRE IN THE FERN and was the prime minister of New Zealand from 1877 to1879). ▷ 5.18

GUADALUPE HIDALGO, TREATY OF
Treaty ending the MEXICAN-AMERICAN WAR (1846–47), signed on 2 February 1848. In return for $15 million and the assumption of $3.25 million debts owed to Americans, the USA gained the Rio Grande boundary for Texas, all of New Mexico and California (the MEXICAN CESSION). ▷ 5.23

GURKHA WAR
(1812–16) War in which British forces invaded NEPAL to deter Gurkhas from raiding northern India. Fierce mountain fighting led to the capture of Gurkha forts in 1815 and a peace agreement (1816). Thereafter the Gurkhas furnished the British army with one of its finest regiments. ▷ 5.21

HADRAMAUT
A region of arid mountains in the south of the Arabian peninsula whose coastline is the Gulf of Aden. It was annexed as a British protectorate in 1888 to guard the approaches to Aden. It became independent as the People's Democratic Republic of Yemen in 1967 and was united with the Yemen Arab Republic to create Yemen in 1990. ▷ 5.14

HAITI
The western third of the island of Hispaniola, the first Caribbean state to achieve independence. Colonized by Spain in 1496 and repopulated with imported slaves, Hispaniola was ceded by Spain to France in 1697. A slave rebellion led by TOUSSAINT L'OUVERTURE in 1791 led eventually to JEAN-JACQUES DESSALINES' declaration of the independent republic of Haiti in 1804. A revolt in the east of the island in 1843 led to the formation of the independent Dominican Republic in 1844. Occupied by US forces from 1915 to 1934, Haiti had a turbulent history under the the Duvalier family (1957–86). ▷ 5.23, 5.24

HAKODATE
Seaport in southwest Hokkaido, Japan. Scene of Commodore MATTHEW PERRY's meeting with the Bakufu convention during his second visit to Japan (1854). Together with SHIMODA, it was the first port open for the purchase of necessities by US ships and as a refuge for shipwrecked American sailors. ▷ 5.20

HAMPTON ROADS, BATTLE OF
Inconclusive naval battle in the AMERICAN CIVIL WAR, the first clash between ironclad ships. The CONFEDERATE ironclad *Virginia* (previously the *Merrimac*) attacked US shipping in Hampton Roads, Chesapeake Bay. The Union ironclad *Monitor* opened fire on 9 March 1862. The *Virginia* returned to Norfolk where it was later broken up to avoid capture by Union forces. ▷ 5.27

HARPER'S FERRY RAID
(16 October 1859) Raid by the JOHN BROWN and 19 ABOLITIONISTS on the Federal arsenal in Harper's Ferry, Virginia (now in West Virginia). Brown's plan was to seize weapons and set up a black fortress in the mountains of West Virginia. Surrounded, he retreated into the engine-house and in the morning marines killed or captured the rebels. ▷ 5.27

HAUSA
People of northern NIGERIA, conquered by FULANI emirs during the 19th century. After

the British defeat of the Fulani (1900–1903), the Hausa came under British rule. ▷ 5.15

HAWAII
Largest of the Hawaiian Islands and a county of the American state of Hawaii. Polynesians settlers from the Marquesas Islands arrived in about AD 400. The island was visited by Captain James Cook, who died there in 1779. The Polynesian kingdom that developed in the 19th century was annexed by the USA in 1898 after American settlers rebelled. ▷ 5.05

HEARNE, SAMUEL
(1745–92) English seaman, fur trader and explorer of northern CANADA, the first man to make an overland expedition to the Arctic (1770–71). He built the first interior trading post for the Hudson's Bay Company on the Saskatchewan River. ▷ 5.25

HEJAZ
Western region of Saudi Arabia, adjacent to the Red Sea, containing the holy cities of Mecca and Medina, where Islam began. It was part of Ottoman empire after 1517. The Hejaz railroad link between Damascus and Medina was attacked during the Arab Revolt (1915–18). Ibn Saud became king in 1926 when NEJD and Hejaz united as Saudi Arabia. ▷ 5.14

HELIGOLAND
Island in the North Sea, 45 kilometers (28 miles) from mainland Germany. It was part of Schleswig-Holstein (1402–1714), then of Denmark. Britain occupied it in 1807, annexed it in 1814, then passed it to Germany in 1890 in exchange for ZANZIBAR. It was an important German base in both world wars and scene of the Battle of Heligoland Bight (27–28 August 1914). Controlled by Britain from 1945, it returned to Germany in 1952. ▷ 5.08, 5.11

HELVETIC REPUBLIC
(Previously the Swiss Confederation) The republic established by the French in 1798 as a centralized puppet state. BONAPARTE conceded local autonomy to the constituent cantons. The republic was dissolved in 1803 and new cantons were added. ▷ 5.07

HERZEGOVINA
See BOSNIA-HERZEGOVINA

HIDALGO, FATHER MIGUEL
(1753–1811) Mexican revolutionary leader who led the rebellion against Spain on 16 September 1810. He failed to capture Mexico City but succeeded in arousing the masses, who fought a vicious guerrilla campaign against the Spaniards (1810–21). Hidalgo himself was captured and executed at Chihuahua. ▷ 5.01, 5.23

HOHENZOLLERN DYNASTY
The royal family of BRANDENBURG-PRUSSIA (1415–1918) and the kaisers of imperial

THE HOHENZOLLERN DYNASTY
KINGS OF PRUSSIA

Frederick I	1701–13
Frederick William I	1713–40
Frederick the Great	1740–86
Frederick William II	1786–97
Frederick William III	1797–1840
Frederick William IV	1840–61
Wilhelm (William) (became Wilhelm I, kaiser of Germany in 1871)	1861–88

GERMAN KAISERS

Wilhelm (William) I	1871–88
Frederick III	1888
Wilhelm (William) II	1888–1918

Germany (1871–1918). Under the Great Elector, Frederick William, Brandenburg-Prussia began the expansion and central-ization that would, under BISMARCK, lead to the formation of the SECOND GERMAN EMPIRE. ▷ 5.09, 5.11

HOLY ALLIANCE
(20 November 1815) Alliance concluded between Austria, Great Britain, Prussia and Russia after the defeat of Napoleon, initially to contain France, prevent a return to power by the BONAPARTE family and support the monarchical order in Europe. It was joined by France in 1818.

HONG KONG
Former British colony off Guangzhou, China. Hong Kong Island was occupied by Britain in 1841 during the OPIUM WARS. Mainland Kowloon was added in 1860. In 1898 China granted a 99 year lease on the New Territories beyond Kowloon. It was the first British possession to be captured by the Japanese in World War II, after a protracted battle (8–25 December 1941). The lease expired in 1997 and the whole of Hong Kong was returned to China. ▷ 5.19, 5.22

HONG XIUQUAN
(1813–64) Chinese revolutionary and leader of the God-Worshippers' TAIPING REBELLION in China (1850–64). His northern army captured Nanjing in 1853 and moved on Beijing. The Taiping reached the Tianjin suburbs before being checked by imperial forces, who now slowly advanced on the southern Taiping strongholds. Hong fell ill in April 1864 and died on 1 June, shortly before the final suppression of his rebellion. ▷ 5.19

HUERTA, VICTORIANO
(1854–1916) Mexican general who in 1913 established a military dictatorship after the FRANCISCO MADERO revolution (1910–11). The American president Woodrow Wilson banned arms shipments to Huerta, and the American

occupation of Veracruz followed in April 1914. Huerta resigned in July 1914 and the USA recognized Venustiano Carranza as president of Mexico. ▷ 5.23

HUNDRED DAYS, THE
(March–June 1815) BONAPARTE's brief return to power after his escape from exile in Elba. After his defeat at WATERLOO he was exiled to the remote Atlantic island of St Helena.

IBADAN EMPIRE
An expansionist west African state located inland, north of Lagos and Benin City. Prominent after its victory over the Ilorin jihadists at Osogbo in 1841, the empire expanded into Ijaye and crushed the Ilesa Revolt (1869–70). Its ruler, the Are Momoh Latosisa (1871–85), aimed to incorporate the YORUBA STATES but he was defeated during the Kiriji War (1877–86). ▷ 5.02, 5.03, 5.15

IBRAHIM PASHA
(1789–1848) Viceroy of EGYPT. His Turco-Egyptian fleet was defeated at NAVARINO, and Syria (which he seized in 1833) was returned to Turkey by the 1840 Convention of London. He was the adopted son of MEHMET ALI and succeeded him because of his senility but predeceased him. ▷ 5.14

IMPERIALISM
Nineteenth-century international system that required the acquisition and exploitation of underdeveloped countries for financial and military advantages. A colonial empire was seen and desired as a mark of world prominence and to a lesser extent as a means of transferring the advantages of western culture to less well-regarded cultures. It caused numerous wars, often presented to the European public as noble and heroic actions, though more frequently times of near genocide. ▷ 5.02, 5.16, 5.18

INDIAN BUREAU
The office for Indian affairs established within the American war department in 1824, trans-ferred to the department of the interior in 1849. It has been one of the most criticized of government agencies, especially for its policy (official until 1934) of assimilating Native Americans and discouraging their own cultures. ▷ 5.26

INDIAN MUTINY
(1857–58, also known as the First National War of Independence) An uprising against British rule in India. It began in January 1857 with sepoys (Indian soldiers under British command) of Calcutta's Dum-Dum musketry depot who refused on religious grounds to use cartridges they believed to be greased with animal fat. Major sepoy resistance broke out at Meerut on 10 May and the mutiny spread across Oudh and central and northern India. The Madras army and most BOMBAY units remained loyal. There was some civilian

involvement and attempts by Muslims to initiate a jihad. After the mutiny the East India Company vanished and QUEEN VICTORIA appointed a viceroy, promising equal opportunity to Indians wishing to hold office. in the Indian civil service. ▷ 5.21

INDIAN TERRITORY
Land to which thousands of American Indians were relocated westward after the Removal Act (1830). It comprised most of OKLAHOMA and parts of Nebraska and Kansas, though these were lost in 1854. On 16 November 1907 the remaining Indian Territory became the state of Oklahoma. ▷ 5.26, 5.27

INDIAN WARS
Wars between the European settlers and the indigenous peoples of North America (1622–1890), during which the Indian population fell by 75 percent to 250,000. There were many hundreds of skirmishes and several pitched battles. Up to 1814, Indians sided with French, British or Canadian interests and after 1830 several groups were in direct conflict with the government of the USA. The fate of all, whether members of the FIVE CIVILIZED TRIBES, the Sioux, Comanche, APACHE or the host of other distinct peoples, was to succumb to the military power of the US Army. The last resistance was the BATTLE OF WOUNDED KNEE (1890). ▷ 5.26, 5.27

INDO-CHINESE UNION
See FRENCH INDO-CHINA

INDUSTRIAL REVOLUTION
A sudden explosion of technological and economic change, initially in Britain (c.1750–1800). It began with the accumulation of trading capital and the mechanization of the woollen and cotton factories of northern England and then of Scotland. Dependent upon the application of steam power, the revolution required factory production and the urbanization of the workforce. It led to population increase and social suffering in the new towns. It was stimulated by the FRENCH REVOLUTIONARY WARS and Napoleonic wars, and the technology was rapidly transferred to the iron and steel industries that in turn stimulated railroad construction. ▷ 5.10

INTERNATIONALS
The International Working Men's Association and its successors. Planning to internationalize the operations of revolutionary socialist and communist activities, the First International (1864–72) met in London under the leadership of KARL MARX. The Second (1889–1940) was based in Paris. The Third (the Socialist International) met in Moscow, initially under Lenin, and in 1933 formed a popular front against the Nazi dictator, Adolf Hitler.

IRISH FAMINE
Famine resulting from the potato blight (caused by the fungus *Phytophthora*

infestans) that struck most of northern Europe from 1845, with particularly consequences in Ireland. The repeal of the CORN LAWS and a program of local relief proved inadequate when the Irish crop failed in 1846. This caused the "great hunger", a famine that brought in its wake typhus and cholera. Penniless and diseased Irish emigrated to North America and parts of Scotland and England in 1847, thousands dying at their destinations. By 1849 the tragedy was beyond the powers of any 19th-century relief organization to relieve. More than a million Irish died between 1841 and 1851; more than 2 million emigrated. It left a legacy of hatred for the British, who were blamed by the Irish for the failure to provide effective relief, and it condemned Ireland to a century of slow economic growth. ▷ 5.05, 5.09

IRISH REVOLUTIONARY BROTHERHOOD
Association descended from the FENIAN BROTHERHOOD. Formed in 1873 it intended at the appropriate moment to wage war against Britain, but lack of unity prevented a clear policy developing and some members chose to use Parliament and the Irish Land League to focus opposition. Membership grew in 1898 (the centenary of the UNITED IRISHMEN REBELLION). In 1916 the brotherhood acted in concert with the Irish Volunteer Force during the Easter Rising in Dublin.

ISANDHLWANA, BATTLE OF
First major battle of the ZULU WAR. On 22 January 1879 Zulu forces led by chief Matyana massacred six companies of the British army's 24th Regiment of Foot. The defeat was largely the result of British overconfidence. The triumphant Zulus then went on to fight the BATTLE OF RORKE'S DRIFT. ▷ 5.17

ISMAIL PASHA
(1830–95) Khedive of EGYPT and grandson of MEHMET ALI. Virtually autonomous by 1872, he expanded Egypt southward. To deal with financial problems, he sold shares in the SUEZ CANAL to Britain in 1875. The Ottoman sultan deposed him in 1879 and his son, Prince Tewfik, became Khedive. ▷ 5.15

ITALIAN UNIFICATION
See RISORGIMENTO

ITURBIDE, AGUSTIN
(1783–1824) Mexican general who led the junta that replaced the Spanish government in Mexico in 1821. He proclaimed himself emperor of Mexico in 1822 and ruled by decree. This prompted ANTONIO DE SANTA ANNA's rebellion in December and led to Agustin I's abdication in March 1823. ▷ 5.23

JACKSON, ANDREW
(1767–1845) President of the USA (1829–37). A soldier and politician, he repulsed the British attack on NEW ORLEANS (1815) and commanded the occupation force in Florida

in 1818. His toughness earned him the name of "Old Hickory". Elected president in 1828 he was re-elected in 1832 as a Democrat. He had no hesitation in expanding the American frontier westward, and he spoke for many Americans when he supported the removal policy for the Indian nations. ▷ 5.26

JACKSON, THOMAS "STONEWALL"
(1824–63) An outstanding CONFEDERATE general in the AMERICAN CIVIL WAR who won his nickname at FIRST BULL RUN (1861) when he defended his position on Henry Hill. He commanded Confederate forces in the Shenandoah valley and won distinction for his tactics in northern Virginia in 1862 and for his skill at CHANCELLORSVILLE (1863). His death from an accidental gunshot wound and subsequent pneumonia was a serious loss for the Confederacy. ▷ 5.27

JACOBINS
The most violent and extreme political group of the French Revolution, formed in 1789 as the Society of Friends of the Constitution. Led by MAXIMILIEN DE ROBESPIERRE they implemented the Reign of Terror. The Paris Jacobin Club was closed in 1794 by the Thermidorian government.

JAMESON RAID
Raid led by Dr L. Starr Jameson (1853–1917), a personal friend of CECIL RHODES. It was designed to support the *uitlanders* (over-taxed foreign residents) in their plan to overthrow the TRANSVAAL president, PAUL KRUGER. The raiders left Bechuanaland on 29 December 1895 but were captured on 2 January 1896. Rhodes had to resign as prime minister of the Cape Colony. ▷ 5.17

JASSY, TREATY OF
(9 January 1792) Treaty between Russia and Turkey signed in Moldavia at the conclusion of their war of 1787 to 1792. Russia restored Moldavia, Wallachia and BESSARABIA to Turkey but kept the land conquered east of the River Dniester and the important port of Ochakov, thus confirming Russian supremacy in the Black Sea. ▷ 5.07, 5.08

JEFFERSON, THOMAS
(1743–1826) President of the USA (1801–09). He drafted the Declaration of Independence and assisted the French in their DECLARATION OF THE RIGHTS OF MAN. During his presidency he approved the LOUISIANA PURCHASE and endeavored to maintain American neutrality during the Napoleonic wars. ▷ 5.26

JENA-AUERSTÄDT, BATTLE OF
(14 October 1806) Battle in BONAPARTE'S campaign against PRUSSIA. Auerstädt is some 22 kilometers (13 miles) north of Jena and the battle involved the two wings of the French army simultaneously confronting the Prussians. Bonaparte's 100,000 troops defeated the Prussians at Jena, while the

French marshal Louis Nicolas Davout, after fighting defensively for six hours, attacked and defeated the second Prussian army at Auerstädt. ▷ 5.08

JOHNSON, ANDREW
(1808–75) President of the USA (1865–69). He was vice-president when ABRAHAM LINCOLN was assassinated. A Democrat, he was anxious to placate the defeated planters of the south, but his Republican CONGRESS passed the RECONSTRUCTION program. Unpopular after he vetoed civil rights acts in 1866, he survived a presidential impeachment. ▷ 5.28

JULY REVOLUTION
Revolution in France (27–29 July 1830). It replaced the Bourbon CHARLES X with the constitutional monarch LOUIS PHILIPPE, whose rule is often termed the July Monarchy. ▷ 5.09

JUNKERS
A term derived from *Jungherr,* referring to officer-cadet sons of PRUSSIAN nobles, later applied to members of the landed gentry in Prussia, the traditional source of the officer class in the Prussian and German armies.

KANAGAWA, TREATY OF
(31 March 1854) The first US–Japan Treaty of Friendship, signed by MATTHEW PERRY at the Japanese port of the same name (now part of Yokohama). ▷ 5.20

KASHMIR
Former state in southwest central Asia partitioned between India and Pakistan and a source of friction since 1948. Once part of the Mogul empire, it has also been occupied by Afghans and Sikhs. It became part of British India in 1846 as a princely state under the rule of the raja of Jammu. ▷ 5.21

KAZEMBE
African kingdom founded in the north of modern Zambia in about 1720 by Kazembe I, a member of the Lunda people. Kazembe III (1760–1805) made the kingdom a focal point of east–west trade: the kingdom's prosperity was reduced by the rise of TIPPU TIP's commercial empire. ▷ 5.15

KHARTOUM
Present capital of SUDAN, it was founded by Muhammed Pasha in early 1820s as a base for the EGYPTIAN army. Captured by the Sudanese nationalist leader, the MAHDI, whose forces killed GENERAL CHARLES GORDON and massacred the Egyptian garrison in 1885, it was retaken by KITCHENER in 1898. ▷ 5.16

KIMBERLEY
South African diamond-mining city. Diamonds were discovered there in 1870 and Britain annexed the area to the Cape Colony in October 1871. Kimberley's diamond mines were amalgamated by CECIL RHODES into the DE BEERS COMPANY in 1888. During the SECOND ANGLO-BOER WAR, Boers besieged Kimberley from October 1899. Relief came on 15 February 1900. ▷ 5.17

KING MOVEMENT
A protest among the Maoris of Taranaki province, North Island, NEW ZEALAND, against land sales to white intruders. Originating in the 1850s, in 1858 it merged into the King Movement for Maori independence led by King Te Wherowhero and his son Tawhiao. This spread throughout New Zealand and led to the FIRE IN THE FERN. ▷ 5.18

KITCHENER, HORATIO HERBERT, 1ST EARL
(1850–1916) British general who defeated the Sudanese MAHDISTS at OMDURMAN (1898), confronted the French in the Nile valley (the FASHODA CRISIS) and methodically overcame BOER resistance in the latter stages of the SECOND ANGLO-BOER WAR. He was the British commander-in-chief in India (1902–09). As secretary of war at the outbreak of World War I, he created the Kitchener armies of volunteers. He drowned when HMS *Hampshire* sank (5 June 1916). ▷ 5.13, 5.17

KLONDIKE GOLD RUSH
GOLD RUSH in the Canadian YUKON TERRITORY beginning in in 1896. Thousands of prospectors arrived, and the town of Dawson City was founded. Gold worth $50 million was extracted between 1896 and 1901. ▷ 5.25

KOSCIUSZKO, TADEUSZ
(1746–1817) Polish soldier who fought in the American revolution and became a US citizen. Returned to Poland to resist Russian attacks, he led the 1794 Krakow Uprising. He contested BONAPARTE's plan to make Poland a Grand Duchy and opposed CZAR NICHOLAS I's CONGRESS POLAND. ▷ 5.08, 5.09

KRUGER, PAUL
(1825–1904) BOER politician and national leader. He took part in the GREAT TREK as a child. He led the independence movement after the British annexed the TRANSVAAL. He headed the provisional government during the FIRST ANGLO-BOER WAR. and was prime minister of the TRANSVAAL (1883–1902). ▷ 5.17

KUBA
Bantu trading kingdom of central Africa established in the 16th century. By 1830 it played a major role in the transcontinental trade in European weapons. Undermined by the rise of TIPPU TIP and by Belgian imperialists, it became part of the BELGIAN CONGO. Exploited Kuban rubber workers rebelled against Belgian rule in 1904. ▷ 5.15, 5.16

KWANGTUNG TERRITORY
Province of southeastern China (modern Guangdong). Its long coastline provided good harbors, five of which (in addition to HONG KONG) opened to trade after the Nanking Treaty (1842). The headquarters of Sun Yixian's Guomindang (Nationalist Party) from 1912, it was occupied by Japan from 1938 to 1945. ▷ 5.19

LADYSMITH, SIEGE OF
British garrison town 185 kilometers (115 miles) northwest of Durban, South Africa. During the SECOND ANGLO-BOER WAR it was besieged for 118 days by Boer troops (from 2 November 1899). The siege was lifted after the Boer withdrawal and the arrival of Sir Redvers Buller's relief column. ▷ 5.17

LAISSEZ-FAIRE
A maxim in economics meaning "let it go" in French. In an industrial society, it signifies that individuals may manufacture and distribute their products without state interference or control. This freedom existed by the end of the 18th century but the appalling conditions in industrial towns and the political unrest among the working classes prompted some state regulation of factories, public health, transportation, social security, education and trade unions during the 19th century. The question of state control of market forces remained a matter of political controversy throughout the 20th century.

LARAMIE, TREATIES OF
Two treaties signed at Fort Laramie, Wyoming, between the USA and the Plains Indians. By the first (1851) the Sioux, Arapaho, Cheyenne and Shoshoni accepted new tribal boundaries and permitted the forts and roads on their land. The second (1868) followed a Sioux uprising after road-builders tried to cross the Bighorn Mountains. It acknowledged Sioux land rights in South Dakota. ▷ 5.26

LAURIER, WILFRID
(1841–1919) First French-Canadian prime minister of CANADA. An advocate of free trade with the USA, he led the Canadian Liberal Party and became prime minister in 1896. Defeated in 1911, he firmly supported Canada's entry into World War I. ▷ 5.25

LAWRENCE, T. E. (LAWRENCE OF ARABIA)
(1888–1935) Archeologist, soldier and writer who invigorated the Arab Revolt against the Ottoman empire. He won the confidence of Prince Faisal and captured the Red Sea port of Aqaba in 1917. He led a valuable guerrilla campaign on the right flank of the British advancing into Palestine (1917–18).

LEE, ROBERT E.
(1807–70) CONFEDERATE general in the AMERICAN CIVIL WAR. Trained as a military engineer, he served in the MEXICAN-AMERICAN WAR and captured JOHN BROWN at HARPER'S FERRY. He resigned from the Union army when Virginia seceded. He fought at SECOND BULL RUN, at ANTIETAM, at Fredericksburg, at CHANCELLORSVILLE and at GETTYSBURG. He

finally surrendered, for the sake of his war-weary troops, at APPOMATTOX. He was paroled after the war and though most of his battles ended in defeat he is revered as one of America's great generals. ▷ 5.27

LEIPZIG, BATTLE OF

(16–19 October 1813) The climax of the 1813 campaigns in Germany during the Napoleonic wars. It was the biggest battle during the wars (370,000 Russian, Prussian, Swedish, Austrian troops; 198,000 French troops) and is also known as the Battle of the Nations. It was BONAPARTE'S first major defeat on a battlefield and began the retreat that ended with his abdication in Paris in 1814. ▷ 5.08

LEOPOLD II

(1835–1909) King of the Belgians (r.1865–1909). An imperialist monarch, he wished to make Belgium a colonial power. He became king of the independent Congo Free State (BELGIAN CONGO), explored by H. M. STANLEY, but the conditions of the Congolese began to arouse international concern. In 1908 Leopold agreed to the annexation of the Congo by Belgium in return for £3.8 million. Much of this money was used to embellish public works in Antwerp and Brussels. ▷ 5.16

LESSEPS, FERDINAND DE

(1805–94) French engineer and cousin of Empress Eugénie of France. He received the contract to build the SUEZ CANAL in 1854, and it was opened to shipping in 1869. He was then asked to build the PANAMA CANAL but his company failed. ▷ 5.23

LEWIS, MERIWETHER

(1774–1809) American explorer and private secretary to PRESIDENT THOMAS JEFFERSON, who asked him to find a transcontinental route to the Pacific. The expedition, begun in 1804 in company with WILLIAM CLARK, was successful, and Lewis became governor of the LOUISIANA TERRITORY. ▷ 5.26

LIBERAL PARTY

British political party, initially of whigs and radicals who endorsed Irish home rule, religious nonconformity and LAISSEZ-FAIRE economics. WILLIAM GLADSTONE headed four Liberal ministries (1868–74, 1880–85, 1886, and 1892–95); Henry Campbell-Bannerman and Herbert Asquith headed Liberal ministries between 1906 and 1916 and strongly favored state intervention. The party's fortunes rapidly declined after World War I.

LIBERIA

West African republic. In 1822 the American Colonization Society (founded in 1816) chose this region to settle freed slaves. Liberia – from the Latin *liber* (free) – became independent in 1847. Its prosperity declined but was reinvigorated by the sale of rubber plantation concessions to the Firestone Company in 1926. ▷ 5.15, 5.16

LIGURIAN REPUBLIC

Republic centered on Genoa, northwest Italy, and founded by BONAPARTE (6 June 1797). It was recognized by the Peace of Lunéville (9 February 1801) and united with France on 4 June 1805. ▷ 5.08

LI HONGZHANG

(1833–1901) Chinese administrator and provincial governor who advocated the modernization of industry. Interested in warship and firearms design, he was the leading spirit of the Self-Strengthening Movement (1870–95). He established foreign language schools, sent teenagers to study at Hartford, Connecticut, opened firearms factories and modern shipyards, and introduced the electric telegraph and railroads. Despite these superficially impressive achievements, there was no industrial coordination, no grassroot enthusiasm as in Japan and no investment capital strategy. Li did not have the resources or will to transform China into a modern industrial state. ▷ 5.19

LINCOLN, ABRAHAM

(1809–65) Sixteenth president of the USA. He joined the Republican Party in 1856 and spoke against the extension of slavery into the new territories, though he confessed he could not see a way of abolishing it. His election as president precipitated the AMERICAN CIVIL WAR. His declared war aim was to preserve the Union, not to end slavery, which he made clear in his GETTYSBURG ADDRESS. However, as the war turned in the Union's favor in 1863 he proposed in his Emancipation Proclamation to free all slaves after the war. Days after the final Union victory, he was shot in Ford's Theater and died the following day, 15 April 1865. ▷ 5.27

LITTLE BIGHORN, BATTLE OF THE

(25 June 1876) Battle of the INDIAN WARS. After attacks by the US Seventh Cavalry at the Washita River (1868), in Montana (1873) and in the Black Hills (1874), Cheyenne and Sioux warriors assembled in 1876 on the Little Bighorn River. LIEUTENANT COLONEL GEORGE ARMSTRONG CUSTER and 212 troopers recklessly attacked the camp without adequate reconnaissance and were annihilated by nearly 3,000 warriors including CRAZY HORSE. ▷ 5.26

LIVINGSTONE, DAVID

(1813–73) Explorer and missionary. Qualified as a doctor by 1840, he joined the London Missionary Society and began working in BECHUANALAND in 1841. He explored the Zambezi River and found the Victoria Falls (1852–56). He explored the Shiré and Rovuma Rivers (1858–63) and was appalled by the extent of the local slave trade. In 1866 he set out to find the source of the Nile but illness forced him to retire to Ujiji where he was found by H. M. STANLEY. He died in Chitambo village (now in Zambia). ▷ 5.15

LOBENGULA

(1870–94) King of the NDEBELE (Matabele) who skillfully protected his kingdom of MASHONALAND against the ravages of European prospectors and traders, though he signed the Rudd Concession (1888) that permitted CECIL RHODES to bring in settlers from 1890. The Ndebele fought a brief war of resistance in 1893 but were overcome by Maxim guns. Lobengula died early in 1894. ▷ 5.15, 5.16

LOUIS XVI

(1754–93) King of France (r.1774–93), who married Marie Antoinette, youngest daughter of the Austrian empress Maria Theresa, in 1770. By 1780 he faced a worsening financial situation caused by inflation, debts and an inefficient taxation system. To improve his personal finances he summoned the Estates General (5 May 1789). Rapidly evolving into the Constituent Assembly, it set in train the French Revolution, abolishing the feudal system and forcing Louis from Versailles to take up residence in Paris. His attempt to escape in 1791, his sympathy with aristocratic émigrés and the support forthcoming from Austria and PRUSSIA led to his execution January 1793. ▷ 5.07

LOUIS NAPOLEON

See NAPOLEON III

LOUIS-PHILIPPE

(1773–1850) King of France (r.1830–48). Descended from Louis XIII, he was an émigré until 1815. In power as a result of the JULY REVOLUTION, his refusal to widen the franchise

BOURBON KINGS OF FRANCE 1774–1848	
LOUIS XVI **1774–93**	
1781	Necker dismissed
1789	Fall of the Bastille
1792	Abolition of the monarchy
1793	Executed
LOUIS XVII **1793–95?**	
LOUIS XVIII **1814–24**	
1815	Battle of Waterloo
1821	Death of Napoleon
CHARLES X **1824–30**	
1830	Capture of Algiers, revolution in Paris, abdication
LOUIS-PHILIPPE **1830–48**	
1848	Revolution in Paris, abdication

precipitated a revolution in February 1848. He fled to England and died in Surrey. ▷ 5.09

LOUISIANA
The entire Mississippi catchment claimed by French explorers. Also the name of the first state to emerge from the LOUISIANA PURCHASE, admitted to the Union in 1812. ▷ 5.26

LOUISIANA PURCHASE
(30 April 1803) Extraordinary land sale that doubled the area of the USA. BONAPARTE agreed with THOMAS JEFFERSON to sell LOUISIANA to the USA for $15 million. ▷ 5.26

L'OUVERTURE, TOUSSAINT
(1746–1803) Black revolutionary leader who joined the slave uprising of 1791 in HAITI and fought for independence in 1800. Arrested by the French, he died in prison. ▷ 5.24

LOZI
African kingdom on the flood plain of the upper Zambezi, established in about 1680. A highly sophisticated kingdom with a central-ized government, it controlled the Zambezi trade and expanded to form the Lozi empire (Barotseland). It fell victim to Kololo raiders in the 1840s but re-emerged under King Lewanika who cooperated with the British in order to maintain his personal control over the Lozi people (1890). ▷ 5.15, 5.16

LUCKNOW
Capital of Uttar Pradesh, northern India, and scene of the siege of a British garrison in the INDIAN MUTINY in 1857. The siege was broken twice by British forces but the city remained occupied by rebel Indian forces. It was not until Sir Colin Campbell returned in 1858 with Bang Bahadur's 10,000 Gurkhas from NEPAL that the British regained the city. ▷ 5.21

LUDDITES
Militant workers who destroyed machinery (stocking frames and shearing frames) in the English textile areas of Nottingham, Yorkshire and Lancashire during the Luddite Revolt (1811–12). They are thought to have been named after a Ned Ludd who broke machin-ery in Leicestershire during a fit of temper. The government decreed frame-breaking a capital offense and sent in 12,000 troops to quell the disorder. Seventeen Luddites died on the scaffold at York in 1813. ▷ 5.10

MACARTHUR, JOHN
(1767–1834) Officer in the NEW SOUTH WALES Corps, Australia, and one of those involved in the lucrative rum trade, the main currency of the colony. When Governor William Bligh attempted to intervene, Macarthur joined a mutiny against him in 1808. Exiled to England, he returned to Australia in 1817 to develop, with his wife Elizabeth, quality strains of sheep at Parramatta. He assumed control of the Australian Agricultural Company in 1827. ▷ 5.18

MACKENZIE, ALEXANDER
(1755–1820) Scottish-born fur trader and explorer of CANADA. He discovered the Mackenzie River in 1789 and was the first European to cross the Rocky Mountains (1792–93) to the Pacific Ocean. ▷ 5.25

MACKENZIE, WILLIAM LYON
(1759–1861) Scottish-born reform politician and newspaper publisher in UPPER CANADA. He led an abortive republican revolt in 1837, and took refuge in the USA, where he spent a year in prison for breaching neutrality laws by agitating against British rule in Canada. In 1847 the colonial government issued an amnesty that allowed him to return to Canada and enter Parliament (1851–58).

MADAGASCAR
Island in the Indian Ocean, first settled by Indonesians, who arrived in the 1st century AD. Africans arrived in the 11th century. In the early 19th century the MERINA united much of the island. Gradual French occupation in the late 19th century caused nationalist revolts (1883, 1894–96) but did not prevent the establishment of a colony in 1896. It achieved independence as the Malagasy Republic in 1960 but became the Democratic Republic of Madagascar in 1975. ▷ 5.15, 5.16

MADERO, FRANCISCO
(1873–1913) Mexican revolutionary and politician who challenged the rule of PORFIRIO DIAZ in 1908. He escaped to the USA and from there directed the revolution. He set up his capital at Ciudad Juárez in 1911 and was elected president in October. He faced a revolt by EMILIANO ZAPATA and was murdered in 1913. ▷ 5.23

MADISON, JAMES
(1751–1836) The fourth president of the USA. Born in Virginia, he served in the Continental Congress and the Virginia assembly. He helped draft the federal constitution and its first ten amendments, becoming secretary of state in 1801, then president (1809–17).

MAFEKING, SIEGE OF
(12 October 1899–17 May 1900) BOER siege during the SECOND ANGLO-BOER WAR of the town of Mafeking, held by Colonel Baden-Powell and a few British troops. In Britain there was widespread admiration for the white garrison but little or no recognition of the ill-fed African defenders who made up the majority. The lifting of the siege was greeted by exuberant celebrations in Britain. ▷ 5.17

MAGERSFONTEIN, BATTLE OF
(10–11 December 1899) Battle in east central Republic of South Africa where the BOERS defeated a British relief column en route to KIMBERLEY during the SECOND ANGLO-BOER WAR. The British general Lord Methuen's troops attacked hill positions near the Modder River and were repelled. ▷ 5.17

MAHDI
The title (al-Mahdi – the guided one) adopted by Muhammad Ahmed (1844–85), a Muslim leader who proclaimed a jihad in 1881 and occupied the SUDAN. He besieged KHARTOUM and killed GENERAL CHARLES GORDON before establishing a theocratic state at OMDURMAN. The Mahdist state survived until 1898 when it was conquered by the British. ▷ 5.16

MAHMUD II
(1785–1839) Sultan of Turkey from 1808, who saw much of the Ottoman empire disappear: BESSARABIA to Russia (1812), Greek indepen-dence (1821–29), the autonomy of MEHMET ALI of EGYPT. He abolished the corps of janissaries (slave soldiers) in 1826 and began the slow westernization of Turkey. ▷ 5.14

MAJUBA HILL, BATTLE OF
(27 February 1881) Battle of the FIRST ANGLO-BOER WAR, fought on a British-held hill controlling a crucial pass in modern KwaZulu-Natal, South Africa. BOER riflemen killed General Sir George Colley and killed or wounded 222 of a British force of 648. ▷ 5.17

MALAY STATES, FEDERATED
Federation between Negri Sembilan, Pahang, Perak and Selangor created in 1896. In 1909 SIAM transferred to Britain her rights to Perlis, Kedah, Kelantan and Trengganu. These became the unfederated Malay states. Johore was also an unfederated state. ▷ 5.22

MANDINKA EMPIRE
Term used to describe the SAMORI EMPIRE, a Muslim state created by Samori Toure in west Africa. It is also referred to as the first (1884–92) and second (1892–98) Dyula empire. They were overrun by French colonial forces in three wars (1885–6, 1894–5, 1898). ▷ 5.15

MANIFEST DESTINY
Doctrine used to justify the expansion of the USA across the North American continent with little or no regard for the lives and cultures of peoples encountered on the way. The phrase was penned by the editor John O'Sullivan who wrote in 1845 that it was America's "manifest destiny to overspread the continent allotted by Providence…" ▷ 5.26

MANILA BAY, BATTLE OF
(1 May 1898) Naval battle of the SPANISH-AMERICAN WAR. Four US cruisers and two gunboats under COMMODORE GEORGE DEWEY attacked ten Spanish warships anchored off Cavite Point in the Philippines. All ten were sunk, captured or disabled, allowing US forces to invade the Philippines. ▷ 5.22

MAORI WARS
Wars in NEW ZEALAND (1843–48, 1860–72). The first arose from Maori resentment over land seizures on the Wairu River and the accidental shooting of Te Ronga, a Maori princess, by white settlers. The second

involved the KING MOVEMENT. Guerrilla warfare and occasional assaults on Maori fortresses went on for 12 years, although fighting was desultory after 1870. ▷ 5.18

MARATHA WARS

Three wars between the British in India and the Marathas, Hindus living in the Deccan region. The Marathas emerged in the 17th century and fought a major war against the Mogul empire (1670–1707). The British waged their First Maratha War from 1779 to 1782 and captured Gwalior. During the Second Maratha War (1803–05) Arthur Wellesley, later the DUKE OF WELLINGTON, defeated the Marathas at Assaye (September 1803) and Argaon (November). The Third Maratha War (1817–18) was a complete victory for the British and the peshwa (Maratha hereditary chief minister) formally surrendered. ▷ 5.21

MARCH TO THE SEA

General WILLIAM SHERMAN'S 1864 advance through central Georgia during the AMERICAN CIVIL WAR, a pitiless destruction of the southern infrastructure and of the people's will to resist. Determined to "make Georgia howl", he captured Savannah and went on to devastate South Carolina in 1865. ▷ 5.27

MARENGO, BATTLE OF

(14 June 1800) Battle fought 1.6 kilometers (1 mile) east of Alessandria in northwestern Italy when 31,000 Austrian troops attacked BONAPARTE'S 23,000 and were initially the victors. A French cavalry attack then broke the Austrians and forced them to flee. ▷ 5.08

MARONITE CHRISTIANS

Monothelite Christian heretics who established their church in 7th-century Syria. Maron, their founder, maintained that Christ had but one will. They united with the Roman Catholic Church in the 12th century. In the colonial period, the Maronite population was much favored by the French, who separated Lebanon, with a slight Maronite majority, from Syria. Growth in the Lebanese Muslim population upset the balance of power, and civil war broke out in 1975. ▷ 5.14

MAROONS

Escaped slaves who settled in the mountains of Jamaica, Hispaniola and other West Indian islands. They raided Jamaican plantations, and the British fought two Maroon wars (1734–8 and 1795–96). The second war led to the exile of 556 maroons to SIERRA LEONE. The name derives from the American Spanish word *cimarrón* ("dwelling on peaks"). ▷ 5.24

MARX, KARL

(1818–83) German founder of international communism. His Communist League met in London and his *Communist Manifesto*, drafted by FRIEDRICH ENGELS, was published in Brussels (1848). Expelled from Brussels, he settled in London in 1849 and wrote *Das Kapital* (Volume I, 1867). Volumes II (1885) and III (1894) were edited by Engels after Marx's death. This work, defining the class struggle and emphasizing the supreme importance economics has in history, exerted a worldwide influence on revolutionaries, political activists and teachers of economics and sociology. ▷ 5.10

MASHONALAND

A region in northwest Zimbabwe, home of the Bantu Shona (Mashona). Acquired by the British South Africa Company, it was the scene of the Chimurenga (1896–1903), a guerrilla war of resistance that ended with the defeat of all the African leaders: Makoni (shot 1897), Mashayamombe (killed 1897), Mangwende, Muchemwa and Mapondera (all three surrendered by 1903). ▷ 5.17

MASINA

Nineteenth-century west African jihad state in modern central Mali. Shaikh Ahmad Lobbo (1775–1845) was a FULANI scholar who sought an independent Masina in which all Muslims could faithfully observe the *sharia* (Islamic law). His jihad began in 1818 and he established his caliphate in 1821. By 1827 he had removed Segu from Bambara rule and created a stable and well-administered Muslim state. It fell first to TUKULOR and then to French colonial rule. ▷ 5.02, 5.15

MASON-DIXON LINE

Boundary defined by the 1820 MISSOURI COMPROMISE between free and slave states of the USA – later seen as the frontier between north and south. Two British astronomers, Charles Mason and Jeremiah Dixon, employed to settle a boundary dispute between Pennsylvania and Maryland, mapped the line between 1763 and 1767. ▷ 5.27

MATABELELAND

Region in modern southwest Zimbabwe and former NDEBELE kingdom created by Mzilikazi (1795–1868) with a capital at Thabayezinduna. Resistance to British penetration began on 20 March 1896 when Ndebele warriors attacked white settlements. CECIL RHODES persuaded leaders to attend the Matopo Hills Conference and peace was restored. ▷ 5.15, 5.16, 5.17

MAXIMILIAN I

(1832–67) Archduke of Austria and emperor of Mexico (r.1864–67). He was persuaded by NAPOLEON III to accept the crown of a new French empire in Mexico, but his power there depended on the presence of French troops. American pressure forced their removal and he was captured by Mexican liberal revolutionaries and shot. ▷ 5.23

MAZZINI, GIUSEPPE

(1805–72) Italian republican who joined the CARBONARI before founding the YOUNG ITALY MOVEMENT in 1831 as the first step toward a united Italy. He liberated Milan during the revolt against the Austrians in Lombardy (1848–49) and then headed the triumvirate governing the new Roman Republic. Most of his supporters favored an Italian monarchy, and Mazzini's influence in Italy waned. ▷ 5.09

MEDICINE LODGE CREEK CONFERENCE

(October 1867) Conference to restore peace on the American plains. More than 5,000 Indians assembled in southern Kansas to meet government representatives, and though most chiefs signed a treaty in which they agreed to live on reservations, they had little intention of abiding by this. Fighting continued and soldiers were soon destroying Indian villages along the Washita River (1868–69). ▷ 5.26

MEHMET ALI

(1769–1849) Viceroy of EGYPT. An ALBANIAN soldier, he was transferred to Egypt in 1799 to fight for the sultan against BONAPARTE. Made governor in 1805 and viceroy (1811–48), he was an imperialist who conquered the SUDAN and founded KHARTOUM in 1823. He became governor of Crete for services to Turkey in the GREEK WAR OF INDEPENDENCE but fought two wars against the Turks (1832–3 and 1839–40). The great powers forced him to surrender his territorial gains. He founded the royal dynasty that ruled Egypt until 1922. ▷ 5.14

MEIJI RESTORATION

Restoration of the Japanese Meiji emperor Mutsuhito after the Tokugawa shogunate was overthrown in 1868. Mutsuhito's name came to symbolize Japan's rapid transformation into a modern industrial state. ▷ 5.20

MENELIK II

(1844–1913) Emperor of ETHIOPIA (r.1889–1913). Italy recognized his status in exchange for Massawa and ERITREA. He introduced western technology but rejected the Italians' desire for a protectorate in 1893 and summoned a national uprising when the Italians invaded in 1894. He won the BATTLE OF ADOWA and forced Italy to recognize Ethiopia's independence (Treaty of Addis Ababa, 1896). ▷ 5.16

MERINA

The inhabitants of Imerina in the center of MADAGASCAR located around their capital Antananarivo. The kingdom of the Merina, acknowledged by the Anglo-Merina Treaty (23 October 1817), embarked on a program to unify the entire island but was challenged by French colonial interests from 1881 onward. A French fleet bombarded the coast in 1883, and after two Franco-Merina wars (1883–85 and 1894–95) France secured its conquest of of the area by 1896. ▷ 5.15

MÉTIS REVOLT

Rebellions by communities of mixed French and Indian (Métis) stock resisting the westward expansion of CANADA. A dispute with land surveyors precipitated a revolt in the RED

RIVER COLONY (modern Manitoba) in 1869 and 1870, and warfare later broke out in Saskatchewan (1885). Both revolts were led by LOUIS RIEL and both failed. ▷ 5.25

METTERNICH, PRINCE CLEMENS
(1773–1859) Austrian diplomat and chancellor. He took Austria into the Fourth Coalition against BONAPARTE and presided over the CONGRESS OF VIENNA. A dominant figure in European diplomacy from 1815 to 1848 (a period often described as the Metternich System), he was forced into exile during the 1848 revolution, returning in 1849. His policy was to develop Austria's interests in Italy and the BALKANS rather than in Germany. ▷ 5.09

MEXICAN-AMERICAN WAR
War deliberately provoked by the American president James Polk (1795–1849). His aim was to secure the Pacific coastline and northern Mexico. Amphibious forces captured California (1846–47) and US marines marched into Mexico City in 1847. Mexico made peace by the Treaty of Guadalupe Hidalgo (1848), suffering huge territorial losses. ▷ 5.23, 5.27

MEXICAN CESSION
The territory ceded by Mexico to the USA after the MEXICAN-AMERICAN WAR, chiefly California and New Mexico. Mexico also surrendered all claims to Texas above the Rio Grande River. The USA gained the Pacific harbors of San Francisco, Monterey and San Diego, more than 1 million square miles of territory and enormous (still undiscovered) mineral wealth. ▷ 5.26

MEXICAN REVOLUTION
Revolution beginning in 1910 under the leadership of FRANCISCO MADERO. PRESIDENT PORFIRO DIAZ dominated Mexico from 1876 to 1911, but after popular protest, Madero's armies occupied Mexico City in 1911 and Porfiro abdicated. After General VICTORIANO HUERTA became president in 1913 Madero was murdered. A casual incident involving US sailors in Tampico in 1914 caused American intervention, followed by mediation brokered by ARGENTINA, BRAZIL and CHILE. The US recognized Venustiano Carranza as Mexican president in 1915. ▷ 5.23

MEXICAN WAR FOR INDEPENDENCE
Revolutionary war beginning in 1810 under the leadership of the priest MIGUEL HIDALGO. When it failed to win control of Mexico City Hidalgo was executed and succeeded by another priest, José Maria Morelos. The Mexican aristocracy was not enthusiastic about this peasant-based uprising and the country only united against Spain when AGUSTIN ITURBIDE became leader and proclaimed independence in 1821. ▷ 5.23

MFECANE
The "crushing", a series of migrations at the end of the 18th century when the Bantu nations east of the Drakensberg Mountains were destabilized by the sudden expansion of the ZULU. This expansion led to almost perpetual warfare and unprecedented insecurity in southern Africa. ▷ 5.15

MISSOLONGHI
City in west-central Greece besieged by the Turks during the GREEK WAR OF INDEPENDENCE and captured in 1826. The poet Lord Byron, who did much to to win British and French support for Greek independence, died here in 1824. ▷ 5.09

MISSOURI COMPROMISE LINE
Boundary authorized by CONGRESS in 1820 in an attempt to settle problems arising out of the balance between slave states and free states admitted to the Union. It balanced the admission of Maine (free) with Missouri (slave) but ruled that LOUISIANA PURCHASE states north of the line 36° 30´ would be free. The Supreme Court declared this line unconstitutional in the 1857 Dred Scott case. ▷ 5.27

MOLTKE, HELMUTH VON
(1800–91) German field marshal who understood the importance of railroads and telegraphs in military operations and organized his general staff accordingly. He directed the occupation of Jutland in the war against Denmark (1863–64), planned the Austrian campaign in 1866, the invasion of France in 1870 and the SIEGE OF PARIS (1870–71). ▷ 5.11

MONACO
Tiny principality located on the Mediterranean coast between France and Italy. Absorbed by France (1793–1814), it was a Sardinian protectorate from 1815 to 1860. An 1861 treaty with France restored the monarchy. Prince Charles III opened the famous casino in 1863. ▷ 5.11

MONDOVI, BATTLE OF
(21 April 1796) Battle of BONAPARTE's Italian campaigns. Following his success at the Battle of Dego (14–15 April), Bonaparte pushed on to attack the Piedmontese at Mondovi. The Piedmontese army scattered, Victor Amadeus surrendered and Piedmont came under Bonaparte's control. ▷ 5.07

MONROE DOCTRINE
Doctrine expounded by President James Monroe (1758–1831) in his annual message to CONGRESS in 1821 in response to a claim by CZAR ALEXANDER I that the Pacific coastline was Russian above the 51st parallel. Monroe stated that no foreign power had the right to colonize the American hemisphere and this became a fundamental principle of US foreign policy. ▷ 5.22, 5.23, 5.24

MONTENEGRO
The medieval SERBIAN province of Zeta. It became independent after the Ottoman conquest of Serbia in the 14th century. From 1516 to 1851 it was ruled by elected Orthodox bishops under loose Ottoman control. It became a secular republic in 1851 and a kingdom in 1910. The Ottomans recognized its independence in 1878 and it fought in the BALKAN WARS. It was occupied by Austria (1915–18) and voted to join the kingdom of the Serbs, Croats and Slovenes (the future Yugoslavia) in 1918. When the country broke up (1990–92) Montenegro remained with Serbia in the Federal Republic of Yugoslavia. ▷ 5.13, 5.14

MORANT BAY RISING
(4 October 1865) A riot in Jamaica, incited by a Baptist preacher, Paul Bogle, outside Morant Bay courthouse. GOVERNOR EDWARD EYRE promptly hanged George Gordon, a mulatto landowner whom he believed was at the root of the insurrection. He declared a state of emergency, killed over 500 Jamaicans and destroyed hundreds of local homes. His over-reaction led to his recall and unsuccessful prosecution. ▷ 5.24

MORGAN, JOHN PIERPONT
(1837–1913) American financier who founded the international bank of J. Pierpont Morgan & Co. in 1860. He controlled major railroad interests, bought out ANDREW CARNEGIE in 1901 and created the United States Steel Corporation. ▷ 5.28

MORMONS
Members of the Church of Jesus Christ of Latter-day Saints, founded at Fayette, New York State in 1830, by Joseph Smith (1805–44). Smith's *Book of Mormon* is accepted by Mormons as a Christian scripture. Mormons form a missionary church with their headquarters in Salt Lake City, Utah, and about 6 million members worldwide. ▷ 5.26, 5.28

MUHAMMED AHMAD
See MAHDI

MUKDEN, BATTLE OF
(10 February–20 March 1905) The last major land battle of the RUSSO-JAPANESE WAR. It was fought in southern Manchuria, on a 64-kilometer (40-mile front). After violent fighting (100,000 Russians and 70,000 Japanese fell) the Russians retired to Harbin. ▷ 5.20

NAMA REBELLIONS
Rebellions (1904–09) in the south of modern Namibia, then GERMAN SOUTH WEST AFRICA. The Nama, opposed to European settlements on their grazing lands, were led by Hendrik Wibooi, killed in 1905. Jakob Morenga succeeded him as guerrilla leader (1905–09). German forces herded the Nama resistance fighters into the Kalahari Desert, where thousands died. ▷ 5.17

NANJING, TREATY OF
(29 August 1842) Treaty signed on board HMS *Cornwallis*, concluding the FIRST OPIUM WAR (1839–42). It ceded HONG KONG to Britain,

opened the TREATY PORTS, and paid indemnities for Britain's expenses in the war. ▷ 5.19

NAPOLEON I
See BONAPARTE, NAPOLEON

NAPOLEON III (LOUIS NAPOLEON)
(1808–73) Emperor of France (r.1852–70). Nephew of BONAPARTE, he was imprisoned after twice trying to seize the French throne (1836, 1840) but escaped to England in 1846. He returned after the 1848 revolution to be elected president of the Second Republic. A coup (2 December 1851) made him emperor from 1852. He foolishly declared war on PRUSSIA after the EMS TELEGRAM, was captured at SEDAN in 1870 and died in exile. ▷ 5.11

NATAL
Now KwaZulu-Natal, Republic of South Africa. It was in the possession of the ZULU when the VOORTREKKERS arrived in 1837. A BOER commando defeated the Zulu at Blood River (1838). Britain, anxious to protect its base at Port Natal, fought the Boers (1842–43) and in 1843 proclaimed Natal a British colony under the supervision of Cape Colony. ▷ 5.17

NATIONAL ASSEMBLY
The assembly of France's Third Estate, meeting in the ESTATES-GENERAL at Versailles, and recognized by LOUIS XVI in June 1789. The name was changed to Constituent Assembly on 9 July 1789. ▷ 5.07

NATIONS, BATTLE OF
See LEIPZIG, BATTLE OF

NAVARINO, BATTLE OF
(20 October 1827) Sea battle between the Turco-Egyptian fleet and a British, French and Russian flotilla commanded by the British admiral Sir Edward Codrington during the GREEK WAR OF INDEPENDENCE. Though under orders not to provoke an engagement, he destroyed the Turco-Egyptian warships, thus guaranteeing Greek independence. ▷ 5.14

NDEBELE
Bantu people of MATABELELAND, in the southwest of modern Zimbabwe. Enemies of the Shona living in the northeast, they fought a resistance war against the British in 1896 and also split black resistance to white minority rule after 1964. ▷ 5.15, 5.16

NEJD
Region in central Arabia occupied by the militant WAHHABI sect, followers of the theologian Ibn Abd al-Wahhab (1703–87). The region was conquered by Ibn Saud in 1905, and after World War I he united the Nejd with the HEJAZ to form the kingdom named Saudi Arabia in 1932. ▷ 5.14

NELSON, HORATIO, LORD
(1758–1805) English admiral. In the course of a brilliant career he lost an eye fighting in

Corsica and an arm during an attack on the Canary Islands. He destroyed the French fleet at the BATTLE OF THE NILE (1798) dooming BONAPARTE's invasion of EGYPT, destroyed the Danish fleet at COPENHAGEN (1801) and won over a century of naval dominance for Great Britain by defeating the Franco-Spanish fleet at TRAFALGAR (1805) where he died aboard HMS *Victory* after being shot by a French sniper. ▷ 5.08

NEPAL
Buddhist kingdom, founded by the Licchavi dynasty in the 4th or 5th century AD in the Himalayan Mountains. It was conquered by the GURKHA ruler Prithvi Narayan Shah and involved in frontier wars with Tibet, China and British India. Nepal's independence was fully recognized in 1923. ▷ 5.21

NEW BRUNSWICK
Maritime province in eastern CANADA. Initially the unpopulated west of Nova Scotia, it became a Loyalist refuge after the American Revolution and a separate colony from 1784. It confederated with Québec, ONTARIO and Nova Scotia to create the DOMINION OF CANADA in 1867. ▷ 5.25

NEW ORLEANS, BATTLE OF
(8 January 1815) Battle in the WAR OF 1812. After an initial naval success, the British were heavily defeated in a poorly conceived attack on GENERAL ANDREW JACKSON's defenses. The battle had no effect on the course of the war which, unbeknownst to the participants, had already ended in the Treaty of Ghent. ▷ 5.25

NEW SOUTH WALES
State in southeast Australia, claimed for Britain by Captain Cook in 1770. Transported convicts first arrived in 1788 (at BOTANY BAY). New South Wales received representative government in 1842 and responsible government in 1856. It joined the Commonwealth of Australia in 1901. ▷ 5.18

NEW ZEALAND
Independent state in the southwest Pacific, originally settled by Maoris from eastern Polynesia in the early 11th century. The first European sighting was by Abel Tasman in 1642. Captain Cook circumnavigated the two main islands in 1769. British colonization was begun by the New Zealand Company (1840–51), though not without stiff opposition from the Maoris (MAORI WARS). It became a self-governing colony until 1907 when it achieved dominion status. ▷ 5.18

NGUYEN ANH
(1762–1820) Emperor of Vietnam (r.1802–20). He opposed the Tayson government and was was aided with weapons provided by the French missionary Pigneau de Béhaine. He defeated the Tayson and reunited Vietnam. He took the name Gia Long when he proclaimed himself emperor. ▷ 5.22

NICHOLAS I
(1796–1855) Czar of Russia (r.1825–55). Shortly after his accession he had to deal with the DECEMBRIST REVOLT and his experience turned him into an autocrat. He formed a secret police and discouraged education, suppressed the Polish nationalist revolt (1830–31) and sent troops into Hungary in 1849. He began the modernization of the Russian army. ▷ 5.12

NIGERIA
West African federal republic, the location of major African empires such as Bornu (1814–93) and SOKOTO (c1808–1903). It was colonized by Britain between 1861 and 1914, achieving independence in 1960. It has undergone several military coups and a civil war (1967–70). ▷ 5.15, 5.16

NILE, BATTLE OF THE
(1 August 1798) Naval battle in Aboukir Bay between HORATIO NELSON's fleet and the French fleet that had brought BONAPARTE's army to Alexandria. Nelson sailed either side of the 17 French warships and destroyed or captured 15 of them. The battle spelled disaster for Bonaparte's Middle East campaign. ▷ 5.07

NORTHEAST FRONTIER AGENCY
Mountainous region in northeastern India occupied by the British (1913–14) to deter Chinese expansion. Under direct British rule, it passed to India in 1947 and was the scene of Indo-Chinese conflict in 1962. The area remained in dispute until 1993. As Arunachal Pradesh (Land of the Rising Sun) it became a union territory in 1972 and an Indian state in 1987. ▷ 5.21

NORTHERN RHODESIA
Former British colony located in south central Africa, part of modern Zambia, and home of the NDEBELE and Shona. It was governed by the British South Africa Company (1889–1924) and then became a protectorate. It was a member of the Central African Federation until independence on 24 October 1964.

NORTHERN TERRITORY
The northern part of Australia, bordering the Timor and Arafura seas, and home of Aborigines first encountered by European mariners in the 17th century. Originally administered by NEW SOUTH WALES, it came under central government control in 1911. Small parts were bombed by the Japanese in World War II. ▷ 5.18

NORTH GERMAN CONFEDERATION
Confederation created after the AUSTRO-PRUSSIAN WAR (1866) and lasting from 1867 to 1871. Member states retained their own governments apart from military and foreign affairs, decided on by the Bundesrat (Federal Council) and the Reichstag, both dominated by PRUSSIA. ▷ 5.11

NORTHWEST ORDINANCE
Passed by the US CONGRESS in 1787 under pressure from Manasseh Cutler (1742–1823) and the Ohio Company, who wished to settle the northwest. It defined the principles of expansion for the USA, regarding all new regions coming under Congressional control as free (i.e. non-slave) areas and potential states of the Union. Any prospective state with 60,000 citizens would qualify for statehood. ▷ 5.26

NORWAY
Kingdom in northwest Europe. It emerged in the late 10th century under King Harald Finehair, reaching its greatest extent in the 13th century when it included Iceland, the Faroe, Orkney and Shetland Islands, the Hebrides and the Isle of Man. It joined the Union of Calmar with Denmark and Sweden in 1397. Norway declared its independence after the Napoleonic wars but was awarded to Sweden by the CONGRESS OF VIENNA. Swedish troops invaded to enforce the union but it retained its own constitution, becoming independent in 1905. Norway was occupied by Germany in World War II. ▷ 5.09, 5.10

O'HIGGINS, BERNADO
(1778–1842) Soldier, revolutionary and liberal dictator of CHILE (r.1818–23). His father was Irish and he was part-educated in England. Allied with JOSÉ DE SAN MARTÍN, he defeated the Spanish forces at the BATTLE OF CHACABUCO (1817) and became dictator of Chile. Criticized as an autocrat, he went into exile in 1823. ▷ 5.23

OKLAHOMA
Southwestern US state, acquired mainly in the LOUISIANA PURCHASE. It became the INDIAN TERRITORY, where Indians were concentrated after the 1830 Indian Removal Act. After the AMERICAN CIVIL WAR, the Indians' annual Okmulgee Council resolved to create an independent Indian state. They failed and Oklahoma was admitted to the Union on 16 November 1907. ▷ 5.26, 5.27, 5.28

OMAN
Southeastern Arabian state, originating in the 8th century. Oman benefited from its strategic position at the mouth of the Persian Gulf to control east African trade, especially ZANZIBAR's trade with Persia and India. Oman declined after the Portuguese seized its port of Muscat but recovered after their expulsion in 1660. It was under British protection from 1891 to 1970. ▷ 5.14, 5.15

OMDURMAN, BATTLE OF
(2 September 1898) Battle in which GENERAL KITCHENER's Anglo-Egyptian army reconquered the SUDAN. Kitchener's forces inflicted a great slaughter on the ill-equipped MAHDIST forces of the Khalifa Abdullah 6.4 kilometers (4 miles) from KHARTOUM. The battle ended with a charge by the 21st Lancers. ▷ 5.15, 5.16

ONTARIO (UPPER CANADA)
Canadian province. Ceded to Britain by France in 1763, it was a refuge for Loyalists during and after the American Revolution (1775–83). Known as UPPER CANADA from 1791 to 1841, it was united with LOWER CANADA (now Québec) from 1841 before the two became separate provinces of the DOMINION OF CANADA in 1867. ▷ 5.25

OPIUM WARS
Two wars (1839–42, 1856–60) between Britain and China. They were not caused fundamentally by the opium trade but by Britain's determination to penetrate China, establish diplomatic relations and arrange advantageous trade. These aims were achieved by the Treaties of NANJING (1842), Tianjin (1858) and Beijing (1860). ▷ 5.19

ORANGE FREE STATE
Province of South Africa, established by BOERS after the GREAT TREK and annexed by Britain in 1848. Recognized as the independent in 1854, it was involved in conflicts with Britain until annexed as the Orange River Colony in 1900. It joined the UNION OF SOUTH AFRICA in 1910. ▷ 5.15, 5.17

OREGON TERRITORY
Northwest region of North America centered on the Columbia River basin, claimed and jointly occupied by both Britain and the USA until the Oregon Treaty (1846) which divided the it along the 49th parallel. The north later became the Canadian province of BRITISH COLUMBIA, the south the American states of Washington and Oregon. ▷ 5.26

OREGON TRAIL
From the 1840s the main emigration route from the eastern to the western USA. The 2,000-mile trail ran from Independence, Missouri, across the Great Plains and Rocky Mountains to the mouth of the Columbia River and took around six months to complete by wagon train. ▷ 5.26

OTTAWA
Capital city of CANADA, in southeast ONTARIO. Originally known as Bytown, after its founder Colonel John By, it was built as a base for the construction of the Rideau Canal in 1826. The name Ottawa was chosen in 1854. ▷ 5.25

OTTO, NIKOLAUS
(1832–91) German engineer who improved the internal combustion engine. In 1876 he invented four-cycle internal combustion, the most common engine type used in automobiles. ▷ 5.10

OYO EMPIRE
Former African trading empire located in modern NIGERIA. It first came to prominence under the Alafin Ajagbo in about 1670. It conquered Dahomey but by the 18th century was torn apart by civil war. An internal jihad caused it to collapse when HAUSA slaves, OYO Muslims and FULANI pastoralists rebelled against the Alafin Afonja (1823–24). The power vacuum left in the region by 1836 led to attacks by IBADAN. ▷ 5.01

PACIFIC, WAR OF THE
(1879–83) War between CHILE and PERU (allied with BOLIVIA) over control of nitrate-producing areas. Chile launched a seaborne invasion of Peru and occupied Lima in 1880. The war ended in 1883 with the Treaty of Ancon, ceding Peru's Tarapac province and Tacna to Chile. Bolivia signed the separate Treaty of Valparaiso ceding its entire coastline to Chile in 1884. ▷ 5.23

PANAMA CANAL
Canal linking the Atlantic and Pacific oceans across 64 kilometers (40 miles) of the Central American republic of Panama. FERDINAND DE LESSEPS was commissioned to build it but the company failed in 1889. Finally constructed by the US Army Corps of Engineers, it opened to traffic in 1914. Annually, 13,000 ships pass through the canal, which the USA is due to hand over to Panama in 1999. ▷ 5.23

PAPINEAU, LOUIS JOSEPH
(1786–1871) Leader of the French Canadians in the legislative assembly of LOWER CANADA, forced to flee to the USA in 1837 when opposition to the British colonial government turned to armed revolt in Montréal. Fourteen rebels were executed. An amnesty in 1847 allowed him to return to Canada from his refuge in France and enter Parliament. ▷ 5.25

PARAGUAY
Republic in central South America, settled by Guarani Indians, conquered by Spain in 1537, later incorporated into the viceroyalty of Rio de La Plata. It won independence from Spain in 1811 but lost South America's biggest war when it fought against the TRIPLE ALLIANCE (1865–70). ▷ 5.23

PARIS, SIEGE OF
(1870) Prussian siege of the French capital begun on 9 September 1870 after their victory at SEDAN during the FRANCO-PRUSSIAN WAR. General Jules Trochu, commander of Paris, faced Prussian bombardment after 5 January 1871 and constant food shortages. He agreed to an armistice on 26 January and Prussians entered the city on 1 March 1871. ▷ 5.11

PARIS, TREATY OF (1898)
Treaty ending the SPANISH-AMERICAN WAR, following the peace protocol agreed at the armistice of 12 August. Spain ceded Puerto Rico, Guam and the PHILIPPINES to the USA. ▷ 5.24

PARIS COMMUNE
Insurrection sparked by the French government's attempt to disarm the turbulent Paris national guard after defeat in the FRANCO-

PRUSSIAN WAR. The government fled from Paris and a central committee called the Commune took control there on 26 March 1871. While the Prussians remained the suburbs, regular French troops entered Paris to suppress the Communards. ▷ 5.11

PARTHENOPEAN REPUBLIC
A French satellite established in Naples in 1799 after General Jean-Antoine-Etienne Championnet's victory over the Neapolitans at Civita Castellana (4 December 1798), swiftly abolished by the Neapolitan peasantry organized into the *Sandifesti* (Army of the Holy Faith) by Cardinal Ruffo in 1799. ▷ 5.07

PATAGONIA
Region in South America stretching some 1610 kilometers (1000 miles) south of the Rio Negro River to the Strait of Magellan. Originally populated by Tehuelche Indians, it was claimed by ARGENTINA who carried out a conquest (1879–80) and shipped the surviving Indians into reservations. The region was then divided between CHILE and Argentina. ▷ 5.23

PATHANS
Members of the Pashto-speaking peoples of Afghanistan and northwest Pakistan. Mostly Muslims, courageous and ferocious in war, they were a constant threat to British security on the Northwest Frontier.

PEDRO I
(1798–1834) Second son of Joao VI of Portugal, and first emperor of BRAZIL (r.1822–31). He promulgated the 1824 constitution and abdicated in favor of his son. ▷ 5.23

PEDRO II
(1825–91) Emperor of BRAZIL (r.1831–91). Son of PEDRO I, he did not assume full powers until 1840. He welcomed the WAR OF THE TRIPLE ALLIANCE, as he believed this would encourage Brazilian nationalism. He was an ABOLITIONIST who helped end slavery in 1888. Republicanism led to his abdication. ▷ 5.23

PENINSULAR WAR
(1808–1814) War for the Iberian peninsula (Spain and Portugal) fought between the ultimately victorious British expeditionary force and invading French armies. It drained BONAPARTE's resources (he called it the "Spanish ulcer") and was characterized by continuous guerrilla warfare as well as pitched battles. Seapower was crucial, enabling Britain to maintain and reinforce a distant army for six years. ▷ 5.08

PERRY, MATTHEW
(1794–1858) American naval officer who fought in the WAR OF 1812, against Barbary pirates (1815–16) and at Veracruz in the MEXICAN-AMERICAN WAR. He is best known for his two voyages (1853, 1854) to open up Japan to trade and for the resulting TREATY OF KANAGAWA. ▷ 5.20

PERU
South American republic, the center of the Inca empire until conquered in 1533 by the Spanish. Its reserves of precious metals made it the most important of Spain's territories in the New World. Spain retained control until 1824 when ANTONIO JOSÉ DE SUCRE won the BATTLE OF AYACUCHO. ▷ 5.23

PHILLIP, ARTHUR
(1738–1814) English naval captain and the first governor of NEW SOUTH WALES. He commanded the first fleet of convicts to BOTANY BAY in 1787 but moved the convict settlement to SYDNEY in 1788. ▷ 5.18

PHILIPPINES
Independent republic, a large archipelago of some 7,100 islands located 805 kilometers (500 miles) off the southeast Asian coast. First inhabited some 30,000 years ago, the islands were claimed for Spain by Magellan in 1521. Spanish settlement began in 1565, and in 1571 the islands were named in honor of Philip II of Spain. An independence struggle began at the outbreak of the SPANISH-AMERICAN WAR in 1898, but Spain ceded the islands to the USA, which had suppressed native resistance by 1901. Under Japanese occupation from 1942 to 1944, the Philippines achieved independence in 1946. ▷ 5.22

PIEDMONT
See SARDINIA-PIEDMONT

PITT, WILLIAM (THE YOUNGER)
(1759–1806) British prime minister (1783–84, 1784–1801, 1804–06). His governments financed the First (1793) and Second (1798) Coalitions against France and introduced important social and administrative reforms. He resigned because of George III's hostility to Catholic emancipation (1801), but returned in 1804 to lead the fight against BONAPARTE. He died in office. ▷ 5.07, 5.08

POLAND, PARTITIONS OF
Partitions beginning with the suggestion of the PRUSSIAN ruler Frederick the Great in 1772 that one third of Poland should be divided between Prussia, Russia and Austria (first partition). Russia gained most territory at the second partition (1793). The third partition (1795) followed TADEUSZ KOSCIUSZKO's 1794 uprising. The fourth partition (1815) saw

THE POPES 1775–1914	
Pius VI	**1775–99**
Pius VII	**1800–23**
Leo XII	**1823–29**
Pius VIII	**1829–30**
Gregory XVI	**1831–46**
Pius IX	**1846–78**
Leo XIII	**1878–1903**
Pius X	**1903–14**

Russia gain territory previously allocated to Prussia. ▷ 5.07, 5.08, 5.12

PORT ARTHUR, BATTLES OF
Two major battles at Port Arthur in the Liaodong peninsula of China. The first (on 21 November 1894, during the SINO-JAPANESE WAR) saw the Japanese storm the fortress; the second (on 8 February–2 May 1904, during the RUSSO-JAPANESE WAR) saw a series of successful Japanese naval actions against the Russian fleet outside Port Arthur prior to a Japanese assault on the fortress, forcing Russia to surrender it. ▷ 5.19, 5.20

PORT JACKSON
See SYDNEY

PORTSMOUTH, TREATY OF
(5 September 1905) Treaty signed in New Hampshire USA, ending the RUSSO-JAPANESE WAR. Japan secured strategic control of southern Manchuria and thus began her expansion on the Asian mainland, a policy to be continued in 1910 and 1914. ▷ 5.20

PRAGUE, TREATY OF
(23 August 23) Treaty concluding the AUSTRO-PRUSSIAN WAR. Highly favorable to PRUSSIA, it dissolved the GERMAN CONFEDERATION, gave Prussia leadership of the NORTH GERMAN CONFEDERATION and permitted Italy, Prussia's ally, to acquire VENETIA. ▷ 5.11

PROMONTORY POINT
Historic point in northwest Utah, where the last spike linking the Union Pacific and the Central Pacific Railroads was driven in on 10 May 1869 to create the first American transcontinental railroad ▷ 5.28

PRUSSIA
Former kingdom in north-central Germany, with its capital in Berlin. A duchy founded in 1511 by Albert I, it passed to John Sigismund, the HOHENZOLLERN elector of Brandenburg in 1611. Frederick William, the Great Elector, (r.1640–88) fully incorporated Prussia and BRANDENBURG and laid the basis of future power by creating a professional army. In 1701 Prussia was recognized as a kingdom by the Holy Roman emperor. Prussian power increased rapidly under Frederick the Great (1740–86) and during the Napoleonic wars. It led the ZOLLVEREIN (customs union) of 1834, held most of north Germany, led the GERMAN CONFEDERATION (1867–71) and formed the heartland of the SECOND GERMAN EMPIRE (1871–1918). ▷ 5.08, 5.09, 5.10, 5.11

QIANLONG
(1735–99) Emperor of the Chinese Qing (Manchu) dynasty (r.1736–96). He was an imperialist who expanded China to include Xinjiang, Tibet. Many southeast Asian kingdoms, including Burma and Annam, were tributaries. He saw China as the center of the world and superior to all lands that fringed its

frontiers. The Macartney mission (1793), requesting increased trade between China and Britain, was rejected on these grounds. Although he brought Manchu power to its peak, his reign was marked by a complacency that left China unprepared to face increased external threats in the 19th century. ▷ 5.19

QUEENSLAND
State in northeast Australia. Its first European settlement was the penal colony at Moreton Bay. By 1895, 50,000 Melanesians (called Kanakas) had been brought in to work on the cane fields. This immigration was stopped in 1904, after Queensland became a state of the Commonwealth of Australia. ▷ 5.18

RAFFLES, SIR STAMFORD
(1781–1826) English colonial governor who went to Penang as an assistant secretary to the East India Company in 1805. He proposed the capture and annexation of Java, describing it as the rice granary of the east, and was made the lieutenant-governor of the island after accompanying the successful invasion in 1811. Java was restored to the Netherlands in 1815 and he became governor of Benkulen (1818–23) and established a British settlement in SINGAPORE. ▷ 5.22

RAJ, BRITISH
The expression, derived from the Hindi *raja* meaning king or prince, was used to describe British rule in India. ▷ 5.21

RAURACIAN REPUBLIC
Territory adjacent to the northwest of Switzerland, centered around Monthéliard, conquered by revolutionary France, given brief republican status (1792–93) and then annexed to the expanding French empire. ▷ 5.07

RECONSTRUCTION
(1866–77) Military administration of the south following the AMERICAN CIVIL WAR. The 1867 Reconstruction Act divided the south into five military districts to restore law and order, aid the reorganization of local government and prepare for the re-admission of rebel states into the American Union. ▷ 5.28

RED CROSS
An international relief agency created by the 1864 GENEVA CONVENTION to help those wounded or captured in war. An armband or flag depicting a red cross was designed to provide immunity from hostile action for stretcherbearers, ambulances and field hospitals.

RED RIVER COLONY
Agricultural colony established in 1811 by the Earl of Selkirk in the valley of the Red River, Manitoba, CANADA. In conflict with ALEXANDER MACKENZIE's North West Company (1816–17) it became a Canadian territory in 1869 and the province of Manitoba in 1870. ▷ 5.25

REINSURANCE TREATY
(1887–90) A secret Russo-German treaty that promised each party neutrality in war unless Russia attacked Austria or Germany attacked France. It was BISMARCK's alternative to the DREIKAISERBUND. ▷ 5.11, 5.12

REVANCHE MOVEMENT
(From the French for "revenge") A movement to recover territory lost to an enemy – a demand in France for a foreign policy aimed at regaining ALSACE-LORRAINE, taken by Germany in the FRANCO-PRUSSIAN WAR. ▷ 5.13

RHINE, CONFEDERATION OF THE
Confederation created by BONAPARTE at the Treaty of Paris (17 July 1806). It joined 16 German states (including Hesse-Darmstadt, Bavaria, Würtemberg and Baden), bringing 8 million Germans under direct French control, an arrangement that lasted until 1813. ▷ 5.08

RHODES, CECIL
(1853–1902) British-born South African businessman and politician. He acquired BECHUANALAND as a British protectorate in 1884, amalgamated the KIMBERLEY diamond workings into the DE BEERS CONSOLIDATED MINES COMPANY in 1888 and became Cape Colony's prime minister in 1890. He resigned because of involvement in the JAMESON RAID and fought at Kimberley during the SECOND ANGLO-BOER WAR. He founded numerous Oxford scholarships. ▷ 5.17

RICHMOND
Originally a trading post, now the capital of the state of Virginia. It was the CONFEDERATE capital in the AMERICAN CIVIL WAR. Despite a skillful defense against superior Union forces, ROBERT E. LEE had to abandon it on 2 April 1865, prior to his retreat to Lynchburg. ▷ 5.27

RIEL, LOUIS
(1844–85) Canadian rebel who led the MÉTIS REVOLT in the RED RIVER COLONY (1869–70). It was crushed by Sir Garnet Wolseley, August 1870. Riel escaped to lead another rebellion in Saskatchewan in 1885 and he was captured and hanged in November 1885. ▷ 5.25

RISORGIMENTO
("Resurgence") The movement for Italian unification (1815–70). The name was not widely used until CAMILLO DI CAVOUR entitled his newspaper *Il Risorgimento* in 1847. Despite the general failure of the 1848 "Year of Revolution", the lone constitutional monarchy of SARDINIA-PIEDMONT, ruled by VICTOR EMMANUEL II from 1849, was determined to unify Italy. With leadership from Cavour, who became prime minister of Piedmont in 1852, and from the outstanding soldier and patriot GIUSEPPE GARIBALDI, Piedmont won a string of military victories that united Sardinia-Piedmont with Parma, Modena, the KINGDOM OF THE TWO SICILIES, part of the Papal States and Lombardy. On

11 September 1870 Italian troops entered Rome, effectively uniting Italy. ▷ 5.09

ROBESPIERRE, MAXIMILIEN DE
(1758–94) French revolutionary who was effectively the country's ruler from 1793 to 1794. An attorney, and a representative of the Third Estate in the ESTATES GENERAL he became leader of the JACOBIN CLUB. Popular with the Paris mob because of his incorruptibility and his support of democracy, he backed the execution of LOUIS XVI, helped to overthrow the more moderate Girondins and controlled the Committee of Public Safety, which conducted a bloody reign of terror. His enemies conspired against him and he was guillotined in 1794. ▷ 5.07

ROCKEFELLER, JOHN D.
(1839–1937) American oil millionaire. With his brother William (1841–1922) he founded the Standard Oil Company in 1870. By 1879 the company controlled nearly 95 percent of American oil refining. A philanthropist, he set up the Rockefeller Foundation in 1913 "to promote the well-being of mankind". ▷ 5.28

ROMANIA
Republic in southeastern Europe. The principalities of Wallachia and Moldavia on the Danube united in 1861 and took the name Romania. Independence was recognized in 1878. Romania joined the Allies in 1916 and gained BESSARABIA and Transylvania. Germany's ally from 1941 to 1944, Romania was a communist people's republic from 1947 until 1989. ▷ 5.07, 5.09, 5.10, 5.12, 5.13, 5.14

ROOSEVELT, THEODORE
(1858–1919) The 26th president of the USA. Assistant secretary to the navy when the SPANISH-AMERICAN WAR began, he raised the ROUGH RIDERS and fought in Cuba. President after the assassination of President William McKinley in 1901, he was elected to a second term in 1905. He supported naval expansion but was defeated by Woodrow Wilson in the presidential election of 1912. ▷ 5.24

RORKE'S DRIFT, BATTLE OF
(22 January 1879) A remarkable defensive battle at a river ford on the Buffalo tributary of the Tugela River in South Africa, in which 137 soldiers – mostly B Company, 2nd Battalion the 24th Foot (Royal Warwickshire) commanded by lieutenants Chard and Bromhead – repelled 4,000 of CETSHWAYO's ZULUS and won 11 Victoria Crosses and nine Distinguished Conduct Medals. ▷ 5.17

ROSAS, JUAN MANUEL
(1793–1877) Argentinian rancher and businessman, governor of Buenos Aires and dictator of ARGENTINA (1829–32, 1835–52). He imposed internal security and brought peace and security in exchange for the loss of personal freedoms. Britain refused to accept his offer to end Argentina's claim to the

FALKLANDS (Islas Malvinas) in return for cancelling Argentina's debts. He intervened in URUGUAY and was defeated at the Battle of Monte Caseros (3 February 1852). ▷ 5.23

ROUGH RIDERS
The First Volunteer Cavalry. Fighting in Cuba in the SPANISH-AMERICAN WAR, THEODORE ROOSEVELT was their second-in-command. Because their horses could not be transported, they fought on foot in Cuba. ▷ 5.24

RUMELIA
A general term, meaning "the land of the Romans", current during the time of the Ottoman empire. It embraced Macedonia and Thrace and centered on Plovdiv. Eastern Rumelia was annexed by BULGARIA in 1885, causing the crisis (1885–88) that led to the REINSURANCE TREATY. ▷ 5.14

RUSSIAN EMPIRE
Founded by Ivan III (r.1462–1505) when he adopted the title czar (caesar) in 1471. Three centuries of steady eastward expansion had carried Russian control to the Bering Sea and Pacific Ocean by 1801. The Russian empire was confirmed by the 1815 Vienna settlement and included CONGRESS POLAND. After the CRIMEAN WAR Russia attempted to liberate Slav peoples under Turkish and Austrian rule, causing several international crises. Her colonists pushed into the Caucasus, Asia, Siberia and North America. With them went the autocratic rule of the czar and the Russian army. An expanding empire caused problems: rebellions by subject peoples and great-power hostility, especially once Russia prepared to penetrate Afghanistan, Persia and Xinjiang. The empire technically fell following the 1917 revolution but in reality survived until the fall of the Soviet Union in 1991. ▷ 5.08, 5.12, 5.19

RUSSO-JAPANESE WAR
(February 1904–September 1905) Struggle for control of Korea and Manchuria, with Japan taking the initiative in order to ensure victory before Russian reinforcements could arrive from the west. Decisive Japanese victories at PORT ARTHUR, Mukden and TSUSHIMA were followed by American mediation and the TREATY OF PORTSMOUTH. ▷ 5.20

RWANDA
Central African kingdom emerging in the 16th century with a Tutsi pastoralist minority ruling a Hutu agriculturalist majority. Colonized by Germany (part of German East Africa, 1890–1916), it was mandated to Belgium by the League of Nations as Ruanda-Urundi. A 1959 Hutu uprising led to independence in 1962. In 1995 and 1996 it was the scene of genocide by the Hutus against the Tutsi. ▷ 5.15, 5.16

SAIGON, TREATY OF
(5 June 1862) Treaty between France and Tu Duc, the last precolonial emperor of Annam (Vietnam), it gave France three provinces of

COCHIN CHINA adjacent to Saigon and opened three ports to western commerce. By 1867 France had occupied the rest of Cochin China. ▷ 5.22

SAMORI EMPIRE
Two MANDINKA empires established by the talented Islamic military leader Samori Toure (c.1830–1900). The first was located between the Tukulor caliphate and the southern forestlands of west Africa. Forced to retreat by the French, Samori Toure established a second empire in the Ivory Coast and Ghana (1894–98) before being captured by the French and exiled. ▷ 5.15, 5.16

SAMURAI
The armed retainers of a Japanese *daimyo* (landowner) and members of a *bushi* (warrior) caste (c.1100–1868). They were members of the ruling class marked out by their appearance and by bearing two swords. Abolished after the MEIJI RESTORATION they were paid off in a lump sum in 1876. ▷ 5.20

SAND CREEK
Scene of a massacre of Cheyenne and Arapaho families (29 November 1864) 65 kilometers (40 miles) northeast of Fort Lyon, Colorado. About 300 Indians were killed by troops commanded by Colonel J. M. Chivington. Black Kettle survived and took his revenge on the South Platte settlements, killing more people than had died in the massacre. ▷ 5.26

SAND RIVER CONVENTION
(17 January 1852) Britain's recognition of the South African Republic: the BOER settlements north of the Vaal River (the TRANSVAAL). ▷ 5.17

SAN JACINTO RIVER, BATTLE OF THE
(21 April 1836) Battle in southeastern Texas during the TEXAN WAR OF INDEPENDENCE. Troops led by General Sam Houston (1793–1863) defeated ANTONIO DE SANTA ANNA who recognized the independence of Texas. ▷ 5.23

SAN MARTÍN, JOSÉ DE
(1778–1850) Argentinian soldier and statesman who played an important part in the independence movements of CHILE and PERU. He crossed the Andes, defeated the Spanish at CHACABUCO and occupied Santiago. He captured Lima in 1821 and proclaimed the independence of Peru. Disagreements with SÍMON BOLÍVAR in 1822 led to his exile. ▷ 5.23

SAN STEFANO, TREATY OF
(3 March 1878) Treaty signed at a small village (now Yesilkoy) on the Sea of Marmara to end the Russo-Turkish War (1877–78). Its creation of a "large" BULGARIA was superseded by the CONGRESS OF BERLIN. ▷ 5.13

SANTA ANNA, ANTONIO DE
(1797–1876) Mexican soldier and president (1833–36) who assisted AGUSTIN ITURBIDE in

securing Mexican independence. While president, he captured the ALAMO but was defeated by the Texans at the SAN JACINTO RIVER. Effectively president one again from 1841 to 1846, he was exiled by an opposing faction in 1855 but was granted an amnesty in 1872. ▷ 5.23

SANTIAGO DE CUBA, BATTLE OF
(3 July 1898) Battle on the southern coast of Cuba during the SPANISH-AMERICAN WAR. A US naval squadron blockaded the Spanish fleet in the harbor and when the Spanish ships tried to break out sank or disabled all four cruisers and three destroyers. ▷ 5.24

SANTO DOMINGO
The eastern part of Hispaniola, which remained Spanish after Spain ceded the western part of the island to France in 1697. It was part of independent HAITI (1804–1809, 1822–44) and became the independent Dominican Republic in 1844. ▷ 5.23

SARDINIA-PIEDMONT
The kingdom formed in 1720 when the House of Savoy exchanged SICILY for the Mediterranean island of Sardinia. The heartland remained the mainland territories of Savoy (southeastern France) and Piedmont (northwestern Italy) to which Genoa was added in 1815. It took the initiative in the RISORGIMENTO. The kingdom, less Savoy (ceded to France in 1860) but with the addition of Lombardy (acquired in 1859), united with other Italian states in 1861 to form the kingdom of Italy, and its king, VICTOR EMMANUEL II, became the first king of Italy. ▷ 5.09

SATSUMA REBELLION
An expression of SAMURAI discontent with the modernizing program of the MEIJI RESTORATION, it was an attempt in 1877 to promote samurai values by armed opposition. Satsuma rebels fought with traditional weapons against Japan's new conscript army and were defeated at Kagoshima in September 1877. ▷ 5.20

SCHLESWIG-HOLSTEIN WAR
War caused by a disputed succession to the duchies of Schleswig and Holstein, previously ruled by Denmark. Austro-Prussian forces invaded Denmark on 1 January 1864 and besieged the fortress of Dybbol. Britain sought to end hostilities but a fresh Prussian attack on 26 June forced the Danes to surrender control. North Schleswig, which had a Danish majority, was returned to Denmark in 1920. ▷ 5.11

SCHLIEFFEN, ALFRED VON
(1833–1913) German general. As chief of the general staff (1891–1906), he devised a strategic plan for a war against both France and Russia. Confident that Russia would be slow to mobilize, he planned a rapid advance

through neutral Belgium to encircle and defeat the French armies. The plan was implemented, unsuccessfully, in 1914.

SEDAN, BATTLE OF
(1 September 1870) Key PRUSSIAN victory during the FRANCO-PRUSSIAN WAR. On 2 September 130,000 French troops and their commander, NAPOLEON III, surrendered at this border fortress town in northeastern France, leaving the way clear for the Prussians to march on Paris. ▷ 5.11

SELIM III
(1761–1807) Sultan of Turkey (r.1789–1806). His attempts to establish diplomatic relations with the great powers failed to preserve his imperial frontiers, while his plans to westernize the army and reform land tenure were unpopular. He was overthrown and executed. ▷ 5.14

SEMINOLE WARS
Two American wars against the indigenous Seminoles, who raided US territory from their homeland in Spanish Florida. In the first (1818) US forces invaded Florida. Later, when the Seminoles resisted removal, a second war (1835–43) led to the destruction of their Everglades stronghold and their removal to OKLAHOMA. ▷ 5.26

SERBS
A Slavic people who settled in the BALKANS in about 600 and in the 14th century briefly controlled most of the region. Defeated by the Turks at the Battle of Kosovo in 1389, Serbia was incorporated into the Ottoman empire. Autonomous within the empire from 1817, Serbia became independent in 1878. An Austrian attack in 1914 – in retaliation for the assassination by Serbian nationalists of the Austrian archduke Franz Ferdinand at Sarajevo, BOSNIA-HERZEGOVINA – precipitated World War I. After the war, Serbia became part of the kingdom of the Serbs, Croats and Slovenes (Yugoslavia from 1931) and, with MONTENEGRO, formed the Federal Republic of Yugoslavia following the break-up of Yugoslavia (1990–92). ▷ 5.12, 5.13, 5.14

SERINGAPATAM, BATTLE OF
(6 April–4 May 1799) British siege of this former capital of Mysore, now in modern Karnataka, southern India. The British began their main assault on 3 May and killed 8,500 defenders, including TIPU SULTAN, in two days of fighting. ▷ 5.21

SEVEN WEEKS WAR
See AUSTRO-PRUSSIAN WAR

SHAKA
(1787–1828) African military genius and king of the ZULUS (r.1816–28). His age-regiments, with new equipment and tactics, revolutionized Bantu warfare (1816). He integrated defeated clans into a Zulu nation capable of

fielding 40,000 warriors (1817). His endless warfare forced some Zulu leaders (e.g. Sobhuza, Mzilikazi) to begin the MFECANE and found their own Bantu nation-states. ▷ 5.15

SHERMAN, WILLIAM
(1820–91) American general who served in the SECOND SEMINOLE WAR, and at FIRST BULL RUN, SHILOH and CHATTANOOGA. He applied the concept of total war in his destruction of CONFEDERATE resources (the MARCH TO THE SEA, 1864–65). He was commanding general of the army from 1869 to 1883. ▷ 5.27

SHILOH, BATTLE OF
(6–7 April 1862) Battle of the AMERICAN CIVIL WAR. The CONFEDERATES made a surprise attack and almost defeated the Unionists but lost their commander and his successor decided to retreat to Corinth because of the arrival of Union reinforcements. ▷ 5.27

SHIMODA
Seaport of western Honshu, Japan, visited by MATTHEW PERRY. Opened to US commerce in 1854, it was a major trading center by 1860. In 1856 the first US consul-general to Japan, Townshend Harris, was based here. ▷ 5.20

SHIMONOSEKI, TREATY OF
(17 April 1895) Treaty signed in Honshu, Japan, after the SINO-JAPANESE WAR. China was represented by LI HONGZHANG. Japan emerged as a major power, gaining Taiwan and a huge indemnity in lieu of the Liaodong peninsula and Lushun (Port Arthur). ▷ 5.20

SIAM
Southeast Asian kingdom, known since 1949 as Thailand. Settled by Thai migrants from central Asia in about 900 it was a unified kingdom by 1351, with a capital at Ayutthaya. Siam gradually lost territory to the colonial powers (to France in 1893, to Britain in 1903) but retained its independence and became a constitutional monarchy in 1932. ▷ 5.22

SICILY, KINGDOM OF
Mediterranean kingdom founded by the Normans when they occupied Sicily and Naples (1059–1194). Its dynastic history is complex. The crowns of Sicily and Naples were separated in 1713 but reunited in 1720. Conquered by the Spanish Bourbons in 1734. Sicily and Naples were again separated in 1806 when the French drove the Bourbons from Naples. When reunited once more under the Bourbons in 1816, it adopted the name of KINGDOM OF THE TWO SICILIES (which had been used informally since the 14th century). The Bourbons suppressed the 1820 revolt of the CARBONARI but they were overthrown by GIUSEPPE GARIBALDI, and Sicily joined united Italy in 1860. ▷ 5.08, 5.09

SIERRA LEONE
West African republic, settled by Mende and Temne peoples in about 1400. About 400

black veterans resettled here by the British in 1787 were followed by blacks from Nova Scotia and MAROONS from Jamaica. It became a British colony in 1808 and a protectorate in 1896, independent in 1961. ▷ 5.15, 5.16

SILESIA
Region in east-central Europe, mainly within modern Poland. Most of area was acquired by PRUSSIA in 1742 as Upper and Lower Silesia; the remainder became part of Czechoslovakia in 1918. After a League of Nations plebiscite (1921–22), Upper Silesia was partitioned between Germany and Poland. ▷ 5.09, 5.11

SINGAPORE
Southeast Asian island republic south of Malay peninsula and a major seaport until destroyed by the Javanese in the 14th century. It was refounded by SIR STAMFORD RAFFLES in 1819 to become a British colony and a major Asian trading center. Captured by Japan in February 1942 and liberated in 1945, it achieved independence in 1965. ▷ 5.22

SINO-JAPANESE WAR
(1894–95) War between China and Japan, fought in Korea and Shandong province, China. China's defense of Korea depended on control of the sea. Japan's naval victory in the Battle of the Yalu River was therefore decisive. Lacking reinforcements, the Chinese army in Korea retreated behind the Yalu, surrendered Port Arthur and fell back on Shandong, thus exposing Beijing to a Japanese pincer movement. The war ended with the TREATY OF SHIMONOSEKI. ▷ 5.19, 5.20

SITTING BULL
(1831–90) Hunkpapa Sioux chief, revered as a mystic. He agreed to make peace with the United States government in the TREATY OF LARAMIE (1868) but opposed gold prospectors in the Black Hills. Regarded as a major figure in the GHOST DANCE movement, he was killed by Indian police. ▷ 5.26

SOCIALISM
A doctrine that public ownership of the means of production and distribution will produce a just and classless society. It has many facets and its quarrelsome divisions have facilitated the rise of 20th century extremist governments, both communist and fascist. European socialist parties remain strong and often head national governments. The Socialist Party of America (1901–20) made little impact on society: its membership peaked at 120,000 (1912) and its leader, Eugene Debs, secured only 6 percent of the presidential vote. ▷ 5.10, 5.18

SOKOTO CALIPHATE
West African empire founded by the FULANI jihadist Usman dan Fodio (1754–1817) who conquered the HAUSA (1804–10). The caliphate is named after its capital at Sokoto (1809) and lasted until the systematic British

conquest (1897–1903), culminating in the death of Sultan Attahiru Ahmed at Yola. Sokoto was absorbed into NIGERIA. ▷ 5.16

SOLFERINO, BATTLE OF
(24 June 1859) Battle between an Austrian army and a Franco-Piedmontese force commanded by NAPOLEON III, who had invaded Lombardy during the wars that preceded the unification of Italy. After several clashes along the Mincio River, heavy casualties persuaded Napoleon III to seek an armistice at Villafranca (11 July 1859). ▷ 5.09

SOMALILAND
Modern Somalia. Its northern region was under Egyptian administration until 1884, when it became a British protectorate. The southern region was part of Italian East Africa from 1889 until occupied by Britain in 1941. The two colonies were united and became independent as Somalia in 1960. ▷ 5.16

SOUTH AFRICA, UNION OF
The united South Africa agreed during meetings in 1908 and 1909 by representatives of Cape Colony, the TRANSVAAL, ORANGE FREE STATE and NATAL. The British parliament approved a constitution in 1909 and the Union was proclaimed on 31 May 1910 as a dominion under the British crown. From the outset the ruling white (British and Afrikaner) minority practiced systematic racial discrimination against the black majority. It introduced apartheid (racial separation) in 1948 and withdrew from the British Commonwealth in 1961, becoming the Republic of South Africa. Moves to abolish apartheid began in 1989 and Nelson Mandela became president in 1994.

SOUTHERN RHODESIA
British southern African colony, named for CECIL RHODES. Homeland of the Shona and NDEBELE peoples. A British protectorate was established in 1888, and white settlement began in 1890. Shona-Ndebele resistance movements were put down between 1896 and 1903. Despite African opposition, it was part of the white-dominated Central African Federation (1953–63). In 1965 the white-dominated government unilaterally declared an independent Rhodesia, but this was only internationally recognized in 1980 when, with the introduction of black majority rule, its name was changed to Zimbabwe. ▷ 5.15, 5.16

SPANISH-AMERICAN WAR
(21 April–12 August 1898) War between the USA and Spain, precipitated by an explosion that destroyed the USS *Maine* in Havana Harbor (15 February 1898). Americans were anxious to liberate Cubans from Spanish rule and the subsequent warfare was in Cuba (San Juan Heights and SANTIAGO DE CUBA) and the PHILIPPINES (MANILA BAY). At the TREATY OF PARIS, Spain ceded Guam, the Philippines and Puerto Rico to the USA, and Cuba became independent. ▷ 5.22, 5.23, 5.24

SPION KOP, BATTLE OF
(19–23 January 1900) Battle of the SECOND ANGLO-BOER WAR. General Sir Redvers Buller tried to smash through BOER defenses on the Tugela River to relieve LADYSMITH. After initial success, the British were driven back with heavy losses. ▷ 5.17

STANLEY, H. M.
(1841–1904) British explorer and journalist commissioned in 1869 by the *New York Herald* to find DAVID LIVINGSTONE. Their historic meeting near Lake Tanganyika led to a brief cooperation exploring the region. Stanley later explored the Congo Basin and signed treaties on behalf of Leopold II to establish the BELGIAN CONGO. ▷ 5.15, 5.16

STOCKTON AND DARLINGTON RAILWAY
The first public railroad in the world. Its commercial success heralded the railroad era. Built and equipped by George Stephenson between 1823 and 1825, it transported coal 36 kilometers (20 miles) from the Bishop Auckland district of County Durham, England, to the port of Stockton for distribution by the coastal trade. ▷ 5.10

STOLYPIN, PYOTR
(1862–1911) Russian politician regarded as a ruthless but reliable minister by NICHOLAS I. He helped to crush the 1905 revolution and was premier from 1906 to 1911. He believed in reform from above but said, "I must face revolution, resist it and stop it." He was murdered in Kiev. ▷ 5.12

STRAITS SETTLEMENTS
The British settlements at SINGAPORE, Malacca and Penang from 1826. Controlled by the East India Company until 1858, then by the British India Office, they became a Crown colony in 1867. Penang and Malacca became part of Malaysia in 1963 while Singapore became independent in 1965. ▷ 5.22

STUART, JOHN MCDOUALL
(1815–16) Explorer of the Australian interior during six expeditions (1858–62). He crossed the continent (1861–62) from Adelaide to Darwin, and the Overland Telegraph Line followed his route in 1872. ▷ 5.18

SUCRE, ANTONIO JOSÉ DE
(1793–1830) South American soldier and politician who assisted in the liberation of BOLIVIA, winning the BATTLE OF AYACUCHO. He was Bolivia's first president (1826–28). In Colombian service, he won the Battle of Tarqui (1829) and was murdered the following year. ▷ 5.23

SUDAN
African republic in the east of the geographical region traditional called the Sudan (north-central Africa immediately south of the Sahara and Libyan deserts and stretching from the west coast to Ethiopia). The republic is

centered on the Nile River valley. Civilizations, influenced by Egypt to the north, developed here in the 2nd millennium BC. Conquered and Islamicized by the Arabs in the Middle Ages, in the 1820s Sudan came under Egyptian rule, which was overthrown by the MAHDI (1884–85). Reconquered and jointly governed by Britain and Egypt (1899–1924, 1936–53), Sudan became semi-autonomous in 1953 and independent in 1956. ▷ 5.16

SUEZ CANAL
Canal linking the Mediterranean with the Red Sea. It cuts through the Suez isthmus in northeastern EGYPT. Built between 1859 and 1869 by FERDINAND DE LESSEPS, it came under British control in 1875 and was nationalized by Egypt in 1956, an event that led to an unsuccessful Anglo-French-Israeli intervention. ▷ 5.06, 5.14

SWAN RIVER COLONY
Colony founded by Captain James Stirling on the Swan River, Western Australia, in 1829, when FREMANTLE and Perth were established. By 1830 4,000 settlers had arrived but 2,500 had left by 1832. Convict ships from Britain brought cheap labour until 1868. The colony became part of the state of Western Australia in 1890. ▷ 5.18

SWAZILAND
South African kingdom. Founded by King Ngwane II in the 18th century, it was expanded by Sobhuza I (c.1793–1838) and his son, Mswati, who survived the encroachments of ZULUS, the Shangane and European imperialists. By 1865 it was a unified state, though it came under British protection and did not achieve independence until 1968. ▷ 5.15, 5.16, 5.17

SYDNEY
Founded in 1788, the first British settlement in Australia. Initially a penal center, it was named after Viscount Sydney, the British home secretary. Quickly developing into NEW SOUTH WALES's principal center of commercial economic and political activity, it became the state capital. ▷ 5.18

SYNDICALISM
(From the French *syndicat* – "trade union") A 19th century political movement that rejected parliamentary and constitutional processes in favor of direct action and the general strike to secure worker control of the state. Popular in France and the USA, it briefly appeared in Britain in 1911 and 1912. It was largely absorbed by communism.

TAIPING REBELLION
An attempt by the Chinese mystical leader, HONG XIUQUAN to overthrow the Qing (Manchu) dynasty in one of the bloodiest civil wars in history – around 20 million people may have died. The rebels aim was to establish the "heavenly kingdom of great

peace", introducing political and religious reform. By 1860 Hong's God-Worshippers had brought one-third of China under their control and established a capital at Nanjing. Qing forces, aided by CHARLES GORDON, captured Nanjing in 1864 and Hong committed suicide. ▷ 5.19

TANGIER CRISIS

Crisis caused by the unexpected visit of Kaiser Wilhelm II to this north Moroccan seaport in 1905 to challenge the apparent French domination of Morocco. It was resolved by the ALGECIRAS CONFERENCE. ▷ 5.13

TEN YEARS WAR

(1793–1830) A Cuban revolt against Spanish rule that won sympathy in the USA. Spain eventually promised reforms, but these were inadequate and a further revolt (1895–98) led to the SPANISH-AMERICAN WAR. ▷ 5.24

TENASSERIM

Region bordering the Andaman Sea in the northwest of the Malay peninsula. It was ceded to Britain, together with the Arakan, by the Burmese king of Ava (Treaty of Yandabu, 1826). ▷ 5.22

TEXAN WAR OF INDEPENDENCE

(1835–36) War of secession from Mexico by American settlers in Texas. Formerly part of the Spanish American empire, Texas passed to Mexico in 1821. The Americans who settled there fought for independence against the Mexican president ANTONIO DE SANTA ANNA, defeating him at the SAN JACINTO RIVER, after which the USA recognized the independence of Texas. Texas was admitted to the American Union on 29 December 1845. ▷ 5.23

THOMPSON, DAVID

(1770–1857) English-born explorer whose expeditions beyond the Great Lakes (1789–1811) opened routes across CANADA, as far as the Columbia River. ▷ 5.25

THREE EMPERORS, LEAGUE OF THE

See DREIKAISERBUND

TILSIT, TREATY OF

(8 July 1807) Treaty signed between Czar ALEXANDER I and BONAPARTE aboard a raft moored in the River Niemen, northern East Prussia. Alexander agreed to a GRAND DUCHY OF WARSAW and a new kingdom of Westphalia and promised to join the CONTINENTAL SYSTEM if Britain refused to make peace. Alexander kept his word until the end of 1810 and the Franco-Russian alliance lasted until Bonaparte invaded Russia in 1812. ▷ 5.08

TIPPU TIP

(1837–1905) ZANZIBARI trader and plantation owner who led trading expeditions into east-central Africa, specializing in ivory and slaves. He ruled a trading empire in the eastern Congo (1869–81). ▷ 5.15

TIPU SULTAN

(1749–99) Sultan of Mysore (r.1782–99), India. He attacked British-controlled Travancore in the Third Mysore War and was forced to take refuge in SERINGAPATAM and make peace. He then initiated the Fourth Mysore War and was killed in the defense of Seringapatam. ▷ 5.21

TOGO, HEIHACHIRO

(1848–1934) Japanese admiral trained in Britain who was commander of the Japanese combined fleet in the RUSSO-JAPANESE WAR. His decisive victory at the BATTLE OF TSUSHIMA (27 May 1905) forced the Russians to accept American mediation. He is regarded as Japan's greatest admiral and has been called the Nelson of the east. ▷ 5.20

TOGO (TOGOLAND)

West African republic. Home of the Ewe since the 14th century, it became a German protectorate in 1885. Regarded by Kaiser Wilhelm II as a model colony, it abolished slavery and built roads and railroads. It was invaded by Allied troops in 1914, mandated to France in 1922 and independent in 1960. ▷ 5.15, 5.16

TONE, WOLFE

(1763–98) Irish politician who sought Irish independence, forming the SOCIETY OF UNITED IRISHMEN in 1791. He persuaded the French to support two rebellions in Ireland (1796 and 1798) though he did not see action in the 1798 rebellion. Captured by the British, he committed suicide in Dublin. ▷ 5.01, 5.07

TONGHAK REVOLT

Political revolt of 1894 in Korea fomented by a religious movement that professed *Tonghak* (Eastern learning). Led by the mystic Choe Cheu (1824–64), the movement had been dissolved by the Korean government in 1892 and forced underground. When the 1894 revolt broke out it was crushed by Chinese troops. Japanese troops arrived, ostensibly to protect trade interests, and the SINO-JAPANESE WAR broke out. ▷ 5.20

TONGKING

Region making up the northern provinces of Vietnam. Invaded by France in 1873, it was occupied in 1883 and united with FRENCH INDO-CHINA in 1887. Occupied by Japan (1940–45), it formed part of North Vietnam in 1954 and became the center of resistance to American intervention in Vietnam during the Vietnam War (1964–75). ▷ 5.19, 5.22

TORRES VEDRAS

Three lines of fortifications constructed by the DUKE OF WELLINGTON in 1810, during the PENINSULAR WAR. Stretching for 48 kilometers (30 miles) from the River Tagus to the sea, they were occupied by Portuguese, British and Spanish troops from 10 October 1810. They were unsuccessfully attacked by the French general André Masséna, who, lacking supplies, had to retreat from Portugal. ▷ 5.08

TRADE UNIONISM

Wage-earners' movements to promote pay and working conditions for the benefit of members. Active in all the industrialized nations, trade unions were usually hampered by the state and employers, and confrontation was common. Mass trade unionism for unskilled workers emerged through strike action toward the end of the 19th century, for example, in the the Great Railroad Strike (USA, 1877) and the Match Girls' Strike (Britain, 1888). The League for Founding Labor Unions became active in Japan from 1897. ▷ 5.10, 5.20, 5.24, 5.28

TRAFALGAR, BATTLE OF

(21 October 1805) Naval battle off Cape Trafalgar, Spain, between a British fleet of 27 ships commanded by HORATIO NELSON and a Franco-Spanish fleet of 33 ships commanded by Admiral Pierre Villeneuve. Though Nelson was killed during the battle, his decisive victory thwarted BONAPARTE's naval plans and secured British control of the seas for over a hundred years. ▷ 5.08

TRAIL OF TEARS

The route followed by 14,000 Cherokee in a forced removal from Georgia to the INDIAN TERRITORY (1838–39). They took the trail in the winter and about 4,000 died. ▷ 5.26

TRANS-SIBERIAN RAILROAD

Russian railroad planned in 1875, surveyed between 1888 and 1890, and under construction from 1891, partly funded by foreign loans. Trains were ferried across Lake Baikal until 1915. The link between Moscow and Vladivostok, via Cita and Khabarovsk, was not completed until 1916. ▷ 5.12

TRANSVAAL

BOER republic located between the Vaal and Orange Rivers. Originally the home of Bantu peoples, it was settled by BOERS during the GREAT TREK and became independent in 1852. Gold discoveries in 1886 attracted *uitlanders* (white non-Afrikaners) and sparked the abortive JAMESON RAID. The Transvaal fought Britain in two ANGLO-BOER wars and joined the UNION OF SOUTH AFRICA in 1910. ▷ 5.17

TREATY PORTS

Ports that the Chinese agreed to open to foreign trade in the 19th century. The first (by the NANJING TREATY) were Guangzhou, Xiamen, Ningbo, Fuzhou and Shanghai, and the total number open by 1900 exceeded 50. ▷ 5.19

TRINIDAD

West Indian island, northeast of Venezuela. Originally populated by the Arawaks, it was ceded to Britain by Spain in 1802 and became part of the colony of Trinidad and Tobago in 1899. With Tobago, it became an independent state in 1962 and a republic in 1976. ▷ 5.24

TRIPLE ALLIANCE (ARGENTINA, BRAZIL AND URUGUAY)

(May 1865) Alliance between ARGENTINA, BRAZIL and URUGUAY against PARAGUAY. Francisco Solano Lopez (1826–70) became perpetual dictator of Paraguay in 1862 and intervened in a dispute between Brazil and Uruguay, invading Brazil (26 December 1864). A change of government in Uruguay led to the Triple Alliance and its war with Paraguay lasted until the death of Lopez. ▷ 5.23

TRIPLE ALLIANCE (AUSTRIA, GERMANY AND ITALY)

(May 1882) Secret treaty that lasted until 1915, masterminded by OTTO VON BISMARCK. It was agreed that Germany and Austria would aid Italy if it were attacked by France. Italy would aid Germany if attacked by France. In 1914 Italy did not go to war, as France was not the aggressor. ▷ 5.13

TRIPLE ENTENTE

Collaboration between Britain, Russia and France from 1907 to 1917. To enhance the ENTENTE CORDIALE, in which Britain settled disputes with France, Britain reached agreements with Russia (the Anglo-Russian Entente, 1907). The Entente powers formed a military alliance on 3 September 1914, agreeing that none of them would make a separate peace with Germany. ▷ 5.13

TRIPOLI

Capital city of the north African state of Libya. Tripolitania was a former Barbary state, feared for its piratical attacks on Mediterranean shipping that caused a war with the USA (1801–05). It was ceded to Italy by Turkey in 1912 and became part of independent Libya in 1951. ▷ 5.14, 5.15, 5.16

TROPPAU, CONGRESS OF

Congress held in Moravia in October 1820 to discuss an international response to revolts in Spain, SARDINIA-PIEDMONT, Portugal and Naples. METTERNICH wanted states involved in revolution to be forced to rejoin the HOLY ALLIANCE. Britain rejected this. ▷ 5.09

TRUCIAL OMAN

Now the United Arab Emirates, located in the southeast of the Arabian peninsula. "Trucial" arises from an agreement (truce) of 1835 not to engage in piracy in return for British support against attacks from tribes in the interior. Trucial Oman was a British protectorate from 1892 to 1971. ▷ 5.14

TSUSHIMA, BATTLE OF

(27–8 May 1905) Decisive naval battle of the RUSSO-JAPANESE WAR, and the first major battle between fleets of armored warships. After sailing halfway around the world, the obsolescent Russian Baltic fleet was annihilated in the Strait of Tsushima by the more modern Japanese fleet. ▷ 5.12, 5.20

TUKULOR CALIPHATE

Caliphate founded by the jihadist Al-Hajj Umar (1794–1864). Located in modern Mali, it stretched from Medina to Timbuktu and absorbed the pre-existing jihadist state of MASINA in 1862. It was conquered by France between 1890 and 1998. ▷ 5.15, 5.16

TUNIS

Capital of the north African state of Tunisia. Captured by Spain in 1535 and occupied by Turkey from 1573 to 1574, it became a French protectorate in 1881. It achieved independence in 1956. ▷ 5.14, 5.15, 5.16

TURKO-EGYPTIAN WAR

Two wars between Turkey and EGYPT. The first (1832–33) arose when the Ottoman sultan rejected MEHMET ALI's demand for Syria in return for his support against Greece. An Anglo-French intervention terminated the hostilities but Egypt retained Syria. In the second war (1839–41) the Turks invaded Syria. Anglo-Austrian intervention led to Egypt's evacuation of Syria and to the Straits Convention (1841). This closed the Bosphorus and Dardanelles to foreign warships in peacetime. ▷ 5.14

TWO SICILIES, KINGDOM OF THE

See SICILY, KINGDOM OF

ULUNDI, BATTLE OF

(4 July 1879) Battle fought at CETSHWAYO's royal kraal following the British defeat at ISANDHLWANA and the defense of RORKE's DRIFT. British victory at Ulundi marked the end of ZULU power. ▷ 5.17

UNITED IRISHMEN REBELLION

Rising against the British government in 1798 by the United Irishmen, formed by WOLFE TONE. They burned Enniscorthy in County Wexford before being defeated at the Battle of Vinegar Hill (21 June 1798). French supporters who landed at Killala Bay (22 August) surrendered to Lord Cornwallis. ▷ 5.07

UNITED KINGDOM

The United Kingdom of Great Britain and Ireland, formed by the ACT OF UNION (1801), which dissolved the Irish parliament and united Ireland with Great Britain. The UK was redefined, after the creation of the Irish Free State in 1922, as the United Kingdom of Great Britain and Northern Ireland. ▷ 5.07

UNITED STATES OF AMERICA

North American federal republic, with its capital at WASHINGTON DC. It declared its independence in 1776 and after fighting a revolutionary war against Britain (1775–83) adopted a federal constitution in 1787, uniting 13 former colonies. It expanded through the LOUISIANA PURCHASE, the acquisition of California and New Mexico by the MEXICAN-AMERICAN WAR, the annexation of Texas and

BRITISH PRIME MINISTERS 1783–1916

William Pitt	Tory	1783–1801	Viscount Palmerston	Liberal	1855–58
Henry Addington	Tory	1801–04	The earl of Derby	Conservative	1858–59
William Pitt	Tory	1804–06	Viscount Palmerston	Liberal	1859–65
Lord Grenville	Whig	1806–07	Lord John Russell	Liberal	1865–66
The duke of Portland	Tory	1807–09	The earl of Derby	Conservative	1866–68
Spencer Perceval	Tory	1809–12	Benjamin Disraeli	Conservative	1868
The earl of Liverpool	Tory	1812–27	William Ewart Gladstone	Liberal	1868–74
George Canning	Tory	1827	Benjamin Disraeli	Conservative	1874–80
Viscount Goderich	Tory	1827–28	William Ewart Gladstone	Liberal	1880–85
The duke of Wellington	Tory	1828–30	The marquess of Salisbury	Conservative	1885–86
Earl Grey	Whig	1830–34	William Ewart Gladstone	Liberal	1886
Viscount Melbourne	Whig	1834	The marquess of Salisbury	Conservative	1886–92
Robert Peel	Conservative	1834–35	William Ewart Gladstone	Liberal	1892–94
Viscount Melbourne	Whig	1835–41	The earl of Rosebery	Liberal	1894–95
Robert Peel	Conservative	1841–46	The marquess of Salisbury	Conservative	1895–1902
Lord John Russell	Liberal	1846–52	Arthur James Balfour	Conservative	1902–05
The earl of Derby	Conservative	1852	Henry Campbell-Bannerman	Liberal	1905–08
Lord Aberdeen	Peelite	1852–55	Herbert Henry Asquith	Liberal	1908–16

PRESIDENTS OF THE UNITED STATES OF AMERICA 1783–1921					
George Washington		1789–97	James Buchanan	Democrat	1857–61
John Adams	Federalist	1797–1801	Abraham Lincoln	Republican	1861–65
Thomas Jefferson	Democrat-Republican	1801–09	Andrew Johnson	Democrat-National Union	1865–69
James Madison	Democrat-Republican	1809–17	Ulysses S. Grant	Republican	1869–77
James Monroe	Democrat-Republican	1817–25	Rutherford B. Hayes	Republican	1877–81
John Quincy Adams	Democrat-Republican	1825–29	James A. Garfield	Republican	1881
Andrew Jackson	Democrat	1829–37	Chester A. Arthur	Republican	1881–85
Martin Van Buren	Democrat	1837–41	Grover Cleveland	Democrat	1885–89
WIlliam Henry Harrison	Whig	1841	Benjamin Harrison	Republican	1889–93
John Tyler	Whig	1841–45	Grover Cleveland	Democrat	1893–97
James Knox Polk	Democrat	1845–49	William McKinley	Republican	1897–1901
Zachary Taylor	Whig	1849–50	Theodore Roosevelt	Republican	1901–09
Millard Fillmore	Whig	1850–53	William Howard Taft	Republican	1909–13
Franklin Pierce	Democrat	1853–57	Woodrow Wilson	Democrat	1913–21

the GADSDEN PURCHASE. Split by the AMERICAN CIVIL WAR, the Union was reconstructed (1865–77) and expanded through the ALASKA purchase and the acquisition of Spanish colonies after the SPANISH-AMERICAN WAR. There are 50 states in the American Union. ▷ 5.26, 5.27, 5.28

URUGUAY
South American republic, originally populated by Charrua Indians. Known as Banda Oriental by Spain it achieved independence in 1811. Briefly part of BRAZIL, it successfully rebelled in 1825 to be recognized as independent in 1828. It participated in the WAR OF THE TRIPLE ALLIANCE (1865–70) against PARAGUAY. Uruguay was riven by conflict between two parties, the Colorados and Blancos, until 1903 and the reforming presidency of Ordóñez brought peace and prosperity. Political instability returned in the mid-20th century, with urban terrorism in the 1960s and military dictatorship (1976–84). ▷ 5.23

UTETERA
Commercial empire, of which TIPPU TIP proclaimed himself sultan, covering – at its peak in 1880 – 25 percent of the modern Democratic Republic of Congo. ▷ 5.15

VAN DIEMEN'S LAND
Modern Tasmania, an island state of Australia. Settled by Aborigines 35,000 years ago, in 1642 it was discovered by Abel Tasman who named it after the governor of Batavia. It was a British penal settlement from 1803 to 1835. Most of the islands aborigines were extermin-ated by Europeans. Officially named Tasmania in 1856, it became an Australian state in 1901. ▷ 5.18

VEGKOP, BATTLE OF
(19 October 1836) Battle between NDEBELE warriors led by Mzilikazi and VOORTREKKERS led by Hendrik Potgieter (1798–1852), fought 36 kilometers (20 miles) south of the Vaal River. The voortrekkers built a defensive laager on top of Vegkop hill and won the first major victory of the GREAT TREK. ▷ 5.17

VENDÉE
Coastal region in western France between La Rochelle and the Loire estuary, from March to October 1793 the scene of a revolt against republican rule, ruthlessly suppressed. The rebellion smouldered with further outbreaks (1795–1800). ▷ 5.07

VENETIA
Region in northern Italy, encompassing Venice and its hinterland, formerly a major independent trading empire. Ceded to Austria in 1797, it was part of BONAPARTE's Italian kingdom in 1805. Restored to Austria in 1815, it became part of unified Italy in 1866. ▷ 5.07, 5.08, 5.09

VENEZUELA
South American republic. Formerly part of the Spanish viceroyalty of New Granada, it pro-claimed its independence in 1811, though this was not assured until after the BATTLE OF CARABOBO. Part of GRAN COLOMBIA until 1830, it has an unresolved boundary dispute with Guyana. ▷ 5.23

VEREENIGING
Town in northeast South Africa 56 kilometers (31 miles) south of Johannesburg. Founded in 1892, it was the scene of peace negotiations that concluded the SECOND ANGLO-BOER WAR (Treaty of Vereeniging, 31 May 1902). ▷ 5.17

VERONA, CONGRESS OF
Congress to discuss support for a French intervention in the revolutions in Spain and its Latin American empire. It opened in Verona on 20 October 1822. By threatening the use of sea power, Britain blocked any move by European powers to intervene in Latin America. This caused so much dissent that Verona marked the end of international cooperation in the CONGRESS SYSTEM. ▷ 5.09

VICKSBURG, SIEGE OF
(1863) ULYSSES S. GRANT's first major victory in the AMERICAN CIVIL WAR. Vicksburg, a key CONFEDERATE fortress on the Mississippi River, surrendered to Union forces on 4 July, leaving

the way clear for Union control of the river, a strategic waterway. ▷ 5.27

VICTOR EMMANUEL II
(1820–78) King of SARDINIA-PIEDMONT (r.1849–61) and king of Italy (r.1861–78). He was anxious to win international support for the unification of Italy. To this end he sent Piedmontese troops to fight in the Crimea in 1855, allied with France in 1859 to expel the Austrians from Italy and ceded Nice and Savoy to NAPOLEON III. In return, he gained Parma, Modena, Tuscany, the Papal Marches and the TWO SICILIES and was crowned king of Italy in 1861. ▷ 5.09

VICTORIA
(1819–1901) Queen of Great Britain (1837–1901) and empress of India (1876–1901). She married Prince Albert of Saxe-Coburg-Gotha in 1840 and had a keen grasp of constitutional and international affairs. After Albert's death (1861) she went into protracted mourning and did not recover her popularity until after BENJAMIN DISRAELI made her empress of India. Her jubilee celebrations in 1887 and 1897 won immense public support. ▷ 5.02, 5.03, 5.13, 5.16, 5.21

VIENNA, CONGRESS OF
(1814–1815) International conference to settle Europe's affairs followed BONAPARTE's abdica-tion. It was interrupted by his return from Elba and by the WATERLOO campaign. The decisions were taken by the major powers Russia, Austria, Prussia and Britain. Its "Final Act" (Treaty of Vienna, 9 June 1815) created the GERMAN CONFEDERATION, the kingdom of the Netherlands and the free city of Kracow. Most territorial redistribution was made to the great powers (e.g. CONGRESS POLAND to the Russian czar); though other significant changes (e.g. the creation of a neutral Swiss Confederation and the union between Sweden and NORWAY) occurred. ▷ 5.09

VILLA, PANCHO
(1877–1923) Mexican revolutionary leader. With EMILIANO ZAPATA he attempted to take

control of the MEXICAN REVOLUTION but they were forced to retreat into northern Mexico. Villa raided Texas and New Mexico, forcing President Wilson to despatch General John J. Pershing (1860–1948) and 11,000 troops in an unsuccessful bid to capture him (1916–17). He surrendered to Mexican troops in 1920 and was murdered in 1923. ▷ 5.23

VITORIA, BATTLE OF
(21 June 1813) Battle of the PENINSULAR WAR. The DUKE OF WELLINGTON routed a French army under Marshal Jean-Baptiste Jourdan (1762–1833) in northern Spain 81 kilometers (50 miles) west of Pamplona, and the French withdrew from Spain. ▷ 5.08

VOLTURNO RIVER, BATTLE OF THE
(1 October 1860) Battle in the Italian wars of independence. GIUSEPPE GARIBALDI defeated Neapolitan troops when they attacked his forces outside Capua, southern Italy, on the Volturno River, where he had taken up position after capturing Naples. ▷ 5.09

VOORTREKKERS
BOERS who took part in the GREAT TREK into NATAL and across the Orange and Vaal Rivers between 1835 and 1836 and over the next ten years. A minority of the Afrikaner population of Cape Colony, they were led by Andries Potgieter, Louis Trigardt (the first of the voortrekkers), Hans van Rensberg, Piet Retief and Andries Pretorius. ▷ 5.17

WAGRAM, BATTLE OF
(5–6 July 1809) Battle fought 18 kilometers (11 miles) northeast of Vienna in the Napoleonic wars. BONAPARTE employed massive artillery support (488 guns) along an 8-kilometer (5-mile) front against an Austrian army commanded by Archduke Charles Louis. The Austrians fell back after heavy fighting and sued for peace (Treaty of Schönbrunn, 14 October 1809). ▷ 5.08

WAHHABIS
Followers of Muhammed ibn Abd al-Wahhab (1703–79) who believed in unitarianism and held that all legal decisions must be based upon the Koran and the Sunna. Led by Muhammed ibn Saud, they influenced much of the Arabian peninsula. His descendant, Ibn Saud, became ruler of the NEJD (r.1900–06) and fought alongside Britain against the Turks in 1915. ▷ 5.14

WAIKATO RIVER
Maori region in North Island, NEW ZEALAND. The Waikato chief King Te Wherowhero and his son Tawhiao were the leaders of the KING MOVEMENT. ▷ 5.18

WAITANGI, TREATY OF
(5 February 1840) Treaty signed in the Bay of Islands, North Island, NEW ZEALAND, by which the Maori ceded sovereignty over their lands. There were two versions of the treaty, one in Maori and the other in English, and the 45 Maori chiefs who signed did not understand they were surrendering their right to customary law over their people. ▷ 5.18

WAKHAN
Strategic region of the Pamirs, northeast Afghanistan, created as a buffer zone between Russia and British India in 1905 by the viceroy Lord Curzon. ▷ 5.12

WAR OF 1812
(1812–14) War between Britain and the USA. After BONAPARTE published the BERLIN DECREES, Britain imposed a blockade of France and seized all US ships that defied it, press-ganged American sailors and ordered US warships to surrender British deserters. Despite British concessions, the USA declared war in 1812. American forces invaded CANADA but were repulsed. Britain retaliated by attacks on coastal towns (including WASHINGTON, burned in 1814) and a naval blockade that ruined New England trade and led to calls for peace. The Peace of Ghent was signed on 24 December 1814, though the news did not reach North America in time to prevent an unsuccessful British assault on NEW ORLEANS. ▷ 5.01, 5.25

WAR OF THE TRIPLE ALLIANCE
(1864–70) Known also as the Lopez War, it resulted from the invasion of BRAZIL by the Paraguayan dictator Francisco Solano Lopez (1827–70). He declared war on ARGENTINA and the TRIPLE ALLIANCE (Argentina, Brazil and URUGUAY) formed against him on 1 May 1865. Fighting centered on the Paraguay River region and after the Battle of Ypacarai (25 December 1867) Lopez fled north to lead a guerrilla war. He was eventually killed by Brazilian lancers. ▷ 5.23

WARSAW, GRAND DUCHY OF
The eastern provinces of Prussia (Prussian Poland) united under the terms of the TREATY OF TILSIT (1807) with Austrian Galicia. BONAPARTE chose the king of Saxony to rule the grand duchy, which the CONGRESS OF VIENNA abolished. ▷ 5.08

WASHINGTON
Capital city of the USA and its seat of government. It includes the District of Columbia, east of the Potomac River. The site was selected by GEORGE WASHINGTON in 1791, and the government moved there in 1800. The Capitol (seat of CONGRESS) and White House were burned by British troops in 1814 during the WAR OF 1812. PRESIDENT JAMES MADISON and his wife had escaped earlier. The damage was soon repaired and Washington grew rapidly in the 19th century, particularly after the AMERICAN CIVIL WAR. ▷ 5.27, 5.28

WASHINGTON, GEORGE
(1864–70) American soldier and statesman, and first president of the USA. He fought in the French and Indian wars (1754–63) and led the struggle against the British in the American Revolution (1775–83). As commander, he held the Continental Army together through a series of defeats and a difficult winter at Valley Forge (November 1787–April 1778). He planned the Franco-American advance on Yorktown and forced Cornwallis to surrender in 1781, effectively ending the war. President of the Philadelphia constitutional convention in 1787, he was elected president of the USA in 1789. He tried to remain neutral in the growing rift between the Federalists and Jeffersonians and retired in 1797, refusing a third term in office. ▷ 5.26

WATERLOO, BATTLE OF
(18 June 1815) The decisive battle of the Napoleonic wars, which led to radical changes in the map of Europe. It was fought 19 kilometers (12 miles) south of Brussels between the French under BONAPARTE and the allies under the DUKE OF WELLINGTON and GEBHARD VON BLÜCHER. Outnumbered, Wellington fought a skillful holding action until Blücher's Prussians arrived late in the day. Bonaparte was forced to retreat and abdicate for the second time. ▷ 5.08

WATTIGNIES, BATTLE OF
(October 15–16 1793) Battle of the FRENCH REVOLUTIONARY WARS. General Jean-Baptiste Jourdan (1762–1833), commanding the Army of the North, defeated an Austrian army and relieved the siege of Mauberge. ▷ 5.07

WEIHAIWEI
Seaport in northeastern Shandong province, China, scene of a Japanese naval victory in 1895, in the SINO-JAPANESE WAR. The Japanese occupied the port until 1898, when Britain leased it. A naval base until 1930, it was again occupied by Japan from 1938 to 1945. ▷ 5.20

WELLINGTON, ARTHUR WELLESLEY, 1ST DUKE OF
(1769–1852) British soldier and statesman. He served with distinction in in India, defeating TIPU SULTAN and the MARATHAS. He led the COPENHAGEN expedition (1807) and was commander of the British forces in the PENINSULAR WAR (1809–14), driving the French out of Spain and Portugal. His greatest victory was over BONAPARTE himself at WATERLOO in 1815. He was made Viscount Wellington after his victory at Talavera (1809), earl after his capture of Ciudad Rodrigo and BADAJOZ (1812) and duke for his invasion of France and his victory at Toulouse (1814). He was prime minister (1828–30) and took charge of London's security during the Chartist demonstrations in 1848. ▷ 5.08, 5.09

WHITE LOTUS REBELLION
(1796–1804) An anti-Qing (Manchu) revolt fomented by the White Lotus sect. It spread to Henan, Gansu, Sichuan, Hubei and Shaanxi. The sect began in the 13th century and was a

quasi-religious body. It claimed that official oppression justified the people's revolt. Qing forces took nine years to crush it. ▷ 5.19

WILBERFORCE, WILLIAM
(1759–1833) English politician, philanthropist and ABOLITIONIST, who in 1788 began a struggle for the abolition of the slave trade, achieved in 1807. His work included the foundation of the Church Missionary Society (1798), the Bible Society (1803) and the Anti-Slavery Society (1825). He died just before Parliament abolished slavery in 1833. ▷ 5.05

WILHELM I
(1797–1888) King of PRUSSIA (r.1861–88), first emperor of the SECOND GERMAN EMPIRE (r.1871–88). He opposed socialist demands and survived two attempts on his life (1878 and 1883). ▷ 5.03, 5.11

WILLS, WILLIAM JOHN
(1834–61) Australian explorer, who, in company with ROBERT BURKE, made the first south–north crossing of Australia (1860–61). It was the best-equipped expedition to date but both men died, together with five others, during the return journey. ▷ 5.18

WITTE, COUNT SERGEI
(1849–1915) Russian politician and the czar's most valued adviser on transport economics. He actively sought foreign investment, master-minded the modernization of Russian industry and advocated the construction of the TRANS-SIBERIAN RAILROAD. He was prime minister (1905–06) and signed the TREATY OF PORTSMOUTH. ▷ 5.12

WOUNDED KNEE
Scene in southwest South Dakota of the massacre of Sioux families, many of them GHOST DANCERS, by the US Seventh Cavalry on 29 December 1890. Colonel George Forsyth, gave orders for all to be taken prisoner. His orders were not implemented and 146 Sioux, including Chief Big Foot, died. ▷ 5.26

XHOSA
A Bantu African nation between the Great Kei River and Natal, South Africa. The Xhosa raided BOER settlements, leading to a series of Kaffir wars culminating in the sixth (1834–35) after which the British authorities absorbed Xhosa land as the province of Queen Adelaide. It became the Crown Colony of Kaffraria (1847–66) and was then integrated into Cape Colony. ▷ 5.01

YEAR OF REVOLUTIONS
1848. At a time of economic recession and poor European harvests, European intellectuals proposed radical changes in state control, advocating liberal, democratically elected governments. Revolutions, generally unsuccessful and sparked off by the February Revolt in Paris, spread to Austria, Hungary, Italy and the German states, where the motives were sometimes nationalistic. There was an abortive revolution in Ireland and a CHARTIST protest in Britain. ▷ 5.09

YEKE
Central African kingdom that emerged in the mid-19th century a result of increasing trade (slaves, copper, ivory) between the Nyamwezi and KAZEMBE. A Nyamwezi group, the Yeke, settled permanently in southwest Kazembe. Disruption of Kazembe trade in the 1860s by the Yeke king Msiri caused political disunity. It was exploited by ZANZIBARI traders such as TIPPU TIP. ▷ 5.15

YELLOW SEA, BATTLE OF
(10 August 1904) Battle of the RUSSO-JAPANESE WAR, fought when Czar Nicholas II ordered Admiral Vitgeft to break out of PORT ARTHUR (Lushun) and join the Vladivostok fleet. Admiral HEIHACHIRO TOGO intercepted him and in the battle Vitgeft was killed and his fleet forced back into Port Arthur. ▷ 5.20

YORUBA STATES
A complex of states in the southwest region of modern NIGERIA, headed by individual Yoruba kings. Populated by the artistically creative Yoruba-Aja, the region was first dominated by the OYO EMPIRE and then split by warfare led by Ife, Ijebu and FULANI warriors (1816–35). The area became the Southern Protectorate of Nigeria in 1900. ▷ 5.16

YOUNGHUSBAND, SIR FRANCIS
(1863–1942) British soldier and explorer who led an expedition into Tibet to establish whether or not the Russians had penetrated the country. On 3 August 1904, after overcoming armed resistance to his visit he entered Lhasa. He found no Russians and after several misunderstandings established diplomatic relations. ▷ 5.21

YOUNG ITALY MOVEMENT
Movement founded in March 1831 by the patriot GIUSEPPE MAZZINI to promote Italian nationalism at a time when Austrian troops were putting down Italian revolts. Intended as an alternative to the unsuccessful CARBONARI, it lacked support from the Piedmontese government and declined after 1835. ▷ 5.09

YOUNG TURKS
Turkish reform movement that began with Turkish expatriates (1900–01) but was taken over by young Turkish officers – pro-German and dedicated to westernization and modernization – in 1908. ENVER PASHA was its most prominent leader. ▷ 5.14

YUKON
Territory in northwest CANADA south of the Beaufort Sea and east of Alaska. In 1898 the discovery of gold on the Bonanza Creek of the KLONDIKE RIVER led one of the world's biggest GOLD RUSHES. ▷ 5.25

ZAIBATSU
Large financial combines that developed in Japan during the latter part of the MEIJI period. They were united by finance, produced a wide range of products and had their own bank. After 1918 and up to 1941 four giant zaibatsu – Mitsui, Yasuda, Sumitomo and Mitsubishi – dominated Japanese trade and industry. ▷ 5.20

ZANZIBAR, SULTANATE OF
Island sultanate adjacent to Tanzania that became the capital (1832–40) of Sultan Seyyid Said of Oman-Muscat (1791–1856, r.1806–56). He transformed Zanzibar into the major East African slave-trade center and this brought him into conflict with the British. Zanzibar came under German control in 1885 but was passed to Britain in exchange for HELIGOLAND in 1890. ▷ 5.16

ZAPATA, EMILIANO
(1877?-1919) Mexican revolutionary leader who rebelled against PORFIRIO DIAZ in the MEXICAN REVOLUTION and took control of the state of Morelos. He opposed General Venustiano Carranza (1859–1920) and was assassinated on 10 April 1919, possibly on the general's orders. ▷ 5.23

ZHANJIANG
Town in Guangdong province, southwestern China, formerly known as Tsamkong. The port and hinterland were acquired by France as a trading sector in 1890. ▷ 5.19

ZOLLVEREIN
A free-trade customs union begun by PRUSSIA in 1819 and, by 1844, embracing all the other German states apart from major ports such as Hamburg and Bremen. It excluded Austria, extended Prussian power and encouraged railroad building to center on Berlin. ▷ 5.09

ZULU
Bantu-speaking people of southern Africa. Most now live in KwaZulu-Natal, South Africa. The name Zulu originally applied only to the clan of SHAKA who subjugated the surrounding tribes to create the Zulu nation in the early 19th century. They were defeated by the British in the ZULU WAR of 1879 and came under British rule in 1887. ▷ 5.15, 5.17

ZULULAND
Homeland of the ZULU until 1887. After the ZULU WAR, it was a British protectorate and in 1897 was annexed to NATAL, now the South African province of KwaZulu-Natal. ▷ 5.17

ZULU WAR
(1879) An attempt by the British to destroy the military power of CETSHWAYO, the ZULU king. It began with a major Zulu victory at ISANDHLWANA (22 January) and was followed by the defense of RORKE'S DRIFT and the final British victory at the royal kraal at ULUNDI on 4 July. ▷ 5.17

Text, timelines and maps

The authors and publishers readily acknowledge the work of a large number of scholars and published works, on which they have drawn in the preparation of this atlas. Many of these works remain in print, and can be used as reliable secondary reading on the many topics covered in this atlas. Among them are the following:

Adams, AE, Matley, IM, and McCagg, WO *An Atlas of Russian and East European History* (London 1967)
Ajayi, JFA and Crowder, Michael (eds) *Historical Atlas of Africa* (Cambridge and New York 1985)
al Faruqi, Ismail Ragi (ed) *Historical Atlas of the Religions of the World* (New York and London 1974)
Almond, M, Black, J, McKitterick, R, and Scarre, C *The Times Atlas of European History* (London and New York 1994)
Ardagh, John with Jones, Colin *Cultural Atlas of France* (London and New York, 1991)
Ashdown, P. *Caribbean History in Maps* (London and New York 1979)
Banks, A *A Military Atlas of World War I* (London 1989)
Barraclough, G (ed) *The Times Atlas of World History* (4th ed , London 1993 and New York 1994)
Bayley, Christopher (ed) *Atlas of the British Empire* (London and New York 1989)
Blunden, Caroline and Elvin, Mark *Cultural Atlas of China* (London and New York, 1986)
Bolton, Geoffrey (ed) *The Oxford History of Australia* (Oxford and Melbourne 1994)
Brown, Dee *The American West* (New York 1994)
Campbell, John (ed) *The Experience of World War II* (London and New York 1989)
Chadwick, Henry and Evans, Gillian R (eds) *Atlas of the Christian Church* (London and New York, 1987)
Cohn-Sherbok, D *Atlas of Jewish History* (London and New York 1994)
Coles, JM and Harding, AF *The Bronze Age in Europe* (London 1979)
Collcutt, Martin, Jansen, Marius and Kumakura, Isao *Cultural Atlas of Japan* (London and New York, 1988)
Cotterell, A *East Asia* (London 1993, New York 1995)
Darby, HC and Fullard, Harold *The New Cambridge Modern History Atlas* (Cambrdge 1970)
Davis, Norman *Europe: a History* (Oxford and New York 1996)
Dear, ICB and Foot, MRD (eds) *The Oxford Companion to the Second World War* (Oxford and New York 1995)

de Lange, Nicholas *Atlas of the Jewish World* (London and New York, 1984)
Elliott, JH (ed) *The Hispanic World* (London and New York 1991)
Fage, JD and Oliver, R (eds) *The Cambridge History of Africa* (Cambridge and New York 1975–)
Fage, J.D. *An Atlas of African History* (London 1978)
Falkus, M and Gillingham J *Historical Atlas of Britain* (London and New York revised ed 1987)
Fernández-Armesto, Felipe (ed) *The Times Atlas of World Exploration* (London and New York, 1991)
Freedman, Lawrence *Atlas of Global Strategy* (London and New York, 1985)
Gilbert, Martin *The Atlas of Jewish History* (London and New York 5th ed 1996)
Gilbert, Martin *Atlas of The Holocaust* (London 1982, New York 1993)
Griffiths, Ieuan L *The Atlas of African Affairs* (London 1984)
Grosser Historischer Weltatlas (3 volumes (Munich 1981)
Hall, DGE *A History of South-east Asia* (London 4th ed 1981)
Handlin, O. *The History of the United States* (New York 1967)
Hartman, Tom *A World Atlas of Military History 1945–1984* (New York 1985)
Hermann, A *Historical and Commercial Atlas of China* (Cambridge Mass., 1935)
Holt, PM, Lambeth, AKS and Lewis, B (eds) *The Cambridge History of Islam* (Cambridge 1970–)
Homberger, E. *Historical Atlas of North America* (London and New York 1995)
Hosking, G *A History of the Soviet Union* (London 1985)
Johnson, Gordon, Bayly, C and Richards JF T*he New Cambridge History of India* (Cambridge 1987–)
Johnson, Gordon *Cultural Atlas of India* (London 1995, New York, 1996)
Kinder, H and Hilgemann, W *Atlas of World History* (2 vols, Munich, London and New York 1974)
Kulke, H and Rothermund, D *A History of India* (London 1990)
Langer, William I. *An Encyclopedia of World History* (5th ed, London and New York 1973)
Lee, K *A New History of Korea* (Cambridge, Mass 1984)
McEvedy, Colin and Jones, Richard *Atlas of World Population History* (London 1978)
Milner, C.A., O'Connor, C.A. and Sandweiss, M *The Oxford History of the American West* (Oxford and New York 1994)
Milner-Gulland, Robin with Dejevsky, Nikolai *Cultural Atlas of Russia and the Soviet Union* (London and New York, 1989)
Moore, RI (ed) *The Hamlyn Historical Atlas* (London 1981)
Murray, Jocelyn *Cultural Atlas of Africa* (London and New York, 1981)

Nile, Richard and Clerk, Christian *Cultural Atlas of Australia, New Zealand and the South Pacific* (London and New York, 1995)
Nock, O.S. *World Atlas of Railways* (London 1978)
Parker, W.H. *An Historical Geography of Russia* (London 1968)
Paxton, John *The Statesman's Yearbook Historical Companion* (London 1988)
Porter, A.N. (ed) *Atlas of British Overseas Expansion* (London 1991)
Pounds, Norman JG *An Historical Geography of Europe* (Cambridge 1990)
Riasanovsky, NV *A History of Russia* (Oxford and New York 5th ed 1993)
Roberts, JM *The Hutchinson History of the World* (London 1976)
Robinson, Francis *Atlas of the Islamic World since 1500* (London and New York, 1982)
Roolvink, R *Historical Atlas of the Muslim People* (Amsterdam 1974)
Schmidt, KJ *An Atlas and Survey of South Asian History* (New York and London 1995)
Schwartzberg, Joseph E (ed) *A Historical Atlas of South Asia* (Chicago and London, 2nd ed 1992)
Segal, Aaron *An Atlas of International Migration* (London and New Jersey 1993)
Shepherd, William R *Shepherd's Historical Atlas* (New York and London, 9th ed 1974)
Sinclair, Keith (ed) *The Oxford Illustrated History of New Zealand* (Oxford and Auckland 1990)
Sinor, D (ed) *The Cambridge History of Early Inner Asia* (Cambridge 1990)
Spence, J *God's Chinese Son* (London and New York 1996)
Spence, J *The Search for Modern China* (London and New York 1990)
Spence JE (ed) *The World Today* (London 1994)
The Times Atlas of the World (London and New York, 8th ed 1990)
Tindall, G and Shi, DE *America, a Narrative History* (New York, 1996)
Twitchett, D and Fairbank, J (eds) *The Cambridge History of China* (15 vols, Cambridge and New York 1978–91)
Vincent, Mary and Stradling, R.A. *Cultural Atlas of Spain and Portugal* (London 1994, New York 1995)
Waller, Philip (ed) *Chronology of the 20th Century* (Oxford 1995)
Webster's New Geographical Dictionary (Springfield, Massachusetts, 1984)
Winter, JM *The Experience of World War I* (London and New York 1988)
Wintle, J *The Vietnam Years* (London 1991)

Artwork

Artwork references have been assembled from a wide variety of sources. Any individual or institution who can demonstrate that copyright may have been infringed is invited to contact Andromeda Oxford Ltd.